Frederic Alexander Fleming stands in front of the family home in Hibernia with his three children, c. 1897. This was the centerpiece of the "old place," and is the most widely recognized image of Hibernia. The Flemings cherished this home/hotel for nearly 100 years before it was torn down in the 1950s. There are older photos of the Fleming home but they do not include any identifiable members of the Fleming family.

The Flemings of Fleming Island

An Historic Florida Family

Scott Ritchie

The Flemings of Fleming Island: An Historic Florida Family

ISBN: 978-1-949810-00-4

The Florida Historical Society Press
435 Brevard Avenue
Cocoa, FL 32922
http://myfloridahistory.org/fhspress

Dedication

Dedicated in memory of my father, William George Ritchie.

Acknowledgements

I want to thank the following individuals who volunteered resources and/or support for this project. My mother-in-law, Marian Fleming, provided a remarkable collection of family photos, documents, and notes, including several file folders of Fleming family research from eminent Jacksonville historian Dena Snodgrass. I will never forget Marian's joy when I gave her the first complete draft of this manuscript. Another Fleming family member, the late Lurana Crowley "Ranie" Austin, shared her own collection of documents and photos.

Robert Jones was the first to encourage me to go farther—to keep digging until I could tell the Fleming family story. At that time, he was Historic Sites Specialist for the Florida Department of State, Division of Historic Resources.

Archivists and librarians everywhere deserve a shout out. I consulted these dedicated professionals, either in person or via email, so many times and in so many places that it's impossible for me to remember them all. Two deserve special recognition: Charles Tingley, Senior Research Librarian at the St. Augustine Historical Society Research Library, and Vishi Garig, Clay County Archivist.

John Diviney, former faculty member at Flagler College in St. Augustine, generously translated many documents from the East Florida Papers. The late Yvonne Cantilo also translated documents.

Bob Gross offered research assistance and moral support, as did Fleming family member Ken Keefe.

Finally, I want to thank my partner, my friend, my wife, Margot. She patiently listened to me rant and rave when I got frustrated. She shared my enthusiasm when I made new discoveries. I read her so many drafts of this manuscript that her eyes glazed over now and then, but she never flagged in her support and encouragement.

Table of Contents

Fleming Family Tree

George Fleming
(1760–1821)
m. Sophia Fatio
(1765–1848)

m. Augustina Cortez
(1806–1832)
Lewis Michael Fleming
(1798–1862)
m. Margaret Seton
(1813–1878)

George C. Fleming m. Mary O. Bennett
(1822–1858)
Louis I. Fleming m. Mary E. L'Engle
(1828–1888)   (1837–1911)
Augustina Fleming m. William Stephens
(1831–1900)   (1827–1904)

Edwin W. Fleming
George C. Fleming Jr.
Mary M. Fleming
Sophia P. Fleming

L. I. Fleming Jr.
Edward Fleming
Theodora Fleming

Charles Seton Fleming
(1839–1864)
Francis Philip Fleming m. Floride L. Pearson
(1841–1908)   (1843–1932)
Frederic A. Fleming m. Margaret P. Baldwin
(1845–1917)   (1862–1921)
William Henry Fleming
(1847–1922)
Matilda Fleming m. Murdoch M
(1849–1922)
Margaret Seton Fleming
(1852–1877)
Isabelle Fleming m. Edward Sudlow
(1855–1934)

Francis P. Fleming Jr.
Charles Seton Fleming
Florida L. Fleming
Margaret Seton Fleming
Peyre G. Fleming

Margaret Fleming (1888–1980)
Augusta Fleming (1889–1975)
Frederic A. Fleming Jr. (1893–1945)
Dorothy B. Fleming (1899–1988)

Mary Jane Fleming
(1800–1856)
m. Solomon Halliday
(1806–1889)

George Philip Fleming
(1803–1851)
m. Mary Gibson
(1810–1887)

Mary Sophia Fleming m. Davis Floyd
(1827–1858)   (1822–1891)

A Partial Fatio Family Tree

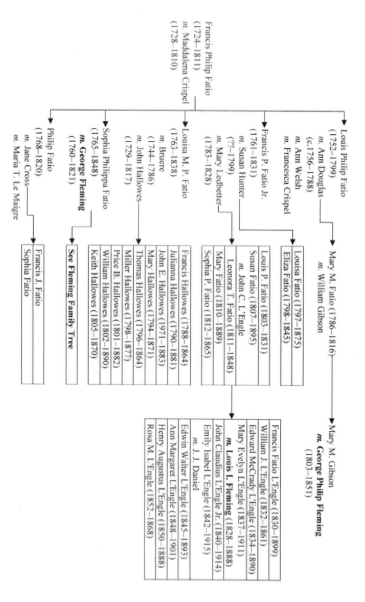

Francis Philip Fatio
(1724–1811)
m. Maddalena Crispel
(1728–1810)

- Louis Philip Fatio (1752–1799)
  m. Ann Douglas (c.1756–1788)
  m. Ann Welsh
  m. Francesca Crispel

- Mary M. Fatio (1786–1816) — m. William Gibson → Mary M. Gibson **m. George Philip Fleming** (1803–1851)

- Francis P. Fatio Jr. (1761–1831)
  m. Susan Hunter (??–1799)
  m. Mary Ledbetter (1783–1828)

- Louisa M. P. Fatio (1763–1838)
  m. Bruere (1744–1786)
  m. John Hallowes (1729–1817)

- Sophia Philippa Fatio (1765–1848)
  m. George Fleming (1760–1821)

- Philip Fatio (1768–1820)
  m. Jane Cross
  m. Maria T. Le Maigre

Louisa Fatio (1797–1875)
Eliza Fatio (1798–1845)

Louis P. Fatio (1803–1831)
Susan Fatio (1807–1895) m. John C. L'Engle
Leonora T. Fatio (1811–1848)
Mary Fatio (1810–1889)
Sophia P. Fatio (1812–1865)

Francis Hallowes (1788–1864)
Julianna Hallowes (1790–1881)
John E. Hallowes (1791–1883)
Mary Hallowes (1794–1871)
Thomas Hallowes (1796–1864)
Miller Hallowes (1798–1877)
Price B. Hallowes (1801–1882)
William Hallowes (1802–1890)
Keith Hallowes (1805–1870)

See Fleming Family Tree

Francis J. Fatio
Sophia Fatio

Francis Fatio L'Engle (1830–1899)
William J. L'Engle (1832–1861)
Edward McCrady L'Engle (1834–1890)
Mary Evelyn L'Engle (1837–1911)
m. Louis I. Fleming (1828–1888)
John Claudius L'Engle Jr. (1840–1914)
Emily Isabel L'Engle (1842–1915)
m. J. J. Daniel
Edwin Walter L'Engle (1845–1893)
Ann Margaret L'Engle (1848–1901)
Henry Augustus L'Engle (1850–1888)
Rosa M. L'Engle (1852–1868)

Note: The purpose of this Fatio family tree is to provide clarity to important interfamily relationships mentioned in the manuscript. Many valued and distinguished Fatio descendants have been omitted due to limitations of the printed page.

Prologue

Fleming Island is located in Clay County, Florida, about twenty miles south of downtown Jacksonville. The island is roughly six miles long and three miles wide, about ten thousand acres altogether. At the southern end of the island, dark, deep water from Black Creek empties into the broad St. Johns River, which flows gently northward along its eastern banks. Doctors Lake, a large cove off the river, rims the northern tip of the island and much of its serpentine western shoreline. The remaining watery boundary of Fleming Island consists of a swamp spanning slightly less than a mile between Black Creek and Swimming Pen Creek. During extremely high tides it is possible to circumnavigate the island in a canoe or kayak; the dense swamp prevents the passage of anything larger. Fleming Island is named for George Fleming, an Irish merchant who arrived in Spanish East Florida in 1783. Seventeen years later, Captain George Fleming received a Spanish Land Grant of one thousand acres on the southeastern end of what would become Fleming Island, where he nurtured a profitable plantation that he named Hibernia in honor of his Irish homeland. For more than two hundred years Hibernia has been home to Captain Fleming's descendants, extending seven generations. Among these descendants are Southern planters, soldiers, and statesmen, including Francis Philip Fleming, the fifteenth governor of Florida. His children and grandchildren tenaciously defended Hibernia through periods of unrest and uncertainty, including the transfer of Florida from Spain to the United States, the Second Seminole War, and the Civil War. The family could not make a living as traditional Southern planters after the Second Seminole War, so the Flemings transformed Hibernia into a winter hotel that became a well-known destination in the early days of Florida tourism and into the twentieth century.

I was linked forever to the Flemings of Fleming Island when I married my wife, Margot, one of Captain George Fleming's many great-great-great-grandchildren. On our honeymoon we made a detour through

North Florida to visit Hibernia. My mother-in-law, Marian Fleming, told us that someday, if we wanted, we could rent the house she still owned there. The place went by the name of Holly Cottage. It was once a part of the Fleming family's winter hotel business, but had been a rental property for over thirty years. Driving down the tree-canopied sand road leading to the house in June 1978, we were struck by three things. One, the heat and humidity were oppressive. Two, the house looked old, dilapidated, and isolated. Three, despite one and two, the setting was absolutely breathtaking. Situated on a bluff on the west bank of the St. Johns River, Holly Cottage was surrounded by massive live oaks, magnolias, water oaks, and pines. Towering cypress trees lined the banks of the river. Hauntingly beautiful Spanish moss hung from almost every tree, swaying gently with the breeze off the river. The river itself is a mile and a half wide, and the views to the southeast extend much farther. Inside, Holly Cottage was dark and dank. The current renters kept the place reasonably clean, but there was no air-conditioning and lots of mildew. The deep porches and heavy tree cover almost blocked out the sun. This place needed a lot of work, so we initially rejected the idea of living there. One year later, after a bitterly cold winter in Colorado, we moved in.

Fast-forward fourteen years, four kids, two dogs, one major renovation, and countless remodeling projects, and we loved Holly Cottage. I came to appreciate the history of Hibernia, the small community where we lived and raised our young children. During those years I met a man named Robert Jones, Historic Sites Specialist for the Florida Department of State, Division of Historic Resources. After a lengthy discussion about Hibernia, and more specifically about my curiosity regarding the history of Holly Cottage, Mr. Jones encouraged me to learn more and to write an application to have Holly Cottage listed on the National Register of Historic Places. Oddly, even though Holly Cottage was a part of Fleming family history, no one knew who had built it. I dabbled into obvious resources in search of information, but nothing published or easily located gave an answer, and the idea languished for several years.

Life took unexpected turns and my family moved to Austin, Texas. Holly Cottage became a rental property once again, but despite the distance, I made a commitment to complete the application to the National Register of Historic Places. My mother-in-law gave me several file boxes of family documents she had saved over the years; this treasure trove of information led me to archival collections at universities, historical societies, the Library of Congress, and the National Archives.

I felt the excitement of historical research using primary documents—the pure thrill of discovering long-lost information that no one else knows. I also endured countless frustrating hours in search of specific information or resources, but finding nothing whatsoever.

After several years of part-time research while teaching in the College of Education at the University of Texas at Austin, I managed to cobble together a history of Holly Cottage. At every major step along the way I shared the story with Robert Jones, who provided invaluable moral support and editorial assistance. I submitted the extensive application early in 2010. Just a few months later, Holly Cottage was listed on the National Register of Historic Places—the only such residence on Fleming Island. It would seem I had completed my project and reached the end of the road, but it was just the beginning. To place Holly Cottage in its historical context, I had learned a great deal about the Flemings of Fleming Island. Their stories harkened back to my childhood fascination with the eighteenth and nineteenth centuries in American history, and Hibernia became my conduit to investigate those times. Now I'm ready to share the stories I've learned. This has been a deeply personal journey—an exciting romp through over two hundred years of history. It all begins with George Fleming.

Before sharing my journey with you, I would like to explain some decisions I made in the course of writing this book. Perhaps the most difficult decision was how to handle the words I used to reference people of African origin or descent in particular historical contexts. Based on books written by scholars who have dedicated much of their careers to the history of East Florida during the Second Spanish Period, I chose to refer to persons of African heritage as "Negroes," primarily because this is the nomenclature of the era, and in this historical context it is in no way an insult or a demeaning term. Moreover, calling these people "African American" during the Second Spanish Period is entirely inaccurate. They were of African heritage, for certain, but they most definitely were not Americans. If they claimed any nationality, it could only be as Spanish subjects, and they were treated as such in East Florida, regardless of their status as slaves or free men and women. I made the decision to adhere to this terminology until after Emancipation, when these men and women were finally given legal status as Americans, albeit still living under the oppressive yoke of injustice and racial prejudice.

Similarly, I chose to refer to persons of mixed race as "mulattos." Historically, this term was applied to anyone who carried even a small fraction of African DNA. In fact, a mulatto man or woman could, for all practical purposes, appear in every way to be white, but he or she was still subject to the same oppressive laws and prejudices as anyone with dark skin.

My decision regarding how to reference native people was much the same. To keep terms in their historical context, I chose to refer to them as "Indians."

I had to make a decision regarding Christian names for the Flemings during the Second Spanish Period. It is difficult for some people to keep in mind that, after the Revolutionary War, Florida was not a state nor even a territory of the United States—it was a part of the Spanish realm. George Fleming was not known as "George" in East Florida; his name was *Jorge*. He and his wife, Sophia Fatio, baptized their children with the names *Luis Miguel, Maria Juana Magdalena,* and *Jorge Philipe*, but after East Florida became a U.S. Territory, they all reverted to the Anglo spellings: Lewis, Mary, and George. For the sake of consistency, I have used only Anglo spellings for Fleming family members.

Finally, the Fleming family includes individuals from three generations who share the first name "George." "George Fleming" could refer to the original George who came to East Florida from Ireland. It also could refer to his son, George Philip Fleming, or his grandson, George Claudius Fleming. The family called the grandson "George C." which sets him apart in the manuscript. To differentiate between George Fleming, the father, and George Philip Fleming, the son, I have chosen to refer to them respectively as "George" and "George Jr."

An Introduction to George Fleming
and His Descendants

George Fleming was an Irishman. This we know with absolute certainty, but we know little of his ancestry or his life before he arrived in Spanish East Florida. Catholic parish records in St. Augustine prove that his parents were Thomas Fleming and Mary Walsh of Dublin, who gave birth to their son in 1760 or 1761. Beyond that, attempts to locate records of Fleming's birth or his Irish family are frustrating. Marian Fleming, one of George Fleming's great-great-granddaughters, dedicated many unsuccessful days in Dublin looking for birth records, emigration records, or other information to trace his roots. After returning home she hired a researcher in Dublin to continue that quest. Between the professional help and my mother-in-law's plucky determination, we know something of George's origins: his father, Thomas Fleming, was a salesmaster in Dublin who owned and operated an inn or a tavern in the Smithfield district known as the Pyde Bull. His business may have included the cattle trade, as well—you will read that George Fleming became a cattleman himself. Mary Walsh was the daughter of John Walsh, a farmer from Kilpedder in County Wicklow. Thomas Fleming and Mary Walsh's marriage contract is dated January 23, 1748, and was recorded in June of 1749. To date, searches of existing birth records from every Catholic parish surrounding the Smithfield district have failed to identify any births or baptisms for children of this couple. Nevertheless, all indications are that this Thomas Fleming and Mary Walsh are, in fact, George's parents, and that he had two older brothers, Thomas and Michael, who remained in Ireland after George emigrated to the New World.[1]

George Fleming's niece, Susan Fatio L'Engle, committed her memories and family history to print late in life. L'Engle tells us that George received a mercantile education, emigrated to America while "quite a young man," and went to work for the Charleston, South Carolina, firm of Napier, Rapelye, & Bennet, a factorage firm dealing in cotton, rice, and other commodities. It would seem rash for a family from the British Isles to ship a teenage son to the rebellious colonies during the Revolutionary War, so it is reasonable to guess that Fleming arrived sometime after the Battle of Charleston in 1780, which resulted in British control of the city. We know for certain that George was in Charleston by early 1783, when he would have been about twenty-two years old. If he arrived in Charleston ready for work then he must have received his mercantile education in Ireland prior to emigrating, which is logical since Thomas Fleming, the salesmaster, was his father and would have prepared him for business. Maybe Thomas Fleming arranged his son's placement at the firm of Napier, Rapelye, & Bennet, and it is likely that another Fleming relative already living in Florida influenced that company's decisions regarding their young employee.

George Fleming traveled to St. Augustine for his firm "after the peace was made, not to reside but to trade with the Spaniards." He arrived in Florida sometime before the 1783 Spanish Census of British Residents in East Florida, which reveals that Fleming was Roman Catholic, a bachelor, and lived on Charlotte Street along with a white servant from his firm.[2] George Fleming had the advantage of a prominent relative in St. Augustine, Charles "Carlos" Howard, who had served the Spanish military for over twenty years and was captain of the Hibernia Regiment. Vicente Manuel de Zéspedes, first governor of East Florida during the Second Spanish Period, relied on Howard because of his extensive military experience, his ability to conduct covert operations and negotiations, and his talent with the French, Spanish, and English languages. Howard became extremely influential during the transfer of power from England to Spain. Without doubt, Howard was in a position to recommend Fleming to conduct business in St. Augustine.[3]

With the exception of these few facts and conjectures, George Fleming's story begins in St. Augustine, Spanish East Florida, in 1784. In his lifetime Fleming rose from a young merchant peddling textiles to private interests and an impoverished government to become a representative and son-in-law of one of the wealthiest and most influential men in all of East Florida. He swore allegiance to the Spanish Crown, attained the rank of captain in the Spanish Urban Militia, and served as a top city official in St. Augustine for many years. His business interests included cattle, timber, planting, and personal representation for citizens of all walks of life in East Florida. In military service he helped defend the province from hostile Indians and insurgencies by foreign powers, even placing himself between friends and business associates who led attacks on Spanish Florida. In his lifetime he received nearly twenty-two thousand acres in Spanish Land Grants for his service to the Crown.

In honor of his homeland, he named one land grant "Hibernia." Hibernia is located on an island along the west side of the St. Johns River about twenty miles south of Jacksonville, Florida. Because of George Fleming, that island became known as Fleming's Island and today is known simply as Fleming Island. Hibernia became home to George's children and his grandchildren, and in the course of over two hundred years, seven generations of the Fleming family have called it home. Among his descendants are Southern planters, soldiers, and statesmen—most notably Francis Philip Fleming, the fifteenth governor of Florida. Family members tenaciously defended their home through turbulent times and economic uncertainty, including during the transfer of Florida from Spain to the United States, the Second Seminole War, the Civil War, and Reconstruction. Fleming's sons, Lewis and George Jr., fought in the Second Seminole War. His four grandsons enlisted with Florida's Confederate armies and saw action in many of the most well-known battles, including Manassas, Gettysburg, Olustee, and Cold Harbor. After the Second Seminole War, the Flemings's only source of income—unreliable cash crops—could not sustain the family, so Lewis Fleming and his wife, Margaret Seton, transformed Hibernia into a winter hotel that became a celebrated destination in the early days of Florida tourism and into the twentieth century. Today Hibernia is a small residential enclave where a few remnants of the Fleming family's rich history still stand to remind us of days gone by.

There are no surviving images or descriptions of George Fleming. Some speculate that he might have had red hair because several of his ancestors share that Irish characteristic. The only personal remnant we have is his signature.

Endnotes

1. Registry of Deeds-Kings Inn, Dublin, Ireland, Deed #91350, January 23, 1748, Marriage contract, Fleming to Walsh, and Deed #525.186.344264, March 14, 1800, Fleming to Fleming. George Fleming used the names Thomas or Michael for his first three children (two of whom died as infants).

2. Grace H. Jarvis, A Spanish Census of Florida in 1783 (Jacksonville, Florida, n.d.).

3. East Florida Papers, reel 85, section 25, (hereafter cited as *EFP* and in the following format: Reel number/section number), Howard to O'Fallon, reel 85, November 20, 1788. Howard stated that Fleming is a relative but gave no further details of the relationship. One historian wrote that Howard was Fleming's uncle without offering a source, but I have been unable to find any evidence to confirm that relationship.

Maps of Fleming Family Land and Residences

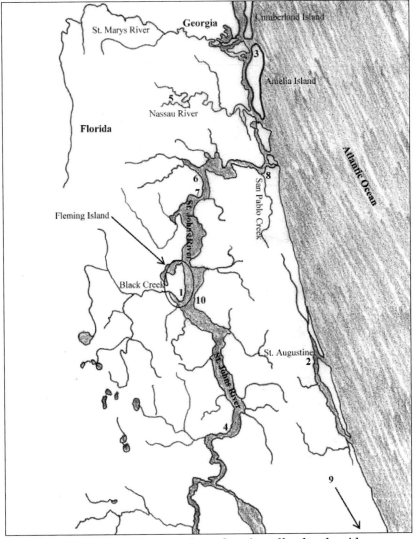

This map indicates the approximate location of land and residences associated with the Flemings of Fleming Island. The key is on the following page. Map by the author.

Fleming Family Lands and Residences

1. Hibernia: George Fleming's 1,000-acre plantation and location of Fleming family homes for more than 200 years.

2. St. Augustine: Location of George and Sophia Fleming's first home, which they kept throughout their lives together.

3. Old Town Fernandina: Land Grant of Block 7, Lot 7, where George and Sophia lived after the Patriot War of 1812–1813.

4. Langley Bryan: George Fleming's 900-acre land grant.

5. Nassau River Grant: F. P. Fatio Sr.'s 10,000-acre grant. Sophia Fleming inherited half this land after her father's death.

6. Panama Mills: Residence of Lewis and Margaret Fleming from approximately 1839 to 1845. Birthplace of Charles Seton Fleming and Francis Fleming.

7. Jacksonville: Sophia, Mary, L. I., and Francis Fleming all owned homes and lived here during their lives.

8. San Pablo Creek: Location of George Fleming's New Hope Plantation, where he and his brother-in-law, F. P. Fatio Jr., planted cash crops. His family frequently resided here from about 1816 until 1821. This is where Fleming died.

9. San Sebastian: George Fleming's 20,000-acre land grant was located approximately 165 miles south of St. Augustine and encompassed both sides of the mouth of the Sebastian River.

10. New Switzerland: F. P. Fatio's plantation where members of the Fleming family frequently visited until its destruction during the Patriot War. F. P. Fatio Jr. rebuilt New Switzerland at the same time Lewis and George Fleming Jr. rebuilt Hibernia. New Switzerland was destroyed forever during the Second Seminole War.

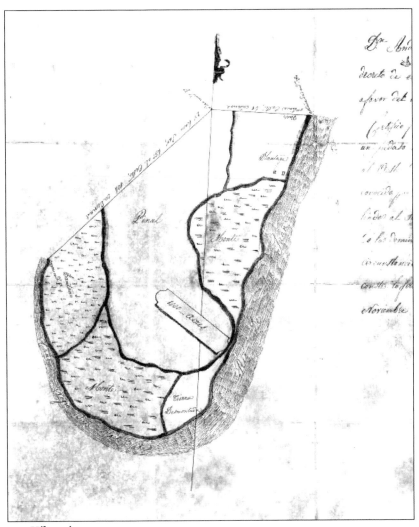

Hibernia

George Fleming's 1,000-acre Spanish Land Grant became the cherished family home. Note the "plantage" (plantation) at the top right, the "tierra desmontada" (cleared land) at the bottom right, the "monte" (hammocks), and "pinal" (pine forests). Map courtesy of State Archives of Florida.

St. Augustine

On July 9, 1784, George Fleming purchased a house (circled) in St. Augustine from his brother-in-law, Luis Fatio. His heirs retained ownership of this home until 1824. The central plaza dominated the center of the town on the Matanzas River. This is just a portion of the 1788 map of St. Augustine known as the "Rocque map." Copy in possession of the author.

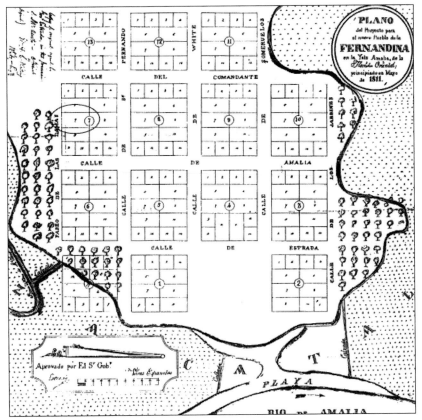

Old Town Fernandina

In 1811 Governor Juan José de Estrada granted George Fleming lot seven, square seven, (circled) in "Old Town" Fernandina, which is located north of present-day Fernandina on Amelia Island. Fleming arranged construction of a home, and this is where his family lived in the aftermath of the 1812–1813 Patriot War. Lewis Fleming's future wife, Margaret Seton, lived on square five. *MWF Collection.*

Scott Ritchie

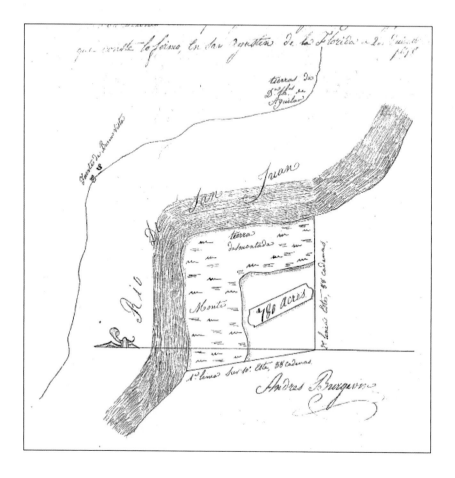

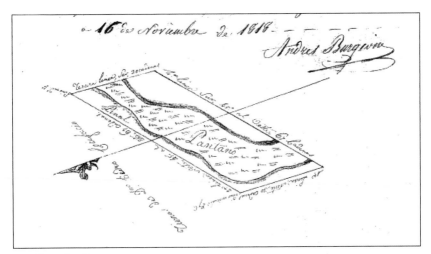

Langley Bryan

George Fleming's Spanish Land Grant north of present-day Palatka consisted of two separate tracts of land: 780 acres along the St. Johns River across from Fort Buena Vista and 200 acres in Coco Swamp. Maps courtesy of State Archives of Florida.

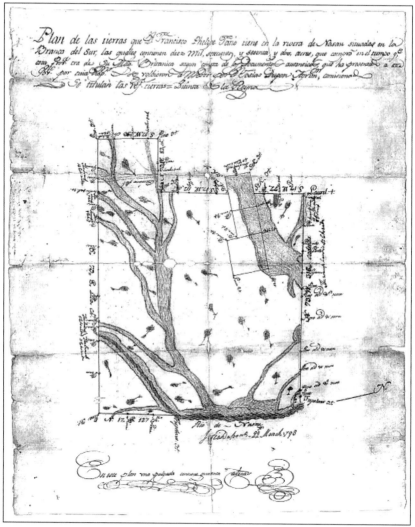

Nassau River

After her father died, Sophia Fleming inherited half of this 10,000-acre tract along the south branch of Nassau River. This was rich timberland where George Fleming and his sons harvested live oak and pine. Map courtesy of State Archives of Florida.

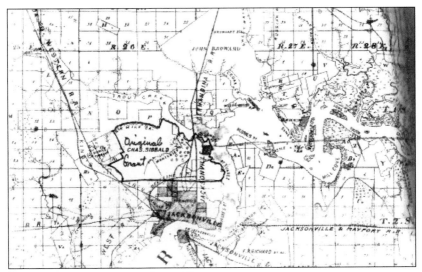

Panama Mills and Jacksonville

Historian Dena Snodgrass used this 1884 map of Duval County to show the location of Panama Mills within Chas. Sibbald's Spanish land grant north of Jacksonville at Sandy Point (the darkly shaded area at the top right of his grant). Fleming family members lived at Panama Mills and in Jacksonville. *MWF Collection.*

Scott Ritchie

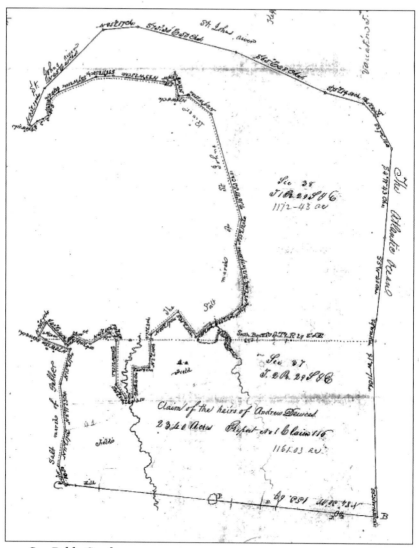

San Pablo Creek

Andrew Dewees received this 2,340-acre Spanish Land Grant. In
1816 he leased it to Sophia Fleming's brother, F. P. Fatio Jr. This
is where George Fleming established his New Hope plantation.
The grant was bounded on the west by San Pablo Creek and salt
marshes, on the north by the St. Johns River, and on the east by
the Atlantic Ocean. This tract of land encompasses most of present-
day Mayport and the Mayport Naval Station. The fields and houses
shown may indicate the location of New Hope. Map courtesy of
State Archives of Florida.

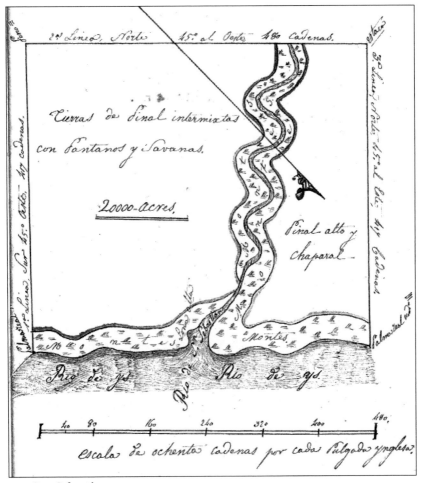

San Sebastian

George Fleming's largest Spanish Land Grant was a 20,000-acre tract located at the mouth of the San Sebastian River along the Indian River. There is no record to tell us if Fleming or his sons ever planted crops or harvested natural resources here. Map courtesy of State Archives of Florida.

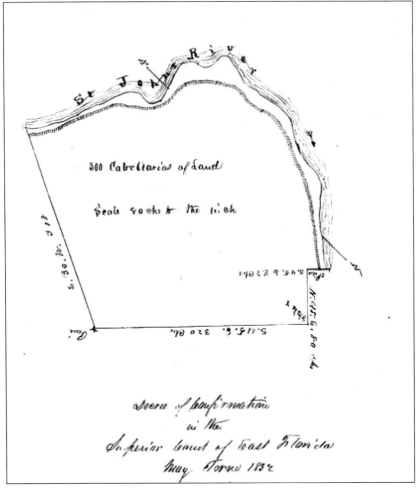

New Switzerland

This unimpressive map of F. P. Fatio's 10,000-acre New Switzerland plantation, which was located directly across the St. Johns River from Hibernia, does not do justice to his vast swath of land abundant in natural resources. Map courtesy of State Archives of Florida.

George Fleming in Spanish East Florida

During the American Revolution, Florida was the only European territory south of Canada that remained loyal to the King of England. As the colonists gradually repelled British forces, some five thousand white British loyalists, along with about eight thousand Negroes, some free but most enslaved, fled northern colonies for St. Augustine in the province known as East Florida. This mass influx fell on an ill-prepared British government and infrastructure. The population of East Florida reached its zenith in 1783 when the British signed both the Treaty of Paris, which officially ended the American Revolution, and the Treaty of Versailles, which returned East Florida to Spanish rule. British loyalists were given eighteen months to depart or swear allegiance to the King of Spain. George Fleming arrived in time to view a mass exodus of British citizens, but, like a handful of other Englishmen, he chose to take advantage of an eighteen-month window and conduct business as the Spanish government struggled to re-establish dominion in East Florida.[1]

Fleming and a white servant assigned by his firm traveled to St. Augustine by ship, carrying with them a cargo of textiles. As he crossed the shallow sandbar at the mouth of the Matanzas River, framed by the shifting white sand beaches of barrier islands on both sides, the imposing Castillo de San Marcos loomed ahead, standing guard over the small riverfront town. Fleming transferred his cargo to the customs house upon arriving, where Spanish officials subjected it to a meticulous inventory. Perhaps his firm had made advance arrangements for his arrival; perhaps not. If not, he had to take the initiative to clear customs, store his cargo, and find lodging for himself and his servant. One way or another, he eventually made his way north of the central city plaza along Carlotta Street to his first Florida home, just a short distance from the Castillo—so close to the river that he could smell low tides, taste the salt air, and feel the sea breeze. Nearly two years pass before he appears in any historical record other than the Spanish census.[2]

Shortly after dark on January 24, 1785, the sound of musket shots ringing clearly across the Matanzas River from the plantation of Jesse Fish on Anastasia Island startled residents of St. Augustine. The gunfire ended abruptly. Soon those near the river heard voices and splashing of oars as boats rowed the short distance to town. Servants from the Fish estate, one of the largest in East Florida, had successfully fended off a pirate attack. The four-man crew of the pirate schooner *Escape* had anchored their ship in an isolated cove shortly after dark. Armed with just two muskets, one pistol, and an old cutlass, they approached the Fish dwellings on foot. The pirates made off with a small quantity of household goods and with Fish's men in pursuit. As they neared the ship, Fish's men fired away and mortally wounded one of the pirates, Thomas Bell. They carried Bell across the river to the guardhouse, where they placed him in the stocks. Francis Philip Fatio was summoned to take Bell's statement. Along the way Fatio selected George Fleming and two others as witnesses. Entering the dimly lit guardhouse they saw Bell confined in the stocks with gaping musket ball holes torn through his side and back. Fleming listened while Bell, bleeding and dying, answered Fatio's questions and confessed his part in the attack.[3] Bell died two hours later. The next day Spanish authorities displayed his body on the gallows, where he would have been hanged if he had survived long enough, as a reminder of the penalty for acts of piracy.

In little more than a year, George Fleming had developed a solid relationship with the man who took Bell's confession, Francis Philip Fatio, one of the most influential men in East Florida. Fatio built a small empire under British rule and chose to remain in Florida after the transfer of power to Spain. He is perhaps best known for his ten-thousand-acre plantation, New Switzerland, that was located on the eastern shore of the St. Johns River about a twenty-mile journey from St. Augustine.[4] Fleming took a particularly active role in Fatio's cattle contracts with the Spanish government. Fresh meat was healthier and, of course, better tasting than salt meat. Feeding the troops and government officials required over four hundred pounds of meat every day, a little less than two head of cattle. At this time sellers in Georgia provided the most reliable source of live cattle. Drovers in teams of three men, usually one on horseback and two on foot, could drive up to one hundred head at a time to the border region for sale to East Florida buyers. A select few influential East Floridians sent their representatives to negotiate purchases and to transport the livestock back to St. Augustine. The profit margins were fatter than the free-ranging cattle, and Fatio was one of just three businessmen holding a special license granting permission for foreign commerce; he once reaped a 250 percent return on a cattle contract with the Spanish government.[5] George Fleming often represented Fatio's business interests in Georgia, and in the summer of 1785 he executed a contract to bring fresh beef for Spanish troops at Castillo de San Marcos and the hospital in St. Augustine. He traveled to Cumberland Island, inspected the cattle, negotiated the purchase, and made arrangements to load the cattle onto a ship for transport to St. Augustine. The trip was not as easy as it might sound.

On July 19, 1785, Fleming left St. Augustine aboard a small ship bound for the crude fort at San Juan. He arrived fourteen days later by way of a mail canoe. This was an unusually long period of time for the approximately sixty-mile trip, but there is no explanation on record for the delay. Fleming carried a letter from Governor Zespédes to the sergeant of the outpost, Antonio Delgado, directing him to "give the distinguished Englishman Mr. Jorge Fleming" anything he might need to reach Amelia Island as soon as possible. Delgado immediately dispatched a small boat to carry Fleming to St. Marys, Georgia. From there Fleming made his way to Amelia Island which, at that time, was a nearly deserted island with only a small military outpost. On August 8th Martin Armassa, commander of the Amelia outpost, gave Fleming a canoe. Fleming assured Armassa that he would have thirty-eight or forty head of cattle ready to board a ship in four days at the latest. Setting off in the canoe, Fleming and his companion plied the currents near the mouth of the St. Marys River to the shores of Cumberland Island.

Within hours of his arrival at Cumberland, Fleming contracted a violent fever and became too ill to carry on. Two days later Armassa received word the illness was passing and that Fleming would get on with his business the next day. One week later, on the night of August 15, Fleming's companion returned to Amelia. He told Armassa that Fleming had managed to get the cattle to Ft. San Nicholas on the St. Johns River for loading aboard a ship, but that Fleming himself was on Cumberland Island and still suffering from a debilitating fever. The tenor of Fleming's message to Armassa creates an image of a man fearful for his life, and most certainly unable to do his work.

At Fleming's request, Armassa crossed over to Cumberland to speak with him on August 27. Still with fever though apparently recovering,

Fleming begged for transport to the militia outpost at San Juan. He had been ill for nearly three weeks, with no doctor and little care in the oppressive August heat. Armassa empathized because he, too, had recently survived serious illness, and ordered the pilot of a small mail boat to take Fleming to the outpost "with all due urgency."

The mail boat made its way to St. Marys, where Fleming boarded the ship *Santa Maria* bound for the outpost at San Juan. Arriving there on the 30th of August, Fleming implored Delgado to delay the ship's departure to St. Augustine one more day on account of his fever. The *Santa Maria* set sail the next morning, experienced favorable winds and tides, and arrived in St. Augustine that evening. All told, it took Fleming nearly a month and a half to fill the contract. Despite the delays, the governor was grateful to Fleming for his service.[6]

It is unclear when Fleming left his Charleston firm to work primarily for Francis Philip Fatio and to pursue his own business interests. His last known transaction involving the firm was in September of 1785. Guillermo O'Kelly, commander of the militia in St. Augustine, needed clothing for his troops, and Fleming said he could fill that need through Charleston.[7] Beyond that, no evidence even hints at continued employment with the firm. Soon all of his business dealings were either as an agent for Fatio or were his own independent ventures.

In March of 1786 Fleming traveled to St. Marys, Georgia, on one of Fatio's sailing ships, accompanied by some of Fatio's slaves. The particular business is unspecified, but less than two weeks later, in St. Augustine, Fleming brokered the sale of a slave from the Carolinas to Juan Bautista Paredes.[8]

Fleming owned a house in St. Augustine by this time, but it was in rough condition and he may never have lived there. In September of 1786 he was making plans to raze the building when the Spanish government, in need of housing for troops and supplies, took an interest in it. Fleming considered the house unfit for habitation, but it suited the militia's needs. Governor Zéspedes directed Commander Engineer Mariano de la Rocque to evaluate the structure. It was thirty feet long, nineteen feet wide, and eight feet tall, and definitely required some repairs. Zéspedes pushed forward with the transaction, sending someone to Cumberland, where Fleming had traveled on business once again, to get the key to the house.[9]

Blinded by Cupid

George Fleming came to East Florida to conduct business—not to make it his home—but by December of 1786 he had cemented his relationship with the Fatio family and was living in their house.[10] One might wonder about the relationship between Fleming's living arrangement and his obvious feelings for Fatio's daughter, Sophia, who was six years his junior. Sophia Fatio was born in London in 1766 and came to British East Florida with her family in 1771, where she would live the rest of her life. She was a "woman of remarkable intelligence and memory," with the dark eyes of her Italian mother, and was educated at home by her parents.[11]

As George and Sophia's relationship blossomed, Carlos Howard urged his younger relative not to marry her, and repeatedly tried to convince him to leave the struggling province of East Florida. Like a proud father, Howard described Fleming as a "young man of healthy principles and respectable conduct," and believed Fleming could build a better life elsewhere. Howard was disappointed, though, because "Cupid wounded [Fleming] with the eyes of Miss Fatio." Howard had nothing against young Sophia, but never liked her father and did not approve of Fleming's association with Fatio. According to Howard, Fatio was "caught up in his own importance" and "if he had the command of a village, the village would be miserable." Finally, despite his lack of respect for Fatio, Howard accepted the relationship and celebrated the pending marriage, "having found that love was more powerful than [his] arguments."[12]

Before George Fleming and Sophia Fatio were married, her parents executed ten pages of legal documents outlining the terms of her dowry. Immediately after the marriage George would receive 4,445 pesos, the equivalent of 1,000 English pounds, paid in hard silver. After two years of marriage Fleming would receive another one thousand pounds silver, along with "other goods," including at least fifteen slaves.[13] Simply for marrying the woman he loved, Fleming received a sum in silver greater than the annual salary of the governor of East Florida, and owned enough slaves to make him a man of means.

Don Jorge Fleming and Dona Sophia Philipina Maria Fatio wed on October 6, 1788. The Catholic bishop in charge of the Diocese of East and West Florida was visiting in St. Augustine at the time, and presided over the service in his private reception room. Other officiates were Don Thomas Hassett, presiding pastor; his assistant, Don Michael O'Reilly; and the priest, Don Pedro Camps.[14] One historian called it "easily the most important wedding of the year," and it surely was the most important event of the year for George Fleming.[15] In the years to come his wife gave him three healthy children, and his personal and economic fortune multiplied.

Sophia Fleming gave birth to five children, three of whom survived to maturity. The joyous occasion of her first child, Thomas Francisco Fleming, on November 27, 1793, was quickly followed by the heartache of his death two months later. Sophia gave birth to her second son on October 23, 1796. He was baptized with the same name as her first son and lived only a little longer. Infant mortality was common at the time, but that would have done little to ease Sophia's pain when her second Thomas died at seven months old. Imagine her combination of hope and trepidation upon the birth of her third son, Lewis Michael Fleming, on May 29, 1798. Next came Sophia's only daughter, Mary Magdalena Jane Fleming, born Mary 27, 1800, who also lived, as did Sophia's youngest child, George Philip Fleming, who was born November 12, 1803.[16] Thankfully, Lewis, Mary, and George lived full lives.

All evidence indicates that the newlyweds continued to live in the Fatio home for the first several years of their marriage. George Fleming was constantly on the move, traveling between St. Augustine, the borderland along the St. Marys River, and Fatio's New Switzerland plantation on the eastern shores of the St. Johns River. It must have been a great comfort to the Fatios that their daughter lived safely with them, bearing the sorrows and the joys of childbirth, while her husband traveled back and forth tending to the family businesses. Sophia Fleming's niece, Susan Fatio L'Engle, wrote that Sophia lived with her parents until their deaths—nearly twenty-three years altogether.[17] She may not have lived in her parents' house all those years, though, because in 1794 George Fleming purchased a house located just one block from the Fatio home.[18] The seller was his brother-in-law, Louis Fatio, who had moved to the Kingdom of Sardinia in 1792 to manage his father's estate there, and never returned to Florida. The house was made of stone and wood, with enclosed living spaces and open-air porches. A few years later, another brother-in-law, F. P. Fatio Jr., purchased the house directly across narrow Charlotte Street from the Fleming home. This gave the extended Fatio family control over prime real estate adjacent to the town plaza. It is reasonable to conclude that George and Sophia lived in their own house, but that Sophia and the children stayed with her parents when her husband was gone on business. St. Augustine was their primary residence, but, like every member of the extended Fatio clan, George and Sophia occasionally stayed at New Switzerland plantation.

F. P. Fatio's business interests were diverse—far too much for one man to manage—so he relied on his sons to handle different aspects of the family business. Louis Fatio tended to business in Italy, while Philip Fatio served the Spanish diplomatic service in New Orleans, where he was in a position to represent the family through his many contacts. With his two oldest sons away from East Florida, Fatio appealed to his third son, F. P. Fatio Jr., to give up his commission as captain with the British Army and move to Florida to serve the family's interests. Fatio's three intelligent and ambitious sons were a great advantage to the family. As for George Fleming, the historian Susan Parker wrote that Fatio enjoyed an "additional stroke of fortune [through] the acquisition of a competent son-in-law."[19] It seems that Fleming was involved in every aspect of the family's business in East Florida. The Fatios and Fleming traded in all sorts of commodities, including spirits, as evidenced by a shipment of wine and brandy aboard the schooner *Mary of Boston* bound for New York in 1799. Fatio and Fleming deemed the spirits—sixty pipes of cognac and three hundred cases of wine—"not a fit article for our place" so they sold it in New York. Put into perspective, that was about 7,400 gallons of brandy, valued at $6,000, and 7,200 bottles of wine, valued at $1,500.[20] The bulk of their business, though, was based on the natural resources of Florida: turpentine, timber, cattle, and agriculture at New Switzerland plantation.

On October 20, 1792, Fleming was with F. P. Fatio Sr. at New Switzerland. Early that morning a group of Negroes found a well-known Indian named Poncho Francisco dead beside a trail on their way to work in the fields. Upon receiving this news, Fatio sent George Fleming and others from the plantation house to investigate. Someone obviously had crushed the man's skull, so they gathered a small group of Indians camping nearby and ushered them to Fatio's house for questioning. Fatio asked an elder among the group what reason someone could have for killing "the poor old Indian Francisco." The elder, who was well known around St. Augustine, replied that two young Indian brothers among his group had killed Francisco, and they were confident the killing was necessary and justified. Francisco had to die, they said, because he was a witch. Just days ago Francisco had given another man some medicine while on a hunt; that man soon vomited blood and died. Later, Francisco bewitched the brothers, causing the fever they currently suffered. Apparently, killing the old witch was the only way to break the spell.[21]

Appointment as Captain of the Urban Militia and Regidor

In September of 1790, Governor Juan Nepomuceno de Quesada formed three urban militia companies and appointed George Fleming, Bernardo Segui, and Miguel Ysnardy as captains. Fleming, who had recently sworn allegiance to Spain, became captain of the Irish militia. His brother-in-law, F. P. Fatio Jr., was his second in command.[22] The urban militia captains also held the title of regidor, and for the next sixteen years they tended to civil and administrative matters related to the governance of St. Augustine.[23] Among other duties, they filed routine quarterly reports of income and expenditures for the town. Regular sources of income included store fees, wharf fees, milk cow fees, pool table licenses, tavern fees, and occasional fines levied against individuals for unspecified offenses. Expenditures for public projects included the purchase of land and construction of a Catholic Church,[24] construction of a bridge,[25] military fortification,[26] and construction and maintenance of a town wharf. Fleming was in charge of finances for wharf construction. His account of the project includes a detailed list of expenses for rental equipment, the names of free Negroes and skilled craftsmen who did much of the work, and the amounts each was paid.[27] It was an ongoing project, requiring regular maintenance and additional construction. A few years later, Fleming managed finances for another project for the wharf, but this one became contentious, with fellow regidores Segui and Ysnardy criticizing Fleming's accounting. In response, Fleming laid blame on the project designers, complaining that it was poorly conceived and poorly planned from the start.[28] Despite the infighting, the project was completed.

The regidores also mediated or settled disagreements between residents and the government. They intervened when town bakers complained about the government's fixed price for bread,[29] and on behalf of citizens about misconduct by fugitive slaves from the United States who had taken refuge in St. Augustine.[30] They held proceedings to address complaints when Francisco Xavier Sanchez was awarded a government meat contract. Eighteen residents argued that Manual Solana made a better offer, so the regidores held proceedings to address the issue.[31]

Along with Fleming's responsibilities to the family business and St. Augustine governance, he also had a role in a Fugitive Slave Agreement between the United States and Spanish East Florida. For years, many slaves escaped from the United States, especially from the Carolinas and Georgia, and made their way to East Florida. Despite the fact most resident Negroes were enslaved in East Florida, runaways from the U.S. often were accepted as free men and women. This motivated more and more slaves to risk the journey south. In 1791 President George Washington authorized the United States to enter into an agreement with East Florida for the return of runaway slaves. Secretary of State Thomas Jefferson signed off on a proposed agreement, and James Seagrove, United States commissioner to the Creek Indians, negotiated the details with Governor Juan Nepomuceno de Quesada in St. Augustine. It is unclear whether or not the agreement was ever signed into law, but for eighteen months "half hearted efforts" led to the apprehension and return of some runaways. Civil and military officers were ordered to take all fugitive slaves to St. Augustine, where they were put to work or incarcerated until an authorized representative arrived to transport them back to their owners in the United States.[32] Seagrove hired George Fleming to act as the Spanish agent to Americans who claimed ownership of runaway slaves. Fleming's duties included providing "the usual allowance of provisions" for runaways who were incarcerated,[33] as well as helping coordinate the return of runaway slaves through the owners' personal agents.[34]

During turbulent times, the regidores' duties as captains of the Urban Militias took precedence. George Fleming took an active role in defending the province at least twice during his early years as a militia captain. In April of 1793, sixteen Indians attacked Edward Turner's plantation, ransacked his house, and set everything afire. One week later, Indians attacked John Silcock's plantation and stole a large herd of cattle.[35] Fear of continued attacks along the St. Johns River in the spring of 1793 prompted militia officers to spring into action, and all St. Johns River planters prepared to defend their plantations. Captain Fleming traversed the region with due haste and compiled a list of men fit to bear arms, as well as an inventory of munitions. F. P. Fatio offered New Switzerland as a gathering place should the Indians attack, although his shrewd offer was probably motivated more by a desire to protect New Switzerland than to protect his neighbors. George Fleming, John McIntosh, Richard Lang, Thomas Stirling, John Leslie, and Andrew Atkinson detailed a plan of defense that they presented to the governor in St. Augustine, who responded with a plan to deliver arms and munitions.[36] The situation did not escalate, however, and the marauding Indians soon withdrew from the area. In less than two years a greater threat to East Florida loomed just over the Georgia border.

Fleming and Florida's French Rebellion

Captain George Fleming took pride in his service during the armed conflict of 1794–95. The historian William Bennett called this "Florida's 'French' Rebellion," and several other historians call it the "Genêt Inspired Invasion." Its origins lay in President George Washington's support of a planned coup of East Florida, engineered by Secretary of State Thomas Jefferson. Jefferson's plan evolved as France and Spain were on the verge of war. Among other things, France wanted to wrest control of the Mississippi River from Spain, and the United States wanted East Florida. Jefferson believed an alliance with France could accomplish both objectives. He enlisted Edmond-Charles Genêt, the French Republic's first minister to the United States, to plan coordinated invasions of New Orleans, East Florida, and West Florida, with the support of French corsairs and rebellious Spanish citizens. The plan included recruiting prominent Anglo citizens of East Florida to support an invasion from Georgia: a force would assemble in Georgia, surge across the border, and overpower the undermanned defenses of St. Augustine. Washington dashed the planned invasion, however, by declaring an official stance of neutrality in the war between France and Spain. Undeterred, Genêt went rogue and pushed forward his plan to attack St. Augustine in April of 1794. At the request of the United States government, French officials intervened, forced Genêt to abandon the attack, and ordered him back to France.[37]

Back in East Florida, though, Genêt's recruits were not about to give up the fight. Among the rebels hellbent on overthrowing Spanish governance were several of George Fleming's fellow merchants and former comrades-in-arms, including John Houstoun McIntosh, who was lieutenant governor of the St. Johns River District, Richard Lang, a militia captain, J. P. Wagnon, William Plowden, and Abner Hammond. They joined troops of Georgians who massed along the border and prepared for the invasion.

At that time, Captain Fleming served under his relative, Carlos Howard, who was lieutenant colonel and commander of Spanish forces along the Georgia-Florida border. Howard held secret meetings with unidentified rebels and learned of the planned invasion. The rebels attempted to dupe Howard into believing they would help fight the invaders, but Howard was not fooled, and in short order all suspected traitors were arrested and interrogated. The arrests of John McIntosh and Richard Lang are well documented. On the evening of January 20, 1794, they were in St. Augustine at Clark's Inn with friends, including two priests. They gathered together, playing cards, where the stakes were cigars and the drinks flowed freely for Lang, if not for all. Lang admitted that during the evening he "got up two or three times to take a drink although he had drunk quite enough."[38] One historian wrote, "So bold were they that McIntosh and Lang talked of the plot while playing cards."[39] Without warning, officials burst into the room, arrested McIntosh and Lang, and hauled them out of the Inn.[40]

Subsequent interrogations of all those rounded up revealed an imminent attack on East Florida from Georgia. Governor Quesada took swift action to defend against an invasion of some seven hundred men, a force far superior to that of the entire East Florida militia. Every white man over the age of fourteen was pressed into armed service, and all male Negroes, both freemen and slaves, labored in preparation. Carlos Howard took charge of defense along the border. Fortunately for Captain Fleming and others at the ready, the arrests of McIntosh, Lang, and their fellow conspirators derailed the attack. Soon thereafter, East Florida officials either released all conspirators for lack of evidence or accused them of minor crimes for which the time already served was sufficient penalty. This was a mistake. Almost immediately, the traitors resumed plans to overthrow East Florida, while George Fleming played a key role in exposing their continued treachery.

In the following months, Fleming supported the ongoing defense of the northern frontier, traveling between Fort San Vizente, near the mouth of the St. Johns River, and St. Augustine to fulfill his duties as a regidor while simultaneously serving Howard's mounted forces as an officer and paymaster for his brothers-in-arms. He continued to conduct Fatio-Fleming family business, which included purchasing cattle in Georgia and organizing their transport to Fort Juana. On one trip to Georgia in late May 1795, Fleming spotted General Elijah Clark in the borderland, and learned that Abner Hammond had joined Clark to plan an invasion of Florida. Fleming quickly communicated this intelligence to Colonel Carlos Howard, who immediately informed the governor.[41] Fleming's timely communiqué was of no avail—for the next three weeks Howard repeatedly warned Bartolomé Morales, who was temporarily in command in St. Augustine while Governor Quesada was ill, of the need for stronger defenses. Due to a lack of funds, and perhaps lack of a sense of urgency, little was accomplished to fortify the border.[42] On June 29, 1795, a rebel force led by Richard Lang overwhelmed the weak defenses at Fort Juana, captured the lone officer and all fourteen enlisted men, destroyed the fort, and stole one hundred fourteen head of George Fleming's cattle.[43]

Immediately following the attack, the St. Augustine Board of War decided to send Fleming to Augusta, Georgia, to deliver an official communication to Georgia Governor Mathews. Acting Governor Morales ordered Colonel Howard to arrange transportation for Fleming, and Howard wasted no time, immediately renting a boat for that purpose.[44] Upon receipt of his orders, however, Fleming declined. His response to acting governor Morales, drafted in Spanish and probably written by his father-in-law, F. P. Fatio, was direct. He could not make the trip for three reasons. First, he was responsible for the purchase, transport, slaughter, and accounting of a Fatio cattle contract, and the government needed the fresh meat for the troops and citizens of East Florida. Second, under the present threat of invasion Fleming needed to defend the family plantation, New Switzerland, where at the time there were more than eighty Negroes—valuable assets highly prized by thieves—and well over a thousand bushels of corn in the field due for harvest. Third, Fleming knew that his enemies were in control of the borderland, and these traitors were well aware that it was Fleming who had identified them and alerted Spanish officials of their presence in East Florida. They already had tried to kill him once, and Fleming knew that William Plowden led a band of men near Fort San Nicholas who were intent on finishing the job. Fleming argued that someone more acquainted with the Indian routes would be better suited for the mission, and presented himself "ready to take arms for the service of the King & the defense of the country according to the employment with which I am honored."[45]

The rebels pressed the invasion by next mounting an attack from McIntosh's Cowford plantation, located near present-day Jacksonville. On July 9, 1795, forces gathered under cover of darkness and traveled the mile or so downriver to cross and make the eastern shore near Pottsburg Creek, where they joined more rebels—including those who had been released from prison just months ago for lack of evidence— then marched on to Fort San Nicholas. Posing as relief forces, they easily gained entry to the fort and overwhelmed the inferior defenders: killing three, wounding many, and taking all survivors as prisoners. Howard received a reconnaissance report late on the evening of July 10 that the rebels were back at McIntosh's plantation, drinking, singing, and bragging.[46]

Howard's quick and decisive action turned the tables. By July 12 he had assembled an impressive armada of four heavily armed ships and led them upriver to retake San Nicholas. Howard ordered the firing of cannons and small arms, which, combined with the sight of his forces, sent the rebels fleeing through marshes—back north across the river to Georgia. In less than a month, all invaders were captured and vanquished from East Florida, or stealthily faded back into their lives as Spanish citizens. The Spanish did not capture the leaders among the traitors, but if they had, their sentence was to be "dragged by the tail of a horse to the plaza in St. Augustine and there hanged; their bodies were then to be quartered and their heads and arms erected in the vicinity of Fort San Nicolas on the St. Johns to serve as a warning to others."[47]

Hibernia

A few years after the Genêt Inspired Invasion, George Fleming acquired a Spanish Land Grant of one thousand acres on an island directly across the broad St. Johns River from Fatio's New Switzerland plantation. There he created his own plantation, which he named Hibernia in honor of his Irish heritage. This is the most fully documented fact of Fleming's life in East Florida, and many sources describe how George and Sophia Fleming, with the labor of their slaves, carved a home in virgin land. Without exception, all such accounts of early Hibernia are based on Margaret Seton Fleming Biddle's description of her great-grandparents:

> At Hibernia George prepared to establish himself with his young bride ... he began to carve a home in this wilderness with the help of slaves and that of his own stout heart ... George and his few slaves hewed a new beginning ... Hibernia was George and George was Hibernia.[48]

Historical documents tell a story quite different from that of his great-granddaughter. Understanding the history of the land that became Hibernia requires an accounting of those who inhabited the land before George Fleming. Not surprisingly, Native Americans roamed the island before any Europeans settled there, though little is known about these people. Two small sites on Fleming Island have yielded ceramics from the St. Johns and Alachua cultures that lived in Clay County from around AD 600 to 1500, and in 1894 C. B. Moore identified a desecrated sand mound near the south end of Fleming Island. Known today as the Hibernia Mound, it is a well documented, and now restored, aboriginal sand mound that may contain human remains.[49]

The first known European residents on present-day Fleming Island arrived during the British Period, 1763–83. In 1769 Admiral Lord Edward Hawke received a twenty-thousand-acre land grant that included the southern portion of Fleming Island, bordered at the south by the confluence of Black Creek with the St. Johns River.[50] British authorities hoped that Hawke would use his power and influence with the Royal Navy to station a warship there to help secure the area for all British landowners in the region. Surveyors mapped Hawke's land in July 1769, and soon thereafter a workforce of Negroes who were managed by an overseer, Alexander Gray, began building a plantation. By 1776 Hawke's Negroes had constructed eight log houses, a kitchen, and a storehouse, and were running a productive plantation which produced 240 bushels of corn that year alone. The native longleaf pine forests around the plantation yielded 154 barrels of turpentine a few years later.[51] Admiral Lord Hawke died in 1781, and his son, Martin Bladen Hawke, abandoned his lands in Florida after the transfer of power from England back to Spain in 1783, approximately the same time Fleming arrived in St. Augustine. Hawke's land grant was vast, but the portion on which he built his plantation encompassed only the land that would become the heart of Hibernia.

Records indicate that the southern portion of Fleming Island remained uninhabited for nine years after Hawke left, until early 1792, when three men took possession of portions of Hawke's land. John McQueen claimed three hundred acres that included all the buildings and fields that had been the main settlement of Hawke's plantation. Andrew Atkinson briefly claimed a six-hundred-acre portion adjacent to the main settlement on the southern end of Fleming Island.[52] Atkinson relinquished that claim, and shortly thereafter, James McGirt, a South Carolina transplant who frequently worked for Francis P. Fatio Sr., took possession of those six hundred acres. Three months later, McGirt negotiated a trade with John McQueen and took possession of the main settlement of Hawke's plantation.[53] With this trade, McGirt consolidated his hold on most of what was to become Hibernia. He improved the plantation and cultivated the land until early in 1794 when McGirt was "compelled" to abandon his property "in obedience to the orders of his superior."[54]

McGirt did not identify his "superior." It may have been the governor because at this time Spanish authorities understood the magnitude of the impending "Genêt inspired" rebellion. As a preventive measure all residents between the north bank of the St. Johns River and the south bank of the St. Marys River were ordered to burn their buildings, harvest or destroy crops, then vacate the land so the invaders would not find useful resources. It seems unlikely, though, that McGirt would interpret this order as relevant to his plantation located nearly thirty miles to the south of that area and on the west side of the St. Johns River. Furthermore, McGirt did not burn his buildings. This gives credence to the intriguing possibility that his ultimate "superior" may have been Francis P. Fatio Sr., who has been described as a "feudal baron," more than ready to wield his power and influence for personal and family gain, and whose New Switzerland plantation was located directly across the river from Hawke's plantation.[55] The close proximity made Hawke's plantation an ideal acquisition for the Fatio-Fleming family, but it is more than proximity and Fatio's well-known arrogance that suggest he may have been the "superior." McGirt was beholden to Fatio for employment, and also for a personal favor—McGirt "owed him." A few years earlier, McGirt's notorious brother, the outlaw Daniel McGirt, was imprisoned at the Castillo de San Marcos in St. Augustine awaiting trial for robbery, horse theft, and raising arms against the government. Fatio defended Daniel McGirt at trial, and even posted a bond to cover expenses that James McGirt had incurred on his brother's behalf.[56] Daniel McGirt was released from prison and from that day forward, "One-Eyed McGirt," as Colonel Carlos Howard called him, lived on the run, committing thefts and property crimes against inhabitants of East Florida, and constantly pursued by the militia.

James McGirt's land remained vacant for two years, at which time local law dictated that it was effectively up for grabs and any qualified Spanish subject could claim it. George Fleming swooped right in and made the claim. In his own words, George Fleming took "actual possession" of the land in 1796, but he did more than just "claim" it as vacant property. Records clearly indicate that Fleming paid McGirt an unspecified amount for the improvements he had made to the plantation.[57] This chain of events resulted in George Fleming's legitimate hold on prime land conveniently across the St. Johns River from his father-in-law's New Switzerland plantation, although he did not legally own it yet.[58]

Coincidentally or not, in late 1795, One-Eyed McGirt stole George Fleming's prized horse. The outlaw McGirt was known to have a weakness for a fine horse, and that may be the only reason he committed this particular crime.[59] It is possible, though, that he believed Fleming and Fatio had conspired to keep James McGirt off of his land, and he wanted vengeance. When Fleming's horse went missing, everyone involved knew One-Eyed McGirt was responsible, so James McGirt and Robert Andrews set out to bring it back. Communicating through an intermediary, James McGirt informed Fleming that "after the most imponderable fatigue and toil" they had recovered the stolen horse. Daniel McGirt conveniently got away, though, riding off on his brother James's horse.[60] Sergeant Ruben Hogan and a band of militiamen captured Daniel McGirt a month later.[61] Once again, he was imprisoned in the Castillo de San Marcos where he remained, often in chains, for over a year. Eventually, he was deported from East Florida and found his way back to South Carolina, where he lived the remainder of his life.

It seems James McGirt never got over the bitter taste of being forced to relinquish his nine hundred acres that included Hawke's plantation. For many years, McGirt, and then his heirs, preserved documents and surveys related to his original claim on the land. In 1828, after Florida became a territory of the United States, James McGirt's heirs claimed the land was rightfully theirs—but to no avail. Government officials were not persuaded by the argument that he had abandoned the land against his will, and ruled against the claim.[62]

After four years of planting and improving that same land, on January 9, 1800, George Fleming petitioned Governor Enrique White for James McGirt's "abandoned" property plus an additional one hundred acres, a total of one thousand acres. James Cashen had previously petitioned the governor for the same land, but withdrew his request after learning that Fleming had paid McGirt for the improvements.[63] Governor White awarded Fleming a conditional land grant two days later. In 1790 the Spanish had created this land grant system, popularly known as "headrights," as a way to encourage non-Spanish residents already living in East Florida to stay, as well as to attract immigrants to develop the interior. Land awards were based on a simple formula. The head of the household could receive a maximum of one hundred acres for himself, plus an additional fifty acres for every person attached to the household, white or nonwhite, free or slave.[64] In order to receive a headright grant, all non-Spanish applicants were required to swear an oath of allegiance to the Spanish Crown. The recipient was then required to develop the land continuously for ten years before receiving unencumbered title.[65]

Fleming's goal was to manage a profitable plantation and eventually acquire clear title to the one thousand acres, but he and Sophia did not make the plantation their home. Sworn statements by Sophia Fleming, Lewis Fleming, and others prove that the family lived in St. Augustine between 1796 and 1812.[66] George Fleming probably took his sons, Lewis and George Jr., to Hibernia to learn the business of planting and cattle. It is certain that Lewis Fleming stayed at his grandfather's New Switzerland plantation for months at a time, and reasonable to assume that all of the Fatio-Fleming clan stayed there on occasion.[67] Considering the fact that Fatio's grand home at New Switzerland was just a short boat ride from Hibernia, they likely took trips to the island from the comfort of Fatio's country estate. To dispel a long-standing Fleming family oral tradition, though, George Fleming did not carve a home for his family in the wilderness; rather, he purchased a working plantation complete with cultivated fields and slave quarters. But, as Jacksonville historian Dena Snodgrass frequently stated, George Fleming did establish the first lasting settlement on Fleming Island.

With help from his father-in-law, George Fleming dedicated himself to improving his new Hibernia plantation while supporting the ongoing operations at New Switzerland. He spent increasingly longer periods of time out in the country at the plantations, and, not surprisingly, records suggest that he likely preferred the comfort of Fatio's fine country home to his own rough accommodations at Hibernia. Fatio's manor house was built of frame construction and was impressively large for its place and time, with approximately twenty-four hundred square feet on two stories, including piazzas, balconies, and well-appointed rooms. One wing of the house was dedicated to the library and study, stocked with over twelve hundred volumes written in English, French, and Italian—some of them highly prized by collectors. Window alcoves surrounded the room, framed by green silk curtains fringed with gold. Each alcove contained bookshelves and a marble table, and servants filled porcelain vases with fresh flowers from the gardens. Later in life, Lewis Fleming commented that the entire house was fitted out in "very handsome style ... everything about the establishment was in the best style of a gentleman of wealth," including fine furniture, paintings, china, silver, and glassware. Some of these items were heirlooms, such as a silver gilt tankard that had been in the family for over three hundred years. All of this was surrounded by the outbuildings, warehouses, sheds, stables, pens, workshops, cabins, and equipment to support a thriving plantation with a workforce of more than eighty enslaved, and some free, Negroes. Fatio's granddaughter recalled that the Spanish referred to the house as "la palacio" (the palace) because of its opulence, and "la castillo" (the castle) because of the turrets on its façade. New Switzerland was "an outpost of European-style civilization on the edge of East Florida's de facto frontier."[68] Soldiers, merchants, Spanish officials, visiting dignitaries, and even travelers from the Indian Nations found shelter and comfort there at one time or another.

Fleming's house at Hibernia, on the other hand, was a sturdy log cabin. His granddaughter preserved an oral tradition that it was a "simple square house for simple primitive housekeeping,"[69] and an eyewitness report supports that description.[70] Fleming's personal inventory of Hibernia depicts a basic working plantation outfitted with only the necessary tools, outbuildings, cabins, equipment, and camp furniture needed by his much smaller labor force of African Americans. Little wonder he preferred to stay with his father-in-law at New Switzerland when he resided in the country.[71]

In October 1800 Fleming traveled to New Switzerland for the cotton harvest there and at Hibernia. Fatio sent his wife a letter shortly after Fleming arrived. The letter was discovered quite by accident nearly 180 years later, in a desk that was donated to the National Society of the Colonial Dames of America in the State of Florida. It provides the following glimpse of life for Fleming and Fatio as wealthy planters along the St. Johns River at harvest time.[72]

On the day Fatio wrote the letter, he and Fleming knew that Indians threatened to ransack isolated plantations, and they believed New Switzerland was targeted for the first strike. In the face of this looming threat, the men carried on with the harvest, fully prepared for a sudden evacuation, if necessary. They harvested across the river at Hibernia first, and then focused on New Switzerland. Constant rain interrupted the harvest and the ginning, but Fleming's crop at Hibernia was now complete and, after ginning, would yield thirty-three bales weighing a total of approximately eight thousand pounds. Fatio had a much larger crop—perhaps one hundred acres—with about one-fourth of that harvested, ginned, and baled. He anticipated a total yield of over twenty thousand pounds at the end of the harvest. Whenever weather allowed, Fleming managed the work of four Negroes at the cotton gins while Juan Gray, a free mulatto who was Fatio's foreman, supervised the ongoing harvest. Negroes soon would load close to thirty thousand pounds of cotton, along with a modest orange crop, aboard one of Fatio's ships for transport to St. Augustine, where much of it was bound for export.

After a demanding day in the fields, the two planters sat down together for a hearty meal. Sources of protein in their diet included fish, fowl, the occasional slaughter of fresh meat, and salted meat, though Fatio suffered some sort of ailment that made salt meat unpalatable. Fatio planned to butcher a lamb the next morning. Negroes would transport half of the fresh meat back to St. Augustine for the family, which included Fleming's wife, Sophia, their two-year-old son, Lewis, and infant daughter, Mary, as well as the Fatio household. Fleming advised that a portion of the lamb "would give the Governor pleasure," and arranged delivery to him. Fatio's garden yielded a bountiful harvest that included salad greens, cabbages, onions, carrots, mustard, beets, spinach, parsnips, and even some asparagus. "I would have liked very much to have some chicory and some blite, as well as some sweet potatoes," wrote Fatio. "Then my garden would be complete for the winter."[73] Cows provided milk, and they had enough tobacco to suit themselves, but Fatio was much vexed that he didn't have "a drop of wine which is a great inconvenience," and asked his wife to send several bottles with the next delivery. Absent the threat of attack by Indians, the letter paints a picture of an idyllic plantation lifestyle. Fatio closed the letter to his wife, writing, "Goodbye, my dear Friend, I am wrapped up in my winter clothes. This cold weather doesn't bother me as it did last year. I am better in mind and spirit, and am of good cheer. Love me without worrying. I shall be happier. But I would not know how, nor would I be able, to love you more."

George Fleming enjoyed his comfortable life as a planter at New Switzerland and Hibernia, but he was still serving as a regidor in St. Augustine. The regidores had a responsibility to ensure fair and honest trade in the city and apparently they fell short in that capacity. Accusations of corruption and favoritism by the regidores were widespread. Military personnel complained that St. Augustine storekeepers, notably Regidor Bernardo Segui, used fraudulent scales to cheat buyers. In August 1804 Governor Enrique White began formulating a plan to dismiss Fleming, Segui, and Pedro Cosifacio (who replaced Ysnardy when he died in 1803).[74] Writing to his superiors, White complained that Segui paid too much attention to his bread contracts and too little attention to his military duties, and Cosifacio lived too far away to attend to his governmental responsibilities and "was related to shopkeepers," implying a link to favoritism and unethical practices. In criticism of his fellow Irishman's lack of attention to government affairs, Governor White wrote that George Fleming "idles his time away in the country," a clear reference to his extended stays at New Switzerland and Hibernia.[75] In September 1806 White replaced all three regidores with the captains of the Third Battalion.[76] By the time it was all done, even the King of Spain himself chimed in on the dismissal of the urban militia captains as regidores of St. Augustine.[77] With this, Fleming lost his civil authority, though he remained a militia captain for the rest of his life.

On August 11, 1811, the extended Fatio-Fleming family lost its patriarch, 87-year-old Francis Philip Fatio.[78] He was born August 6, 1724, near Vevey, Switzerland, to a family of wealth and education. Fatio attended the University of Geneva for a while, then left the study of law to pursue a military career as a lieutenant in the Swiss Guard. He fought during the War of Austrian Succession, for which the King of Sardinia made him a vicomte. After the war he married Maria Magdalena Crispel, of Italian heritage, and purchased an extravagant estate in Sardinia near present-day Nice, France, but he was a restless soul with an adventurous spirit.[79] With his growing family he relocated to Switzerland once again, and then to England, where they remained for ten years until opportunity presented itself in the newly acquired British colony of East Florida. Fatio forged an alliance with other gentlemen to obtain large tracts of land in Florida, chartered a ship, and in 1771 set sail for the New World. The Fatio family arrived in St. Augustine with their servants and an astounding collection of personal possessions. Mr. Fatio initially purchased a large stone house on an entire block of land at a prominent location adjacent to the bay and the town plaza, and later constructed his remarkable country home at New Switzerland.[80] During the Revolutionary War, Fatio volunteered his services to the British and served as a staff officer in Charleston, South Carolina. He spoke German, French, English, and Spanish, and he was an astute businessman who masterfully exploited East Florida's natural resources during both British and Spanish rule. He was known to feign ignorance of the very resources that kept him wealthy in order to guard his business interests.[81]

Fatio lost his beloved wife on August 10, 1810. As his own last days approached, Mr. Fatio's wish was to be buried by her side. This, however, did not come to pass. Maria, a Catholic, was laid to rest in the cemetery at St. Augustine Cathedral Basilica. Her husband, a Protestant, was denied eternal rest by her side, despite vigorous lobbying by his Catholic son-in-law, George Fleming.[82] Instead, the family committed his body to the family plot in New Switzerland. F. P. Fatio Sr. was greatly adored and admired by his extended family, and oral traditions tell us his mind was sharp to the end. He may have been glad to leave this Earth when he did, because he did not have to witness the unprecedented disaster that struck both Hibernia and his New Switzerland plantation two years later.

The Patriot War of 1812–1813

In 1810 George Mathews, a former governor of Georgia and then an agent of the United States government, held clandestine meetings with five prominent East Floridians for the purpose of inciting revolt against Spanish rule. After those meetings Mathews traveled to Washington to speak with President James Madison. Prior to his appointment with the president, Mathews sent a letter to Secretary of State Robert Smith summarizing intelligence gathered. Mathews wrote that he found men in East Florida ready to support a revolt in East Florida, but that they would expect the United States government to pay debts owed them by the Spanish, as well as reward them with land for their support.

Mathews's letter included the mysterious statement (using his own unique spelling): "The Gentlemen of influence in East Florada in our intrest, donnot wish there names commited to paper—but I am at liberty to mention them in a conference with the President or you." During the meeting Mathews revealed the names. Someone wrote them down and filed them along with Mathews's letter. The "Gentlemen of influence" were John Houstoun McIntosh, Fernando de la Maza Arredondo, Andrew Atkinson, Lieutenant Justo Lopez, and George Fleming.[83]

In 1811 Congress passed a secret act authorizing the acquisition of East and West Florida, and Mathews prepared for an invasion. He organized a group of Georgians who called themselves "Patriots" to join U.S. troops and attack East Florida. John Houstoun McIntosh, forgiven for his part in the 1795 Genêt Inspired Invasion but seemingly ever intent on purging the Spanish from East Florida, joined the force. Fleming, Arredondo, Atkinson, and Lopez reversed course and remained loyal to the Crown. Thus began what historian James Cusick called "The Other War of 1812," and others have called "The Patriot War."[84]

On March 17, 1812, United States and Patriot forces took Fernandina without firing a shot.[85] The invaders marched unimpeded up the St. Johns River, so Fleming was forced to abandon his Hibernia plantation to inevitable destruction. It is unclear whether Fleming actually participated in the evacuation of Hibernia or delegated the operation. Either way, he evacuated his slaves—his most valuable property—as well as his free Negroes, and left everything else behind. This was not as simple as it sounds. It required ferrying approximately thirty men, women, and children of mixed ages across the river to New Switzerland. From there it is likely that many of them walked to

St. Augustine, a distance of more than twenty miles across the "Fatio road," while others rode on carts or wagons.[86]

To take East Florida the invaders had to control St. Augustine and on March 25, 1812, they established an offensive position outside the well-defended city walls. Within days President Madison officially disassociated the United States from the attack and revoked Mathews's commission. Nevertheless, the Georgia invaders and a large contingent of United States troops continued their conquest. One day Sophia Fleming climbed atop a roof to see what she could of the enemy camp beyond the city walls. As she watched, they lowered their Georgia flag and raised the Star and Stripes.[87]

Captain George Fleming claimed to be one of the first to commit his personal resources in defense of the city. In St. Augustine, he housed and fed his slaves under circumstances he described as a "cantonment of continual military duty." Fleming's able-bodied slaves and free Negroes "were armed with rifles in the defense of King and country" throughout the siege. Fleming also commanded Prince Whitten's highly esteemed company of Negro soldiers, though he never went into the field with the black troops.[88] Four years later, Fleming would profit handsomely for his part in defending St. Augustine.[89]

The Patriots set up camps at various locations along the St. Johns River to support the assault on St. Augustine. Troops from at least two camps embarked on regular excursions to Hibernia in search of provisions and whatever supplies they could scrounge. A force of invaders stationed at Six Mile Creek went to Fleming's plantation multiple times. They stole hogs, cattle, corn, and potatoes for their camp. During one excursion they killed ten or twelve head of cattle and took provisions of different kinds. Another company of "marauders," as the Spanish referred to them, built a blockhouse at the confluence of Julington Creek and Davis Creek. Their orders were to collect provisions and forward them to troops camped outside of St. Augustine. To that end, they frequently sent troops to Fleming's Island in the summer and fall of 1812, possibly as often as a dozen times. Traveling in a large boat, ten or twelve men took anything they could find, including cattle, hogs, and corn. Each trip they usually killed one or two cattle and one or two hogs, butchered the livestock on the island, then carried the meat back to the Blockhouse.[90]

George Fleming's old friend, Edward Wanton, was at Hibernia for a period of time during the Patriot invasion. Wanton has been described as a scholar who spent much time reading and writing.

He was fiercely loyal to the Spanish Crown and helped recruit a war party of Seminoles to attack the invading forces. Patriots held Wanton personally responsible for brutal Seminole attacks against their troops and took revenge. They ransacked his plantation at Pupo Point and kept him in chains for months.[91] Sometime after his release, Wanton returned to his home only to learn that the insurgents were nearing his residence once again, so he moved across the river to Fleming's plantation, hoping to avoid another confrontation with the Patriots—but that was not to be.[92]

Colonel Samuel Alexander led a contingent of marauders along the St. Johns River in the fall of 1813, wreaking havoc upon the plantations of Spanish loyalists. Alexander purported to be among the Patriots intent on liberating East Florida from Spain, but in the eyes of the Spanish he was a mercenary who stole slaves for profit. While Wanton slept in Fleming's log house on November 9, armed insurgents "burst open the door" and kidnapped three Negro children and a white boy named Jerry. They left Wanton at Hibernia without a boat. Two of the Negro boys escaped from the marauders and made their way back to Hibernia. Wanton immediately sent them on foot to reach a Spanish garrison and signal the alarm, but they were captured along the way and confessed that Wanton had sent them to alert the Spanish.

The furious insurgents came after Wanton, who somehow had been forewarned of their "bloody intentions." As he sat quietly at Fleming's house reading a book on November 16, a party of six men made a sneak attack. Wanton spied them in the nick of time and immediately fled on foot. They fired two shots at him but neither made its mark, and Wanton disappeared into the thick forest. Tense moments ensued as Wanton scurried away with his would-be captors in pursuit. To his great relief, Wanton made a clean escape. A few days later, Wanton discovered a barely seaworthy canoe that the invaders had hidden. He made his way back to his own plantation, only to find that the marauders had taken all of his slaves and his provisions. Wanton wrote that Colonel Alexander had intended to steal slaves from Hibernia as well, but that was not possible since Fleming had moved them to St. Augustine. He also reported some cattle still remained in Hibernia, and the houses, outbuildings, and fences were intact, but that was short-lived.

Across the St. Johns River at New Switzerland, F. P. Fatio Jr. was in charge of his deceased father's estate. The younger Fatio's strategy for his plantation was quite different from that of his brother-in-law, George Fleming. Rather than abandon his property, he subjected the plantation to a sort of protection racket by offering New Switzerland as a place of refuge for the Patriot troops, and they often availed themselves of the comforts of the estate. Fatio hoped their presence would ensure safety, and he was, indeed, safe from the Patriots, although they steadily appropriated his various resources, and their intermittent presence did not protect him from Indians. Seminoles attacked New Switzerland in August of 1813, and his family barely escaped with their lives. In their absence Patriot troops continually looted the plantation. During one raid a group busted open Fatio's trunk and discovered evidence that revealed he had served the British during the Revolutionary War. Many of these invaders had fought the British for American independence, and they went wild with rage. In a merciless fury, they broke open the family vault, removed the remains of F. P. Fatio Sr., desecrated his body, and scattered his bones across the grounds. Friends of the family later gathered up the bones and reinterred them.[93]

Despite the damage inflicted on Spanish citizens and their property, the siege of St. Augustine failed and the Patriots gradually withdrew from East Florida, but not before Patriot marauders and/or Seminoles reduced Hibernia and New Switzerland to ruins and ashes. In years to come, United States commissioners conducted investigations to determine exactly who stole property and who torched plantations throughout East Florida during the Patriot War of 1812–1813. That investigation relative to Hibernia and New Switzerland is a part of the story of George Fleming's heirs, but one result of the inquiry is relevant now—the Fleming and Fatio plantations were a total loss. Fleming's material losses consisted primarily of slave quarters, a log house, livestock, crops, planting equipment, and such tools as were needed for slaves to manage their lives in the remote setting. Fatio's losses were staggering and included all the trappings of a ten-thousand-acre plantation, dozens of slaves, and a finely appointed manor house. Neither George Fleming nor his brother-in-law attempted to rebuild or resume planting operations on their plantations for nearly ten years.[94]

Fernandina and San Pablo

In 1811 George Fleming received a grant of a town lot in Fernandina subject to a few conditions. Fleming could not sell the property without permission of the Spanish government. He was required to build a house within six months, and he had to conform to a building restriction: fences or gardens visible from the street must not "injure the regularity or beauty of the town." Sometime in 1814 the Fleming family moved to their Fernandina house located on Square 7, Lot 7.[95] Sophia complained of the high cost of living. Eggs cost one dollar per dozen. A portion of butter ran from seventy-five cents to a dollar. Butcher's meat was costly at twenty-five cents per measure. Her brother, F. P. Fatio Jr., had moved his family to nearby St. Marys, Georgia, where the cost of living was equally exorbitant.[96] Both families were accustomed to opulent lives as successful planters, so it's no surprise that George Fleming and his brother-in-law desired a return to the land, and within a short period of time the Fernandina town lot was but a small plum among the Fleming family's land holdings.

They still held the rights to Hibernia on Fleming's Island and in 1811, after the death of F. P. Fatio Sr., they inherited an undivided half interest in over ten thousand acres of prime timberland along the south branch of Nassau River.[97] In 1816 Fleming's possession of Hibernia spanned twenty years. He easily fulfilled the headright grant requirement of working the land for ten consecutive years, and moved aggressively to secure ownership. Governor José Coppinger awarded clear title, but that was just a start for Fleming. Next, he petitioned for even more land and was granted 980 acres known as Langley Bryan, comprised of two separate tracts located nearly thirty miles upriver from Hibernia on the west side of the St. Johns River, directly across from Fort Buena Vista and just north of present day Palatka, Florida.[98] Fleming believed he deserved more. On September 9, 1816, Fleming presented a Memorial to Governor Coppinger in which he explained that he was "one of [the] oldest vassals in this province and of the first and most faithful." He cited Spanish law regarding a "distinction between noblemen and commoners and those that were of less rank and merit," placing himself among the aristocracy of East Florida. Fleming wrote that his "public and well known services ... have not been called to your highnesses' attention due to them being so obvious." He described his "undeniable support of the Spanish Government over the prolonged period of thirty-five years that Your Majesty have [sic] existed in this Plaza [St. Augustine]." Fleming reminded the governor of his service during times of war, especially in the defense of St. Augustine during the Patriot War of 1812 and during the Genêt Inspired Rebellion of 1795. In return for his faithful service, Fleming specifically requested twenty thousand acres of land along the Atlantic coast centered at the inlet of the San Sebastian River. Governor Coppinger responded immediately, writing "with respect to the constant and well known services that the requestor alleges, and in merit of the reasons that are presented, all very deserving of the highest consideration, I award to him, with no exceptions, property in the name of His Majesty ... the 20,000 acres of land that is expressed in the earlier solicitation."[99]

After three stokes of a pen George Fleming now owned nearly twenty-seven thousand acres of land in East Florida, as well as houses in St. Augustine and Fernandina.

In the midst of these land acquisitions, Fleming mortgaged Hibernia for one thousand pounds and began anew as a planter along the St. Johns River.[100] Surprisingly, he didn't rebuild at Hibernia or create a plantation on any of his newly acquired land. Instead, F. P. Fatio Jr. leased John Forbes's plantation along the eastern banks of Pablo Creek just a short distance south of its marshy confluence with the St. Johns River. Fatio made Fleming a party to the deal, and they worked together for the benefit of both families.[101] They chose the name Nueva Esperanza, or New Hope, for their new plantation—probably because the leased land represented a new beginning. A contemporary account of the area tells us the land was fertile:

> The land in the neighbourhood [sic] of Pablo is held in such high estimation, that many productive settlements have been made, and are now making. The plantation of Mr. John Forbes, on which Messrs. Fatio and Fleming now work their hands, and those of Don Bartolo, Messrs. Fitch & Chairs, and Mrs. Baker, are the most conspicuous.[102]

It appears that the Fatios resided primarily in Fernandina and the Flemings resided primarily at New Hope, though both families split their time between the two.[103] As he had done most of his life in Florida, George Fleming was constantly on the move, traveling between St. Augustine, New Hope, and Fernandina to conduct business and serve the province. One of his services was to deliver mail from St. Augustine to prominent citizens on Amelia Island and in Fernandina, and while at New Hope, Fleming played a key role in Spain's last attempt to retain control of Fernandina. That story is important, not only because it is a part of George Fleming's life, but also because the disastrous outcome resulted in the United States taking permanent control of Fernandina.

In January of 1817 Governor Coppinger caught wind of a planned invasion of Fernandina. He enlisted Fleming at New Hope to deliver an emergency communication to Francisco de Morales, commander of Fernandina defenses. Coppinger directed Morales to "always concern himself with the defense and conservation of this Plaza and Province."[104] In the event that invading forces attacked Fernandina, he ordered Morales to fight until two-thirds of his men were wounded or killed.[105] Knowing that a fight was coming, Fleming evacuated his family to St. Augustine.[106]

On June 29, 1817, adventurer Gregor MacGregor assembled fifty-four men at St. Marys, Georgia, and prepared to take Fernandina by force. MacGregor claimed to be motived by altruism. He published newspaper columns boldly proclaiming his objective of freeing East Floridians from Spanish tyranny.[107] In truth, his motivation seems to have been profit. His band of "sailors, adventurers, and street brawlers" wanted the spoils of war, including cheap or free land.[108] Armed and ready, they boarded small boats and traveled the short distance to the shores of Amelia Island. The force disembarked on a beach, then marched three miles to Fernandina. Nearly one mile of that trek was an arduous slog through marsh and muck at times as deep as their waists. These men must have been physically taxed by the strenuous march in the Florida heat as they approached the defenses at Fernandina, which included some eighty-four armed men sheltered behind fortifications. One newspaper account tells that "they might have been blown to atoms" but for the cowardice of the Spanish commander, Francisco de Morales, who surrendered without a fight.[109]

During the next month, Governor Coppinger held secret meetings in St. Augustine with George Fleming and others to plan a counterassault and retake Fernandina. The Spanish built an attack force largely comprised of Negro troops from Havana and volunteers from the East Florida northern militia. On August 30, 1817, Governor Coppinger directed Fleming to return to New Hope "with the greatest brevity possible," where he was to provide lodging and supplies for officers and troops in support of the battle plan "that I have manifested to you verbally and most confidentially." He also ordered Fleming to enlist his nineteen-year-old son, Lewis, and his friend, William Travers, to "take any measures necessary" to gather containers, carts, and canoes to support attack.[110] Within days MacGregor learned what the Spanish were about—all honor and bluster laid aside, MacGregor abdicated command to Jared Irwin and fled Fernandina.

On September 7 a band of Spanish militia under command of George Clarke rendezvoused at Cedar Point, about eighteen miles south of Fernandina on the mainland. His men were ill equipped, so the next morning Clarke ordered them to hold position while he hastened to New Hope where Fleming gave him additional arms, a barrel of gunpowder, and ammunition. Almost simultaneously two small Spanish launches arrived on the St. Johns River. Clarke got another thirty guns and food supplies from them before returning to his men.[111] On September 9 Commander Thomas Llorente arrived at New Hope, his horses utterly exhausted from the hard push north to join the militia. Fleming offered aid, including the use of his own horses, which prompted Llorente to tell the governor that Fleming "accommodated us perfectly and I am much obliged to him."[112] Llorente's small band boarded the launches and joined the militia lying in wait at Cedar Point. Fleming, the elder captain of the militia, remained at New Hope, prepared to support whatever situation might come his way.

The morning of September 13 promised a glorious victory for the East Floridians, but in short order the counterassault devolved into an unmitigated failure. It began when Spanish ships moved into position off Fernandina while the troops took McClure's Hill, including abandoned enemy cannon, just south of town. At three o'clock in the afternoon, the boats and the cannon on the hill began firing on the town. The invaders fired back from four locations. Their ineffective shelling lasted until dark, with little or no damage on either side. Then a shot fired from town went long over McClure's Hill and landed among the Spanish troops massed on the other side, killing two and wounding several. Almost immediately the Spanish commander, a major with the Royal Regiment of Havana, ordered retreat. According to the historian T. Frederick Davis, the Florida militia commanders were "maddened by the cowardice of the Spanish commander," and believed they could move to a new position and take the town under cover of night. The chain of command was clear, though, and they had no choice but to follow orders and withdraw from Fernandina. Thus began a protracted retreat that extended over many days. The northern militia, disgusted by Spanish leadership, almost immediately returned to their homes. Llorente's orders were to evacuate the area by way of Pablo Creek, which he accomplished with great difficulty. Some troops rested for a while at New Hope and a few deserted, never to be seen again. Two weeks later at least one soldier was still at Fleming's place with a leg wound, though most had found their way back to St. Augustine.[113]

Fernandina became a haven for pirating and smuggling. On December 2, 1817, President James Monroe described Amelia Island as "... a channel for illicit introduction of slaves from Africa into the United States, an asylum for fugitive slaves from the neighboring States, and a port for smuggling of every kind."[114] By one account more than a thousand slaves were sold illegally into Georgia during this time.[115] With the situation spiraling rapidly out of control, United States forces seized control of Fernandina. Gregor MacGregor threatened another invasion in the spring of 1818, which prompted the United States to act swiftly and strike a bargain with Spain for possession of both East and West Florida.

After the battle to retake Fernandina, George Fleming quietly fades from the historical record. He purchased twelve hundred acres from Bernardo Segui in January of 1819 then sold it to Belton A. Copp in August of 1821.[116] In 1819 Fleming purchased three thousand acres of land from Brigida Gomez then turned around and sold it to Thomas Fitch that same day.[117] He purchased fifty-one acres at Dames Point, plus another ninety-five acres at Clapboard Creek from Joseph Grey, then immediately sold both tracts to Juan Flagg Brown. He sold five hundred acres of his San Sebastian land to Andres Burgevin.[118] It appears that Fleming acted as an agent on some of these land deals, while others were personal land speculation. In 1819 he gave power of attorney for his oldest son, Lewis, to travel to Cuba to collect debts.[119] While in Cuba, Lewis accepted a position with the firm of Forbes & Lawrence and did not return to Florida for three years. He never saw his father again.

The year 1821 marked several major events for the Flemings. This is the year that President James Monroe signed the Adams-Onís Treaty, which transferred Florida from Spain to the United States. George Fleming was now sixty years old and his entire family faced the prospect of pledging allegiance to a new country. Shortly after United States officials took charge in St. Augustine, Fleming and F. P. Fatio Jr. sent some of their Negroes with an overseer upriver from New Hope to New Switzerland and Hibernia, where they began reconstruction of the plantations that had lain fallow for nearly nine years.[120] They likely made some progress with that project before George Fleming died on October 11, 1821. Fleming family tradition holds that he met his death at Hibernia, and a popular novelist created a fictional cause of death— falling from his horse while galloping home from his south fields.[121] Thus far, though, George Fleming's actual cause of death remains a mystery and the obituary written days after his death tells us he died at New Hope. In the obituary, Fleming's friends described him as an honest and generous man, and "few men left their sphere of life attended with more just regret." Fleming was known for his "frankness and philanthropy," and "even a stranger ... will gratefully cherish the recollection of his kindly favors." Everyone who knew him could "truly sympathise [sic] in the grief of his disconsolate widow and children, who will long deplore his loss."[122] Indeed, they would. Not only would they mourn the death of their affectionate father and husband, they also had to cope with the loss of his business savvy and resolve his personal affairs. The lives of Sophia Fleming and her children, Lewis, Mary, and George Jr., were beset by major changes during the next several years, including a series of lawsuits. But first they had to bury their patriarch.

Even though George Fleming was a Catholic, the family did not commit him to sacred ground at the Cathedral Basilica in St. Augustine, possibly because clergy had denied that privilege to F. P. Fatio Sr. Instead, the family loaded his body aboard a boat, traveled nearly forty nautical miles up the St. Johns River, and laid him to rest in Hibernia, where his tombstone faces east across the river toward New Switzerland and the resting place of the man he admired so much. His gravesite is the oldest documented in the cemetery at St. Margaret's Episcopal Church in Hibernia, but it likely is not *the* oldest. It is probable that some of Fleming's Negroes, and possibly even Lord Hawke's Negroes, had previously buried their dead at the same site because there are dozens of undocumented African American gravesites in the back of the cemetery. Fleming family oral traditions tell us these are the graves of Fleming slaves.

We may never know if George Fleming chose Hibernia for his final resting place, or if his wife and children made the decision for him. Either way, the choice makes clear the family's determination to continue his work to rebuild Hibernia and make it their home.

Endnotes

1. Throughout his life in Spanish East Florida, Fleming was known by his Spanish name, Jorge Fleming.

2. The Spanish Census of 1783 provided the first record of Fleming's presence in St. Augustine, including his occupation, his purpose for coming to East Florida, his residence, and the fact that a white servant accompanied him.

3. Helen Hornbeck Tanner, *Zéspedes in East Florida 1784-1790* (Jacksonville: University of North Florida Press, 1989), 59; Joseph Byrne Lockley, *East Florida 1783-1785: A File of Documents Assembled, and Many of Them Translated* (Berkeley: University of California Press, 1949), 439-41; South Carolina Department of Archives and History, "Moultrie, Gov. William, Message, With Enclosures, Transmitting A Letter From Don Vincent Emanuel De Zéspedes, Spanish Governor of East Florida, Concerning A Pirate Gang Operating Along The Coast And Enclosing A Deposition of Thomas Bell, Captured Pirate," Series S165009, Message 0340. http://www.archivesindex.sc.gov/.

4. Gertrude N. L'Engle, *A Collection of Letters, Information, and Data on Our Family*, vol. 1 (Jacksonville, FL: privately published, 1951).

5. Susan R. Parker, "The Cattle Trade in East Florida, 1784–1821" in *Colonial Plantations and Economy in Florida*, ed., Jane G. Landers (Gainesville: University Press of Florida, 2000), 150-68.

6. The account of Fleming's cattle mission is from *EFP*, 45/32, Zéspedes's letters to and from Delgado and Armassa, dated between July 19, 1786 and August 31, 1786.

7. *EFP*, 66/35, Guillermo O'Kelly to Zéspedes, September 15, 1785.

8. *EFP*, 45/32, Manuel Torres to Governor Zéspedes, March 9, 1786; *EFP* 130/68, George Fleming to Governor Zéspedes, March 20, 1786.

9. *EFP*, 45/32, Letters between Governor Zéspedes and Martin Armassa, September 26-30, 1786; *EFP*, 130/86, Fleming to Zéspedes, March 20, 1786.

10. Donna Rachal Mills, *Florida's First Families: Translated Abstracts of Pre-1821 Spanish Censuses*, vol. 1 (Maryland: Heritage Books, 2011), 4.

11. Gertrude N. L'Engle, *A Collection of Letters, Information, and Data on our Family*, vol. 2 (Jacksonville, FL: privately published), 57-58.

12. *EFP*, 85/25, Carlos Howard to Diego O'Fallon, November 20, 1788.

13. *EFP*, reel 169, Fatio to Fleming Dowry, July 12, 1788. This reel of microfilm includes handwritten page numbers at upper right. See pages 855-63; L'Engle, *A Collection of Letters*, 1:194.

14. Historical Records Survey, State Archives Survey, *Translation From Records at the Catholic Bishop's Residence, St. Augustine, Florida*

Scott Ritchie

(Jacksonville: Works Progress Administration State Office, 1931). Copy in *Marian Wilkin Fleming Collection* (hereafter cited as *MWF Collection*).

15. Tanner, *Zéspedes in East Florida*, 175.

16. *Roman Catholic Records, St. Augustine Parish, White Baptisms*, Register Books II & III (St. Augustine, FL: St. Augustine Historical Society Research Library). Throughout this manuscript I will refer to George Philip Fleming as "George Jr."

17. L'Engle, *A Collection of Letters*, 2:58.

18. *Escrituras*, SAHS, Deeds for years 1793 and 1794, Book 369, 303.

19. Susan R Parker, "Success through Diversification: Francis Philip Fatio's New Switzerland Plantation," in Landers, *Colonial Plantations*, 71-72.

20. "Packet of documents carried by the schooner *Mary of Boston* from St. Augustine to New York in 1799," in James G. Cusik, "Hello, Sailor!" *El Escribano* 47 (2010): 32-33.

21. *EFP*, 47/32, Francisco P. Fatio to Don Juan Nepomuceno de Quesada, October 20, 1792. Translated by John Diviney.

22. *EFP*, 8/2, Juan Nepomuceno de Quesada to Luis de las Casas, September 22, 1790. Pedro Cosifacio also was a captain of the Urban Militia, but his name shows up infrequently in the documents; *EFP*, 163, August 31, 1790. Both George Fleming and F. P. Fatio Sr. became citizens of Spain.

23. The East Florida Papers include at least forty-five documents related to Fleming's work as a regidor. Collectively, these reports span hundreds of pages—far too many to translate for a writer who must hire others for that task. Even so, English language abstracts of the reports provide a glimpse of the regidores' varied responsibilities and some of the unique challenges they faced.

24. *EFP*, 83/45, Detailed proceedings of purchase of land for parish church, February 11, 1792.

25. *EFP*, 147/4, Miguel de Ysnardy to Governor of Florida, June 30, 1802.

26. *EFP*, 25/15, Governor of Florida to Gonzalo Zamorano, August 29, 1791.

27. *EFP*, 146/74, Jorge Fleming to Governor of Florida, December 13, 1797.

28. *EFP*, 147/74, Jorge Fleming to Governor of Florida, March 6, 1800.

29. *EFP*, 166/86, Bakers John Martin Struder, Jean Girare, Jean Grisnao, and Juan Villalonga to the Governor, April 15, 1791.

30. *EFP*, 83/45, Fleming, Ysnardy, and Segui to Governor of Florida, February 12, 1792.

31. *EFP*, 118/63, Proceedings on contract for meat with government and public, December 17, 1796.

32. Richard K. Murdoch, "The Return of Runaway Slaves, 1790–1794," *Florida Historical Quarterly* 38:2, (1959).

33. South Carolina Department of Archives and History, "Pinckney, Gov. Charles, Message, With Enclosures, Concerning The Progress Of Simeon Theus, Commissioner To Adjust State Claims Against The U.S. and Transmitting An Agreement Between the Federal Government And The Governor Of East Florida Concerning Fugitive Slaves, A Letter From the President Of The Colonial Assembly Of Santo Domingo Expressing Gratitude For A Loan, And Laws Of France Concerning Shipping," Series S165009, Message 0554, http://www.archivesindex.sc.gov/onlinearchives/search.aspx.

34. Several documents in the East Florida Papers are related to Fleming's work in this capacity. See for example: *EFP*, 41/27, James Seagrove to George Fleming, August 21, 1793; *EFP*, 174/29, Bryan Morel to Governor, October 17, 1791.

35. Cormac A. O'Riordan, "The 1795 Rebellion in East Florida" (masters thesis, University of North Florida, 1995) 99. http://digitalcommons.unf.edu/etd/99.

36. *EFP*, 48/32, William Pengree, April 28, 1793; F. P. Fatio to Governor Quesada, May 3, 1793; Andrew Pleym to Governor Quesada, May 4, 1793; Fleming and others to Governor Quesada, May 6, 1793.

37. Political power in France shifted during Genêt's brief tenure as first minister to the United States. His stubborn insistence on pressing forward with attacks against British and Spanish interests made him a counterrevolutionary in the eyes of the new French leaders. He likely would have been executed if he returned to France, so he appealed to Washington for political asylum. To his good fortune, Washington was sympathetic. Genêt became a naturalized U.S. citizen and lived in New York for the rest of his life.

38. Charles E. Bennett, *Florida's "French" Revolution, 1793-1795* (Gainesville: University Presses of Florida, 1981), 119. Among those at the card game were Father Michael Crosby, Father Francis Esteban, Father Constantine McCaffrey, the innkeeper, and his wife.

39. Susan Parker, "Invasion Scare Terrorized Residents in 1794," *St. Augustine Record*, January 15, 2006, http://staugustine.com/stories/011506/com_3578636.shtml.

40. Lang and McIntosh were shipped to Cuba and briefly imprisoned there. Others were imprisoned in the Castillo in St. Augustine.

41. *EFP*, 51/32, Carlos Howard to Acting Governor Bartolomé Morales, May 30, 1795.

42. *EFP*, 9/2, Quesada to Luis de las Casas, June 9, 1795; *EFP*, 51/32, Howard to Morales, June 23, 1795.

43. *EFP*, 51/32, Pedro Carne to Carlos Howard, June 30, 1795.

44. *EFP*, 52/32, Morales to Howard, July 1, 1795, and Howard to Morales, July 2, 1795.

45. *EFP*, 52/32, Jorge Fleming to Bartolomé Morales, July 3, 1795.

46. Bennett, *"French" Revolution*, 190; "Extract of a letter from Cow-Ford, St. John's River," *Federal Intelligencer and Baltimore Daily Gazette*, September 1, 1795, 3, www.genealogybank.com.

47. Bennett, *"French" Revolution*, 198.

48. Margaret Seton Fleming Biddle, *Hibernia: The Unreturning Tide* (New York: Vantage Press, 1971), 24-26.

49. Florida Master Site File, Division of Historical Resources, File #8CL4, Hibernia Mound. C. C. Moore wrote that early Florida tourists desecrated many Native American mounds in search of souvenirs. Sadly, some of the early visitors to the Fleming family hotel in Hibernia may well have contributed to the destruction of this important, and possibly sacred, site.

50. During the British Period, Black Creek became known as Hawke's River.

51. Kevin S. Hooper, *The Early History of Clay County: A Wilderness that Could be Tamed* (Charleston, SC: History Press, 2006), 60-61.

52. *EFP*, 175/99, Andrew Atkinson to Governor, January 3, 1792, and Atkinson to Governor, August 8, 1795; "Heirs of George Fleming, 1000 Acres on Fleming's Island, Confirmed by Commissioners," *Florida Memory Project*, http://www.floridamemory.com/Collections/SpanishLandGrants/.

53. "Heirs of James McGirt, unconfirmed Claim of 300 acres at Hawke's Plantation," *Florida Memory Project*, http://www.floridamemory.com/Collections/SpanishLandGrants/. McGirt traded a 300-acre tract of land located eight miles north of St. Augustine for John McQueen's 300 acres at Hawke's plantation.

54. Ibid.

55. Susan R. Parker, "I Am Neither Your Subject Nor Your Subordinate," in Jacqueline K. Fretwell and Susan R. Parker, (eds.), *Clash Between Cultures: Spanish East Florida, 1784-1821*, El Escribano (1988).

56. *EFP*, 111, Item 1790-28, Continued Prosecution of Daniel McGirt, November 30, 1790; *EFP*, 25/15, Governor of Florida to Gonzalo Zamorano, July 29, 1791; *EFP*, 132, Item 1791-1, Daniel McGirt Requests Postponement, August 27, 1792.

57. "Susannah Cashen Grant, Confirmed Claim of 500 acres on Fleming's Island, W. side of St. Johns River," *Florida Memory Project*, http://www.floridamemory.com/Collections/SpanishLandGrants/.

58. Heirs of George Fleming, Confirmed Claim of 1000 Acres on Fleming's Island.

59. Thomas J. Kirkland and Robert M. Kennedy, *Historic Camden* (Columbia, SC: The State Company, 1905), 300.

60. *EFP*, 53/32, Andrew Atkinson to George Fleming, January 1, 1796.

61. Ibid., 10/2, Juan Nepomuceno de Quesada to Luis de las Casas, February 3, 1796.

62. Heirs of James McGirt, *Florida Memory Project*, http://www.floridamemory.com/Collections/SpanishLandGrants/.

63. Susannah Cashen Grant, Confirmed Claim. James Cashen subsequently received a Spanish Land Grant of 500 acres immediately to the north of Fleming's grant.

64. Jane Landers, *Black Slavery in Spanish Florida* (Urbana, IL: University of Chicago Press, 1999), 74.

65. Heirs of George Fleming, Confirmed Claim of 1,000 Acres on Fleming's Island.

66. Fleming Patriot War Claim, depositions of Sophia Fleming, Lewis Fleming, Sophia Fatio, and Louisa Fatio.

67. Fatio Sr., Patriot War Claim, deposition of Lewis Fleming.

68. Parker, *Neither Your Subject Nor Your Subordinate.*

69. Biddle, *Unreturning Tide*, 24.

70. Fleming, Patriot War Claim.

71. The description of Fatio's home comes from: L'Engle, *A Collection of Letters,* vol. 1; Fatio Jr., Patriot War Claim; L'Engle, *Notes of My Family*; Florida History Online, *New Switzerland*, www.unf.edu/floridahistoryonline.

72. William Scott Willis, "A Swiss Settler In East Florida: A Letter Of Francis Philip Fatio," *Florida Historical Quarterly* 64:2 (1985). Professor Willis was a Fatio-Fleming in-law through his marriage to one of their descendants.

73. This may have been strawberry blite, also known as strawberry spinach, a native American plant cultivated for its sweetish berries, spinach-like leaves, and for the red dye derived from the berries. Chicory provides leaves for salads, and its roots were baked, ground, and used as a substitute for or additive to coffee.

74. *EFP*, 44/31, Correspondence between Governor and Josef de Ortega, August 5-13 and September 19, 1804.

75. Jean Parker Waterbury, "Where Artillery Land Crosses Aviles Street: The Segui/Kirby House," *El Escribano* 24 (1985): 1-37.

76. *EFP*, 15/5, Governor to Secretary of Grace and Justice, September 30, 1806.

77. *EFP*, 18/10, Doc. 1807-A, King of Spain, November 30, 1807.

78. L'Engle, *Notes of My Family*. Mrs. Susan Fatio L'Engle was a daughter of F. P. Fatio Sr. and preserved many details of his life.

79. At that time Nice was still a part of Italy.

80. The Fatio home was located at the present-day site of A1A Restaurant in St. Augustine, Florida.

81. Parker, "Success through Diversification," 74.

82. *EFP*, 38/25, Miguel O'Reilly to Juan Jose de Estrada, July 19, 1811.

83. "Mathews to Robert Smith, n.d." in J. C. A. Stagg, et al., eds., *The Papers of James Madison, Presidential Series*, vol. 3 (Charlottesville: University of Virginia Press, 1996), 123-24.

84. James G. Cusick, *The Other War of 1812: The Patriot War and the American Invasion of Spanish East Florida* (Athens: University of Georgia Press, 2007).

85. Ibid., 125.

86. Fleming Patriot War Claim, depositions of Lewis and Sophia Fleming.

87. Fatio Jr., Patriot War Claim, deposition of Sophia Fleming.

88. Frank Marotti, *The Cana Sanctuary: History, Diplomacy, and Black Catholic Marriage in Antebellum St. Augustine, Florida* (Tuscaloosa: University of Alabama Press, 2012). Marotti quotes the testimony of Juan Antonio Florencio in the Patriot War Claim of Prince Whitten.

89. "George Fleming Memorial to Governor Coppinger," September 9, 1816, translated by John Diviney, Heirs of George Fleming, Confirmed Claim of 1,000 Acres on Fleming's Island.

90. Fleming Patriot War Claim, depositions of Jesse Long and John Bowden.

91. Cusick, *Other War of 1812*, 217.

92. *EFP*, 84/45, Edward Wanton to George Fleming, November 24, 1813.

93. Cusick, *Other War of 1812*, 239; Marotti, *Cana Sanctuary*, 51-55.

94. Fleming Patriot War Claim, deposition of Sophia Fatio.

95. "Heirs of George Fleming, A Town Lot in Fernandina, Lot 7, Sq. 7, Confirmed by Commissioners, American State Papers, Vol. 4, Page 286, Report 8, No. 6, 1825," *Florida Memory Project*, http://www.floridamemory.com/Collections/SpanishLandGrants/. It is important to note that this is not present-day Fernandina, Florida. It is "Old Town" Fernandina, which is located north of that city.

96. Fatio Jr., Patriot War Claim, deposition of Sophia Fleming.

97. L'Engle, *A Collection of Letters*, vol. 1. See page 194 for a copy of F. P. Fatio's assets and will. Fatio left the Nassau River tract to his daughter, Sophia Fatio Fleming, through her husband, George, and to his granddaughter, Mary Fatio, through her husband, William Gibson. Mary Fatio was the only daughter of Sophia's oldest brother, Louis, whose wife died while Mary was quite young. Louis left Florida forever in 1792 but did not take his daughter with him. Sophia Fleming took the primary responsibility of raising and caring for her niece.

98. "Heirs of George Fleming, Confirmed Claim for 980 Acres 'Langley Bryan' opposite Fort Buena Vista, American State Papers, vol. 4, 160-97, Report 1, No. 25, 1824," *Florida Memory Project*, http://www.floridamemory.com/Collections/SpanishLandGrants/.

99. "George Fleming Memorial to Governor Coppinger," September 9, 1816, translated by John Diviney, Heirs of George Fleming, Confirmed Claim of 20,000 Acres on San Sebastian River. This acreage encompasses present day San Sebastian, Florida.

100. *EFP*, 116/58, Evaluation of property of Jorge Fleming, April 3, 1816; *EFP*, 166/85, Guillermo Lawrence, April 6, 1816.

101. Emily L. Wilson, ed., *Florida Historical Records Survey, Selected Abstract from Superior and Circuit Court Case Files*, vol. 1, (St. John County, Florida, 1939), 97. Forbes thought he had made a clean purchase of this land from Andrew Dewees's widow, Catherine Chicken, but after Spain transferred East Florida to the United States the Dewees heirs sued to get the land back. They prevailed in a lengthy court battle.

102. James Grant Forbes, *Sketches, Historical and Topographical, of The Florida; More Particularly of East Florida* (New York: C. S. Van Winkle, 1821), 77, https://books.google.com/books.

103. L'Engle, *Notes of My Family*, 39.

104. *EFP*, 63/32, Governor to Fleming, Jan. 22, 1817.

105. "Amelia Island," *Daily National Intelligencer* (Washington, D.C.), vol. 5, iss. 1478, October 3, 1817, 3, www.geneaologybank.com.

106. L'Engle, *Notes of My Family*, 39.

107. Gregor MacGregor, "Inhabitants of the Northern and Western District of East-Florida," *Yankee* (Boston, MA) vol. 6, iss. 33, August 8, 1817, 2. MacGregor's proclamation was dated July 12, 1817. It appeared in multiple newspapers around the country.

108. Richard G. Lowe, "American Seizure Of Amelia Island," *Florida Historical Quarterly* 45:1 (1966).

109. "Amelia Island," *Pilot* (Cazenovia, NY), vol. 10, no. 480, October 15, 1817, 2, www.genealogybank.com.

110. *EFP*, 63/32, Governor to Jorge Fleming, August 30, 1817.

111. Ibid., Jorge Clark to Governor, September 10, 1817.

112. Ibid., Thomas Llorente to Governor, September 9, 1817.

113. T. Frederick Davis, "MacGregor's Invasion of Florida, 1817," *Florida Historical Quarterly* 7:1, (1928).

114. Ibid.

115. Richard G. Lowe, "American Seizure Of Amelia Island," *Florida Historical Quarterly* 45:1 (1966).

116. Clarence Edwin Carter, ed., *Territorial Papers of the United States:* vol. 22, *The Territory of Florida, 1821-1824* (Washington, D.C.: USGPO, 1956).

117. Deed Book H, St. Johns County, Florida, 358-59.

118. *Escrituras*, St. Augustine Historical Society Research Library, (1819-1821): 2897-2900.

119. Ibid., 2886-87.

120. Fleming Patriot War Claim, testimony of Sophia Fatio; L'Engle, *A Collection of Letters*, 1:59.

121. Eugenia Price, *Margaret's Story* (New York: Lippincott & Crowell, 1980), 9. Ms. Price extensively consulted Fleming family members and Jacksonville historian Dena Snodgrass for her historical novel about Margaret Fleming, which resulted in many readers accepting fictionalized events as factual.

122. "Obituary," *City Gazette and Daily Advertiser* (Charleston, SC), vol. 42, iss. 13479, November 6, 1821, 2.

Starting Anew–The Fleming Family Copes
with the Death of George

Lewis Fleming was still in Cuba working for the mercantile firm of Forbes & Lawrence when his father died. There he fell in love with Augustina Alexandra Cortes. Augustina was born in Havana in 1806. Her family had strong ties to East Florida, and both her father and grandfather knew George Fleming well. Her father, Dimas Cortes, was a treasury official and schoolteacher in St. Augustine for many years before moving to Cuba sometime after 1800. Her grandfather, Bernardo Segui, was George Fleming's fellow regidor in St. Augustine for sixteen years. Given these connections it is unlikely that the initial meeting between Lewis and Augustina was a coincidence. They were married in Havana in 1821 or 1822 when Lewis was twenty-two or twenty-three years old, and Augustina was just fifteen or sixteen.[1]

Lewis returned to Florida with his bride in 1822 and joined his mother and his siblings for the task of rebuilding the Hibernia plantation. Fortunately for them, they had the great advantage of advice from Sophia's brother, Francis Fatio Jr., who continued rebuilding his New Switzerland plantation directly across the river. Even with Fatio's guidance, starting anew would not be easy. The Flemings owned slaves to perform the labor, but expenses associated with building a home and a plantation on land untilled for many years would be substantial. They probably had some cash and liquid assets, but it appears those didn't last long because during the next ten years they faced a series of financial challenges. Those difficulties can be attributed, in part, to Florida's recent status as a Territory of the United States and George Fleming's complicated estate. One condition of the transfer of power from Spain stipulated that the United States must honor all valid Spanish land titles, but the process of proving title was costly and time-consuming. Another condition of the treaty stipulated that the United States would reimburse Spanish citizens for damages inflicted by U.S. troops during the Patriot Invasion of 1812–1813, but the U.S.

government moved at a snail's pace to honor that commitment. Final adjudication of Fleming's estate was impossible until those affairs were settled, and any profit they might have reaped through sales of their extensive landholdings was stymied.

To raise cash Sophia, Lewis, George Jr., and Mary Fleming, along with Francis Fatio Jr., executed a mortgage with Henry W. Hills and Jacob Wilcox on April 18, 1823, for the sum of $3809.70. Together, the Flemings and Fatio pledged properties in St. Augustine as collateral to secure the bond. The Flemings promised their Charlotte Street home. Francis promised his property located on St. George Street two lots north of Treasury Lane. Both reneged on their commitment to pay the first installment of $1904.80, plus interest, due on October 18, 1823.[2] This was the largest of several debts that plagued the family. The Flemings' various creditors sued for payment several times in the following years, and court-appointed officials traveled almost annually to Hibernia to serve one summons after another. The surviving court records are incomplete, so the final outcomes of many cases remain a mystery.

At his death, George Fleming owed Father Miguel Crosby $286. Father Crosby's son, Thomas, sued for payment on October 2, 1823. Lewis and his mother responded to the suit from Hibernia and promised to pay the full amount before June 1, 1825. More than two years after failing to keep that promise, Lewis and Sophia were summoned to appear in the St. Augustine courthouse on April 9, 1827. The debt with interest was now $313.56.[3]

A merchant named Squire Streeter sued Lewis Fleming, who was summoned to appear in court on February 26, 1824. Streeter claimed that Lewis had not paid him $178.26 for goods delivered, and presented a detailed invoice of the items. A hostile Streeter complained that Lewis had never paid a previous debt despite repeated promises to do so. The merchant clearly had had enough of the promises and accused Fleming of "contriving ... and intending to deceive and defraud." Lewis entered a plea of not guilty and engaged Cox & Lancaster, attorneys, to represent his case.[4] The invoice submitted in this case provides a glimpse of goods Lewis purchased for use in Hibernia, and suggests a family living in high style while not paying debts. Among the items were some ninety-five yards of assorted cloth including gingham, calico, black broadcloth, a small amount of Florentine silk, bombazette (a thin wool cloth), and other varieties too difficult to transcribe from Streeter's scrawled handwriting. The cloth was accompanied by a variety of trimmings, threads, and needles. These represented approximately seventy-five dollars of the total bill. There were seven silk handkerchiefs and three pairs of black silk gloves billed at seventy-five cents each. The two most expensive items were a tortoise comb and a hat, each valued at $5.50. These likely were for his wife, Augustina. Two bottles of brandy and four bottles of wine cost one dollar each. There were only a few food items, including some sugar, four loaves of bread, and a small quantity of cheese. The total invoice is for $144.26 in goods, plus $34 that Streeter paid to another man on Fleming's account.

At the same time, Hills and Wilcox pressed their case against the Flemings and Fatio, and on March 25, 1824, both promised payments. Fatio said he would pay $572.22 and the Flemings promised a payment of $635, a total well below the balance due. However, those payments were not forthcoming, and two months later Hills and Wilcox petitioned to foreclose on the mortgage. Francis and Sophia, Lewis, George Jr., and Mary Fleming all were summoned to appear in the St. Augustine courthouse on May 27, 1824. The court took the entire summer before arriving at a decision. In the end, the Flemings were either unable to pay their mortgage, or more willing to part with their old home in St. Augustine than with their money. The city marshal, Waters Smith, put the Fleming property up for public auction January 4, 1825.[5] We might consider this a public embarrassment for the Flemings, but it actually may have been a shrewd business decision. The Flemings and Fatio each pocketed approximately $1900 in exchange for their houses, which sold at auction for much less than that.

Two years later Margaret Cook claimed that Lewis and George Jr. owed her $452. Once again, a court-appointed official traveled to Hibernia to deliver a summons. Upon receipt of that summons George Jr. and Lewis signed a promise to pay the full amount.[6]

A completely different sort of lawsuit began in 1828 because of events that took place two years earlier. According to court documents, Lewis and George Jr. leased a large tract of land to Sarah and Domingo Acosta. This was the 980-acre land grant known as Langley Bryan that their father received in 1816, plus an additional 170 acres. Specifically, the lease included 200 acres of arable land, 200 acres of pastures, 550 acres of woodland, 100 acres of marshlands, and 100 acres of swamp. On the land were two live oak hammocks and a house that likely included associated outbuildings. There are no records to tell us who built the structures or when they were built. The lease period was for seven years beginning on January 1, 1826.

A scant ten days after the lease agreement, Lewis and George Jr. traveled upriver to the property. In the legal language of the court documents, they "ejected, expelled and remanded" the Acostas and their group from the property, and eleven months later still denied them access. The suit went on to claim "other wrongs and injuries" by the Flemings to the Acostas and claimed one thousand dollars for the damages.

The image of Lewis and George Jr. invading the Acosta's small camp requires some speculation. They probably traveled upriver on a plantation boat powered by some of their Negroes. They pulled ashore at a clearing on the west bank of the St. Johns River, stepped out onto the sandy bottom at the river's edge, and stormed headlong into the camp. The Flemings had a history of arming their slaves and free Negroes, so it is possible some of those men stood ready to support them. Lewis and George Jr. allegedly brandished weapons and shouted threats of bodily harm if the Acostas didn't leave immediately. For their part, the Fleming brothers pleaded not guilty. Their attorney, John Drysdale, defended their actions, and claimed that the whole incident didn't happen that way. This case dragged on for over three years, during which time the Acostas summoned at least thirteen witnesses to testify on their behalf. The surviving court documents are incomplete so we don't know the outcome of the case, and we may never know the truth of the matter.

While that case was ongoing, Andrew McDowell successfully sued Lewis and George Jr. for $187.34. The brothers did not pay, so the court seized five hundred acres of the Langley Bryan tract, which were valued at $625. Marshall Waters Smith offered the property at public auction, but no one bid the full value so the auction was rescheduled for a later date. At the second auction the Flemings' friend, Nehemiah Brush, purchased the tract for half the appraised value.[7] This appears to have been a sweetheart deal, because years later the Flemings again owned the entire Langley Bryan Land Grant. Brush must have sold it back to them.

While still defending himself in the Acosta case, and in the wake of the loss of five hundred acres of land, Lewis Fleming traveled to St. Augustine to settle his debt to William Taber. Lewis presented Taber a written bill of exchange in which he directed his cotton factor, Richard Carnochan, Esq., of Charleston, to pay Taber $157.78.[8] Fleming instructed Carnochan to make the payment ninety days later and charge it to Lewis's account. Taber accepted the bill of exchange, probably because he knew that Carnochan was in St. Augustine, and tried to collect payment that same day. Carnochan refused to accept the bill or to pay any amount whatsoever. Almost immediately, Taber protested to Fleming who "then and there faithfully promised to pay the debt when requested to do so." A month later Fleming still had not paid so Taber sued him.[9]

To close out what must have been a difficult decade for the Flemings, Andrew Lowe, a cotton factor in Savannah, sued for payment due. Marshall Waters Smith published notice that he would confiscate two of Lewis and Sophia Fleming's slaves and sell them at public auction to satisfy the debt.[10]

Life wasn't all debts and lawsuits for the Flemings throughout the 1820s. They experienced the joy of marriage, the birth of healthy children, the sorrowful loss of infants, and, according to family oral histories, eventually prospered at Hibernia. Augustina Fleming gave birth to her first son, George Claudius Fleming, on October 22, 1822, in St. Augustine. He became know as "George C." in the family to distinguish him from his uncle. Her second son, Luis Francisco Isadore Fleming, was born April 4, 1825. He became known as "L. I." to distinguish him from his father. Augustina Fleming gave birth to two other children in the 1820s, Alexandro Manuel Fleming on January 6, 1828, and Walter Smith Fleming on August 29, 1829, but neither of these babies survived infancy. George Fleming Jr. married his first cousin once removed, Mary Magdalena Gibson, in St. Marys, Georgia, on July 26, 1827.[11] George Jr. took his young bride back to Hibernia, and in less than a year she gave birth to their only child, Mary Sophia Fleming.

Hibernia became a productive plantation with cash crops of cotton, corn, and oranges. Prosperity was impossible, though, without slaves and free Negroes to work the fields, and Indians were an ever-present threat to the labor force, frequently enticing slaves to escape and live among them, or stealing them outright. This was an ongoing problem when Florida became a U.S. Territory, and the former Spanish citizens expected the federal government to do something about it. The 1823 Treaty of Moultrie was supposed to confine Indians to about four million acres of interior Florida and leave the established plantations free of their presence. Indians found it impossible to sustain their lifestyle within the treaty boundaries, though, and roamed freely throughout East Florida. In 1824 Sophia Fleming, George Fleming Jr., and Francis Fatio Jr. joined approximately fifty-seven prominent East Floridians and petitioned the federal government to either correct the Indian problem or reimburse them for lost slaves.[12]

Two years later the situation with the Indians was worse. Planters along the St. Johns River, including Lewis Fleming, George Fleming Jr., Francis Fatio Jr., and his brothers Philip and Lewis, sent a Memorial to President John Quincy Adams. They complained that Seminoles and members of other tribes roamed Florida at will, killing cattle and hogs, robbing plantations, and enticing slaves away from their owners. The Floridians implored the president to provide armed forces to "scour the swamps in the Indian boundary" to recover slaves and make the region safe. The planters threatened that without U.S. military intervention they might be "driven to make reprisals on the Indians which may end in a war of extermination."[13] Tensions between settlers and Indians escalated so much that the East Florida citizenry organized a militia. Joseph M. Hernandez, Brigadier General of the First Brigade of the Florida Militia, appointed Lewis Fleming to the position of brigade inspector on December 2, 1829. At the same time he chose John Lee William as assistant adjutant general, Charles Robiou as brigade quartermaster, and William Travers and Samuel Williams as aids de camp, ordering that "they will be respected and obeyed accordingly." The First Brigade trained in preparation to defend St. Augustine and the surroundings against Indian depredations.[14]

During the next few years the Flemings in Hibernia and the Fatios in New Switzerland lost loved ones. On October 22, 1831, Augustina Alexandra Cortes Fleming gave birth to her only daughter, also named Augustina Alexandra. That joyous occasion for the family was tempered by the mother's frail condition following the birth. Her health failed during the next couple of months, and she died in 1832 at the age of twenty-six. She was laid to rest in the family cemetery just a few feet away from the father-in-law she had never met, where her grave is the second oldest on record in the cemetery.

Across the river in New Switzerland, the Fatio family lost its patriarch. Francis Philip Fatio Jr. died at the age of seventy-two on March 15, 1832. His son, Louis Fatio, became master at New Switzerland, but he died just six months later. His nephew, Colonel Miller Hallowes, filled that void. Miller Hallowes was the fourth son of Francis's sister, Louisa Martha Fatio. Louisa first married when she was just fourteen years old, but her husband, Captain Bruere of the British army, died soon afterward. She next married Colonel John Hallowes, also a British officer, and lived her entire adult life in Great Britain. In 1792 the Hallowes family was stationed in Dublin, Ireland, for nearly twelve months. While there she reached out to George Fleming's Irish mother, Mary Walsh Fleming. We might know more about the

Flemings' Irish ancestry through Louisa Hallowes, but Mrs. Fleming showed no interest in getting to know her in-laws. Louisa "called [Mrs. Fleming] twice, drank tea once and begged they would come and see me, but they never favored me with a call ... I fancy that they did not wish to be acquainted, so I dropped them, of course."[15]

Colonel Miller Hallowes was in England on a leave of absence from General Simón Bolivar's army in South America when his uncle died. His mother owned an undivided one-half interest in New Switzerland, so he resigned his commission with Bolivar, moved to Florida, and took up the life of planter and master at New Switzerland.[16] Francis Fatio's daughter, Susan, and her husband, Lieutenant John C. L'Engle, also had a plantation house on New Switzerland land, and the extended Fleming-Fatio family needed to rely on each other more than ever. During the next three years tensions mounted between planters and the Indians, and sporadic violence was commonplace. The St. Johns River valley became a very dangerous place to live, and even the weather conspired against its inhabitants.

Endnotes

1. *U. S. and International Marriage Records, 1560-1900* (Provo, UT: Yates Publishing, 2004), www.ancestry.com; Biddle, *Hibernia: The Unreturning Tide.* Both of these sources confirm that Lewis Fleming and Augustina Cortes were married in Cuba but do not provide the date. I searched Cuban marriage records available at the St. Augustine Foundation, Flagler College, but could not locate the official record of their marriage.

2. SAHS, Civil Cases, File #123-17, Wilcox/Hills vs. Fleming, 1823-1824.

3. Ibid., File #98-55, Crosby vs. Fleming, 1823.

4. Ibid., File #162-27, Streeter vs. Fleming, 1824.

5. Ibid., File #123-17, Wilcox/Hills vs. Fleming, 1823-1824. This folder contains original documents as well as public notices printed in the newspaper regarding the case.

6. Ibid., File #100-27, Cook vs. Fleming, 1827.

7. *Waters Smith, Marshall, to Nehemiah Brush, Deed of Sale at Public Auction,* St. Johns County Records, St. Johns County, Florida. Subsequent land records suggest that at some later date the Flemings purchased the property back from Brush.

8. Throughout the South most planters relied on a "factor" to sell their crops. Cotton factors performed a variety of other services for their clients, including purchasing goods, buying and selling slaves, and even arranging to send their children to boarding schools. Richard Carnochan also was a member of the Board of Directors at a Charleston bank.

9. SAHS, Civil Cases, File #169-69, Taber vs. Fleming.

10. *Florida Herald and Southern Democrat*, vol. 8, iss. 4, December 16, 1829, 3.

11. Jordan Dodd, *Early Georgia Marriage Index 1786-1850*, www.archives.com. Mary Gibson was a grandchild of Sophia Fleming's brother, Louis Fatio. Mary Gibson's mother was Mary Fatio Gibson, whom Sophia nurtured and raised when Louis Fatio moved to Italy.

12. "Petition To Congress By Inhabitants of East Florida, March 8, 1824," in Clarence E. Carter, ed., *Territorial Paper of the United States*: vol. 22, *The Territory of Florida, 1821-1824* (Washington, D.C.: USGPO, 1956), 857-58.

13. Ibid., "Memorial To The President By Inhabitants of St. Johns County, March 6, 1826," 462-63.

14. *Florida Herald and Southern Democrat* (St. Augustine), vol. 8, iss. 4, December 16, 1829, 2, www.geneaologybank.com.

15. L'Engle, *A Collection of Letters*, 2: 28. The information about Louisa Hallowes's unsuccessful attempts to get to know George Fleming's mother

and siblings is contained in a letter she wrote to her brother, Philip Fatio, on September 6, 1795.

16. Ibid., 37.

The Second Seminole War and the
Second Destruction of Hibernia

Planters and Indians alike suffered through the most severe freeze on record in North Florida from February 2 through 9, 1835. Jacksonville recorded temperatures as low as 8°. The St. Johns River was frozen "several rods from shore" [one rod is 16.5 feet] and people reportedly walked a considerable distance across the ice. The extreme cold totally destroyed "entire groves across the state, killing both mature and young citrus trees."[1] Before the freeze, Lewis Fleming's cousin at New Switzerland, Miller Hallowes, managed a thriving orange grove of about fifteen hundred trees, some of them remarkably abundant. Hallowes reported that his highly esteemed slave, Dublin, harvested nearly eleven thousand oranges from just three trees.[2] This reliable source of income was lost forever at Hibernia and New Switzerland. The freeze also destroyed Indians' crops and wild forage, forcing them to encroach more boldly onto land claimed by white settlers. In the following months increasingly heinous violence by both Indians and white men led to all-out war.

With initial reports of violence, the publishers of the *Florida Herald* in St. Augustine urged calm. They assured their readers that the Treaty of Payne's Prairie required Indians to move west of the Mississippi River, and reports of resistance were "altogether unfounded."[3] Two weeks later the editors reported that Indians fired on some people along the Ocklawaha River, but "we are assured that there was no evil intentions on the part of the Indians."[4] Two months later, the editors rebuffed reports that Seminoles attempted to murder a white man, saying it was only a matter of a quarrel between parties.[5] Then on June 19 near the Hogtown settlement, a small party of seven or eight Indians secretly went hunting outside their designated borders and killed a cow. Seven white men came upon five Indians butchering the cow, somehow disarmed them, and set about flogging them with cow-whips. The Indians' companions charged the scene, raised a war whoop, and fired on the whites. The whites returned fire killing one Indian and mortally wounding another. In acquiescence to the demands of settlers, Indian leaders later turned over five of their tribe to white authorities but they were released because no one appeared to press charges.[6]

In August of 1835 Mikasuki Indians shockingly avenged the Hogtown incident. They killed Private Dalton, a mail carrier, while he traveled his regular route between Ft. Brooke at Tampa Bay and Camp King. They scalped Dalton, disemboweled his body, and threw it into a pond. As if that were not enough to make a statement, they cut his mule into pieces. The *Florida Herald* decried the "savages" who did a war dance on Dalton's scalp.[7] This may have been the final act that ultimately pushed the Florida militia into action.

There was never any doubt that Lewis and George Fleming would join the fight. Their father had served the Spanish militia in defense of East Florida and they would volunteer to serve the Florida militia and fight the Indians. Lewis made his feelings clear on this matter when he wrote, "If a man will not protect the country he lives in he should leave it … a man should be a man."[8] His brother George Jr. likely shared the same passion for his homeland. Fleming family service in the Second Seminole War may have been a foregone conclusion at the time, but learning the story of their service more than one hundred seventy-five years later is difficult.

Oral traditions tell us that Lewis served on General Richard K. Call's staff, and that he was cited for bravery in the Battle of Wahoo Swamp. The family has no oral tradition whatsoever regarding George Fleming Jr.'s Seminole War service. Sadly, neither man's service is well documented in historical records. The Fleming family preserved one important letter written by Lewis Fleming at the onset of the Second Seminole War, as well as a couple of brief stories from those years. Hours of research at various archival collections, including the St. Augustine Historical Society, Clay County Archives, Duval County Archives, the Florida State Archives, and the National Archives, provided frustratingly little information. These sources, along with a few newspaper reports in 1835 and 1836, offer just enough information to present a broad account of Fleming service in the Florida militia during the Second Seminole War, as well as a description of what Lewis Fleming experienced during the Battle of Wahoo Swamp.

George Fleming Jr. first mustered in as a corporal with Lieutenant Elijah Bleach's detachment of Captain James E. Hutcheson's company, a part of the 2nd Brigade of Florida Militia commanded by Colonel John Warren of Jacksonville. He was one of nineteen mounted soldiers in his company of thirty-four men who served from November 10, 1835, through March 5, 1836.[9] In October of 1836 George Fleming Jr. submitted a claim seeking payment for "one horse taken into service," valued at $150. The claim was rejected because the horse had been "impressed" into service along with its owner and rider.[10] Territorial Governor Richard Call ordered George Jr. back into service again on December 3, 1836, for a period of two months and twenty days. He served as a private among Captain James Dell's mounted troops in the 1st regiment, 2nd brigade, again under command of Colonel Warren. Private Fleming rode his own sorrel horse throughout this period of service.[11]

Lewis Fleming does not appear in any of the surviving muster rolls for the Second Seminole War. Even so, he was in the field under Colonel Warren's command in December of 1835. He fought in the Battle of Wahoo Swamp late in 1836, and he was on active duty of some sort through at least January of 1837. Evidence suggests that Lewis served on Warren's staff, possibly as a brigade inspector—the same position he held with the St. Augustine militia six years earlier. One contemporary writer described "gentleman citizens" who apparently never mustered into service but nonetheless accompanied Colonel Warren into battle.[12] Perhaps that explains Lewis's absence among the muster rolls. Regardless, Lewis Fleming wrote a letter while on a militia campaign in late 1835. During that time he traveled to and from the Jacksonville area in service to both Colonel Warren and General Richard K. Call, recruiting troops and preparing them to join the militia in the field. Fleming was in the vicinity of what historians generally regard as the first battle of the Second Seminole War, and provided one of the few surviving accounts, albeit secondhand, of events that day.

The Battle of Black Point

General Hernandez ordered Warren's troops out of Jacksonville on December 2, 1835, leaving only sufficient men to protect the immediate area.[13] On December 18, 1835, Lewis Fleming began the day with Colonel Warren at Fort Crum, a tenuous redoubt constructed by Captain Thomas Harn on the west side of Paynes Prairie approximately six miles west of Micanopy.[14] Ten days later, Fleming was in Newnansville and wrote his friend, attorney R. B. Gregory of Jacksonville, to recount the events of December 18–20. Fleming did not witness the Battle of Black Point firsthand, but he may have spoken with soldiers who were on the scene, possibly including his brother, because Corporal George Fleming Jr.'s company of mounted troops engaged the Seminoles that day.[15]

The battle began on December 18 not long after General Clinch ordered Colonel Warren to "scour the country" by way of Wacahoota and the plantation of Captain Gabriel Priest.[16] Warren divided his regiment, sending a greater number to scout for the enemy and a small guard to take the wagons to Micanopy via a route around the southern edge of Paynes Prairie.[17] At a place called Black Point, which is a spot of high ground near the east end of the prairie, a group of Indians swept down, firing upon the poorly defended wagons. The outnumbered wagon guard retreated to the middle of the prairie to take up a defensive position. They took enemy fire, suffered causalities, and saw their cowardly commanding officer turn his horse and flee the scene. Some of the Seminoles pressed the attack while others totally plundered the wagons. Two other militia companies not far away on the prairie heard the firing and charged to the fight. The Indians took up a strong defensive position on a thick hammock, thus preventing an effective counterattack. All the reinforcements could do was carry away the dead and wounded. One man died on the spot and ten days later four others died from mortal wounds. Three men survived their injuries.

General Call arrived in Newnansville that same day with two hundred seventy-five men and joined Colonel Warren's regiment. Call took command and on December 20 marched to Micanopy with a combined force of six hundred militiamen. About a mile from the town the advance guard encountered a party of seven Seminoles who had just burned a home. The Indians fired on the militia and then retreated to a defensive position in the swamp. This time the militia did not hesitate. Fleming wrote that the men "dismounted and charged the swamp like Lions" killing six of the enemy. One escaped, which Fleming thought just as well because "he would inform his brethren that the White [sic] men were not afraid to attack them in their dens."

Fleming summarized the current situation. The Indians had burned twenty-two houses, and approximately four hundred women and children "in the greatest distress" had taken refuge in Newnansville. Fleming witnessed this firsthand. He had been in Newnansville about seven days "organizing the 6th Regiment and sending off the men as soon as they arrive to join Gen'l Call." He confided in Mr. Gregory that he was glad to see General Call in command rather than Colonel Warren, but that he had "little hopes of the regular troops doing any thing [sic]." Fleming had ten or twelve more days of work in Newnansville, after which he would be off to "parts in Jacksonville and Mandarin" to recruit more men for the militia.[18]

Seminoles Attack New Switzerland

Seminoles wreaked havoc on the area around Hibernia and New Switzerland. In early July 1836 they had stolen over four thousand head of cattle along the east side of the St. Johns River. Colonel Leigh Read implored citizens of Florida to defend themselves, writing "If you do not go to fight them, they will come to fight us; if we do not destroy their crops, they will destroy ours; if we do not burn down their towns, they will burn down ours; if we do not capture their wives and children, they will scalp, they will murder, *they will butcher ours* [his italics]." In closing he urged the people of Florida, "Let them to the field with the watchword and battle cry—of Florida! Florida, Florida, single handed!!"[19] His rallying cry came too late to save the plantations at New Switzerland and Hibernia.

On June 10, 1836, Captain Peck commanded the U.S. steamer *Essayons*, a small supply ship that he courageously guided throughout the dangerous territory of the St. Johns River basin during the Second Seminole War. Steaming along the river he saw a small boat coming out from New Switzerland. On board were Miller Hallowes and his close neighbor, Dr. Simmons. Early that morning some Negro children warned Hallowes that Indians lurked nearby. Hallowes took shelter inside his home. While he spoke with Dr. Simmons, Indians fired on them through a window. A bullet passed through Hallowes's ear, struck his skull, and lodged in his neck. He blacked out and fell on the spot, but quickly recovered. Simmons and some Negroes hustled him to a boat at the end of the landing and shoved off into the river. The Indians gave chase and fired again but failed to hit their targets. One account of this event tells that Simmons returned fire.[20] Hallowes and Simmons were making their way to Hibernia for safety when Captain Peck picked them up. In short order those on board the steamer saw flames and smoke from both Hallowes's and Simmons's places.[21] The Indians burned their homes and their cotton houses, destroying valuable crops in the process, and making off with some two thousand dollars worth of plunder from Hallowes's place.

Captain Peck made way to "George & Lewis Fleming's plantation" at Hibernia where he "took off their families and negroes [sic], and proceeded to Picolata." At that time their families consisted of their mother, Sophia, their sister, Mary, George Jr.'s wife, Mary, and four children. George Claudius was thirteen years old. Louis Isadore was eleven years old. Little Augustina was just four years old. Their cousin Mary Sophia was nine years old. It is important to emphasize that the accounts of this event specifically mention that only "their families and negroes" were taken aboard the *Essayons*. There is no mention of Lewis or George Jr. being present at the time. Perhaps they stayed behind to defend the plantation, but if they did it seems likely that Captain Peck would have noted that. The greatest likelihood is that both of them were away from Hibernia serving the militia in defense of their homeland.

About five o'clock that evening, Captain Peck returned downriver to New Switzerland. As he approached the landing Peck saw a Negro hailing the ship and dispatched a small boat to pick him up. The man reported that some thirty Indians were at that very moment behind the Negro houses. They had been whooping and dancing in front of Hallowes's house as it burned. He also reported that a large band of Indians were on their way down both sides of the river and "had expressed their intention of destroying all the settlements on the river." In fact, they had already torched Susan Fatio L'Engle's plantation house at New Switzerland. They also destroyed the plantation of Lewis Fleming's close friend William Travers, which was located at the mouth of Governor's Creek on the west side of the St. Johns River.[22]

Several sources report that Indians destroyed the Fleming plantation at Hibernia during the Second Seminole War. Nearly all such reports cite Biddle's *Unreturning Tide*, John Mahon's *History of the Second Seminole War*, or Dena Snodgrass's 1945 interview of Gertrude N. L'Engle.[23] Each of those accounts is incorrect in some way.

Biddle's account suggests that Indians destroyed Hibernia sometime between 1845 and 1849, which is highly unlikely.[24] Mahon's book does not specifically mention Hibernia, and only tells us that most plantations along the west side of the St. Johns River were destroyed or abandoned. Miss L'Engle tells us that both Hibernia and New Switzerland were burned to the ground early in 1836, but New Switzerland was destroyed in June.

Despite inaccuracies in family oral traditions, and the lack of a firsthand report, it seems likely that Hibernia was, indeed, much devastated—if not totally destroyed—during the war. The historical record includes numerous references to the fact that the Fleming family lost a great deal during these years. Moreover, Sophia Fleming was the lead signatory of a Memorial presented to the U.S. Congress requesting a special commission of process claims for losses suffered during the Second Seminole War.[25] It could be that Indians actually ransacked and burned Hibernia, but it also could be that the fields went fallow and buildings fell into disrepair when the Flemings abandoned Hibernia for fear of their lives in June of 1836. The family did not return to live in Hibernia for nine years, and the war was not over for Lewis and George Fleming.

The Battle of Wahoo Swamp

In November of 1836 the central command received intelligence of the movements of a large band of Indians. A combined force of nearly 2100 men, including Floridians, Tennesseans, and Creek Indians, marched out of Fort Drane to track them down.[26] Colonel John Warren was in command of the 2nd Florida Mounted Volunteers with Major Lewis Fleming among his troops.

The men camped near the Cove of the Withlacoochee River, an area of roughly one hundred thirty-five square miles between the Withlacoochee River and the Tsala Apopka Chain of Lakes. This region was a significant stronghold of Osceola and other leaders of the Seminole resistance. The next day Colonel Warren's mounted troops crossed the river to scout for the enemy, which wasn't as simple as it sounds. The river spanned about 220 yards and required swimming their horses for at least fifty yards. Dense swamp clogged both sides. The horses trudged through mucky swamp bottom, forded and swam the river, and then emerged through swamp again where they found trails and signs indicating the Seminoles had left the area some days ago. Scouts believed that the enemy most likely had gone to Wahoo Swamp, but may have moved south.

Colonel Pierce's command, with Colonel Warren's mounted troops and the Creeks, marched south and west of the river in pursuit. The remainder of the army marched north, where they engaged the enemy in two spirited skirmishes, facing several hundred Indians, inflicting more punishment than they received, and driving the enemy into Wahoo Swamp. The troops reunited as planned, reassembled, and marched in formation to Wahoo Swamp on November 21, 1836. Pierce positioned Colonel Warren's mounted troops, including Major Fleming, on his right. Major Gardner's artillery battalion and middle Florida foot soldiers took positions immediately to the left of Pierce. Lieutenant Colonel Brown and Major Morris were at the far left, in command of the Creek volunteers. The Tennessee brigade under Colonel Trousdale was to the far right of Warren. The troops marched five miles in this configuration and closed within four hundred yards of the swamp when the Seminoles revealed themselves on the edge of a hammock, making war whoops and challenges to battle.

Gardner's foot soldiers moved up in two lines just twenty paces apart to within 130 yards then halted as Tennessee moved to support them on the extreme right. Gardner's men then advanced "coolly and steadily," entered the hammock without firing a shot, then opened up with a devastating barrage. The Indians backed deeper into the hammock while the Floridians chased them for perhaps a mile or more.

Pierce joined the attack at the center of the field supported by Warren's mounted troops. Major Fleming was among those who "commenced a spirited and vigorous fire." They endured galling return fire from the enemy, all the while holding their ground and returning a more lethal barrage than they received. Lt. Colonel Brown led his Creek volunteers over firm ground on the left. Some of his men attempted to cross a small stream to push the attack when Major David Moniac, the first Native American graduate of West Point, was gunned down midstream. His comrades watched his lifeless body sink below the water's surface and abandoned all attempts to cross the stream. All the while, Colonel Trousdale led his Tennesseans on an unfortunate trail to the right that took them into a clogged morass of swamp a half-mile across. The men struggled through black mud and water that sometimes reached their chests for nearly three-quarters of an hour. After that grueling slog the Tennesseans were exhausted, soaked, and covered with mud. Nonetheless, they threw themselves into the fight alongside Pierce and Warren.

Around three-thirty in the afternoon, four hours after the beginning charge, the Seminoles ceased fire and pulled back deeper into the swamp. Creek volunteers reported hearing the Seminole chiefs assure their comrades that the white men would not follow. They were right. Pierce wanted to press the attack, but after consultation with the Tennessee officers he agreed to form a rear guard, gather the dead and wounded, and pull back. The exhausted men were short on ammunition, short on food, and on the verge of starvation. They had begun this campaign from Ft. Drane with inadequate supplies and were now on half rations, with no corn or grain at all for the horses.[27] By ten o'clock that night, they had made their way back to camp. The next morning they marched to Volusia to resupply.

A few days later Colonel Pierce filed his official report, thus giving rise to the Fleming family legend that Lewis was cited for bravery in the battle. As was common practice among commanding officers in the aftermath of battle, Pierce singled out many men for their gallantry under fire. He wrote that Colonel Warren, Lt. Colonel Mills, Major Fleming, Captain Walker, and others, all "behaved throughout the day with great energy and bravery." Remarkably, Warren's command did not suffer any casualties that day. And, to be clear, Major Lewis Fleming received no citation for bravery, just the praise and admiration of a commanding officer on the battlefield that day.[28]

The last known mention of Lewis Fleming's service during the Second Seminole War comes from a quartermaster's report for forage. Lewis purchased corn and hay from Lieutenant George Watson for two horses during his period of service from December 3, 1836, through January 31, 1837.[29] His brother, George Jr., mustered out of Captain Dell's Company on February 23, 1837 then mustered in one last time, serving as a mounted private in Captain James G. Mason's company under Colonel Warren from March 18, 1837 through June 12, 1837.[30]

Some history buffs believe that Lewis Fleming suffered a near-deadly, permanently debilitating wound during the Battle of Withlacoochee on December 31, 1835. That is a fiction concocted for a popular novel titled *Margaret's Story*, but it is reported as a fact on several websites about the Flemings of Fleming Island. The author of the novel, Eugenia Price, worked closely with historian Dena Snodgrass to weave her story around a factual framework, which lends her book an air of authenticity. In the course of her research, Ms. Snodgrass discovered the case of a man named Fleming who suffered a severe gunshot wound to the ankle during the Battle of Withlacoochee. Snodgrass wrote, "Could he [Lewis] have been the Fleming who was wounded? We think this would fit well into the story to have him wounded."[31] It is a good story, yes, but there is no reason to think that man was Lewis Fleming. The medical assistant who treated this man named Fleming wrote that he recovered fully and "to all appearances [was] not in the least distressed," belying the fictitious conclusion in the novel that Lewis Fleming endured a painful limp for the rest of his life.[32] More importantly for the historical record, Lewis Fleming wasn't even with Colonel Warren in the Battle of Withlacoochee. He was in Newnansville, more than sixty miles away.

While the Fleming brothers were out on the Seminole War campaigns, their families had to find refuge somewhere. They went to Picolata after fleeing Hibernia in June 1836. After that, all evidence

Scott Ritchie

suggests they resided in Jacksonville and Fernandina. Fleming family oral tradition tells us that L. I. Fleming, just twelve years old at the time, carried dispatches from Jacksonville to Middleburg "during the excitement and terror of the war." The story goes that he rode hard for four hours, delivered the official papers, and returned safely.[33] If this is true then he probably rode to Garry's Ferry, the site of much militia activity near present-day Middleburg and the disease-infested refuge for hundreds of settlers during the war. This story suggests that the Flemings, better off and better connected than most settlers, may have resided in Jacksonville at the time. It is also possible that they temporarily relocated to their house in Fernandina, safely removed from Seminole attacks. A temporary residence in Fernandina helps explain the most significant development in Lewis Fleming's life during those years—his marriage to Margaret Seton in 1837.

Margaret Seton was born in Fernandina, Florida, on November 7, 1813, the daughter of Charles Seton and Matilda Sibbald Seton. Lewis Fleming was well acquainted with both the Setons and the Sibbalds before Margaret was born. He and Charles F. Sibbald, who was Margaret's uncle, were schoolmates.[34] During the Fleming family's residency in Fernandina following the Patriot War, they partook of social life and regularly interacted with the Setons, Sibbalds, and other residents of the small town. The Flemings lived, quite literally, just around the block from the Setons when Lewis attended a party hosted by Charles Seton. What started as a festive celebration ended in violence.

Seton hosted the celebration and ball at the home of Mrs. Catalina Baker on the evening of May 22, 1814. The invitees were primarily non-Spanish citizens, including Lewis's uncle, F. P. Fatio Jr., and James Cashen, who owned land adjacent to Hibernia on Fleming's Island. Seton also invited a Spaniard, Francisco Ribera, Commander of Amelia Island. This was a time when tensions ran high between Spanish and non-Spanish residents in Fernandina, and Ribera claimed he accepted the invitation because he believed his presence at the ball would prevent any mischief by angry Spaniards. When he arrived, Ribera felt he was received "with the greatest indifference," and was further offended because he was not given a dance card for the quadrille, a type of square dance executed by a set number of partners. When the second dance started Ribera defiantly "took [his] wife by the hand and stood up to dance." At that point, Seton and others "reprimanded" him because "all the couples were already set." Ribera became convinced that he was invited only as a way to insult him. He checked his impulse to challenge Seton to a duel and instead left the ball.

Shortly after that two Spaniards, Corporal Jose Maseyra and

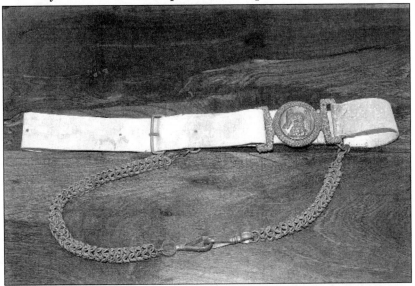

Fleming family members have preserved this militia officer's belt for many years. Based on identification by several experts, it most likely belonged to Lewis Fleming, which suggests the possibility that he wore it during the Battle of Wahoo Swamp. *MWF Collection, photo by the author.*

schooner pilot Diego Ojeda, burst into the party while several other Spaniards stood ready outside. As the shocked partygoers watched, Maseyra and Ojeda stormed across the room then "snatched the musical instruments and broke them over the musicians' heads." Next they drew their swords and set about swatting and smacking anyone they could catch. Mayhem ensued as Seton and his friends protected the ladies and hastened everyone out of the house. A couple of hours later, Maseyra returned to the house and shouted more threats. Seton and Ribera both sent multiple letters of protest to Governor Sebastian Kindelan, who quickly removed Ribera from his position as Commander of Amelia Island.[35]

Lewis Fleming was sixteen years old and couldn't possibly have been smitten with Margaret at the time—she was a small baby only thirteen months old. But when the Flemings abandoned Hibernia for safety during the Second Seminole War, Margaret was a young woman nearly twenty-three years old. It was during this time that Lewis Fleming's courtship of Margaret Seton led to marriage. They wed sometime in the first half of 1837, probably in Fernandina, and possibly at her parents' residence. There was no church in the town at that time, but the South Carolina Conference of the Methodist Episcopal Church, Margaret's religious denomination, posted a minister in Fernandina who presided over worship services in private homes.[36] Margaret was fifteen years younger than her husband, and just nine years older than her new stepson, George C. Fleming.[37]

Lewis Fleming acted as a leader to try and restore some measure of safety from Indian attacks in northeast Florida. On behalf of himself and other planters, he wrote a Memorial in late 1837 to the officer commanding the 2nd Division of the Florida Militia:

> ... the borders of Duval, Nassau, and Columbia counties are left defenseless, ... we think there has not at any time been a greater necessity than the present; that a small party of Indians devastating and murdering in their course, can penetrate to any part of the above counties; that in cultivating their plantations, in security to their property, and danger to their lives is constantly felt by the planters, and the undersigned request that one or more companies of Florida volunteers be stationed between the head waters of Black Creek and the St. Mary's River, in order to afford the citizens that protection they so much need.

Military personnel promptly answered, noting that the forty-four men who signed the Memorial were "among the most prominent worthy and intelligent citizens in East Florida." Two days later Colonel John Warren ordered Captains Isaac Bush and John Price of Duval County to each raise a company of mounted Florida volunteers, but eight more years would pass before Lewis took his family to once again live at Hibernia.[38]

George Fleming's Patriot War Claim

Between 1834 and 1844 the Fleming family pressed their case against the United States government for damages at Hibernia during the Patriot War. George Fleming filed his original claim for losses in 1817. The Adams-Onís Treaty, which transferred Florida from Spain to the U.S., stipulated that the United States must make restitution for the damages caused by operations of American troops during the invasion. Throughout the 1820s Congress did its best to renege on that agreement. All the while Spain and Florida protested vigorously. For nearly twelve years the Flemings' claim sat idle, one among many others, until an Act of Congress on June 26, 1834, cleared the way for nearly two hundred claimants to press suit. This accounts for almost every free citizen of East Florida at the time of the Patriot invasion. Regarding the claims, the process, and eventual awards (or lack thereof) the historian James Cusick wrote:

> As a moral fable, the claims cases reflected almost as poorly on American justice as the conflict itself, for many destitute families that were genuinely impoverished by the Patriot War received little in the way of restitution, while some of the richest inhabitants of Florida, including those who had been active rebels, ate up the lion's share.[39]

The Fleming claim seemed subject to unfavorable bias at various times during its adjudication, and they may have brought some of that on themselves. George Fleming filed his original claim in 1817 for a total of $9680. On November 15, 1834, Lewis Fleming filed an amended claim for $17,650, stating that his father had omitted "many items of great value." His mother explained that her husband was "naturally careless" with personal accounting, and was "more so than usual" in this instance because he thought "no part of said account would ever be paid." Lewis Fleming and his mother despaired that both the plantation overseer and the timber foreman, who could best testify to the amended claim, were deceased, but they identified friends and family members to testify on their behalf. Between 1835 and 1837 officials took depositions from Lewis Fleming's cousins, Louisa and Sophia Fatio, and his old friend, Farquhar Bethune, as well as Zephaniah Kingsley, Seymour Pickett, Francis Sanchez, and James Hall. With the exception of Farquhar Bethune, these were poor choices.

Judge Robert Raymond Reid of Jacksonville, who was well acquainted with the Flemings, initially ruled on the claim. He wrote that serious loss "is sufficiently proved," but that the "particular property lost and its value" is so imperfectly established as to "embarrass very much" the total amount claimed. Reid awarded just $6379. He opined that six of the deponents "prove little or nothing," and that he relied solely on Farquhar Bethune's testimony because "he is a man of strict integrity and correct judgment." Reid acknowledged that George Fleming likely did file his original claim with no expectation of payment, and that it probably did not reflect the actual losses, but that "with such testimony I could not decree more and might be justified in decreeing less." To make matters worse, the United States Secretary of Treasury, Levi Woodbury, objected to Judge Reid's award, in part because testimony did not prove the losses were the direct result of acts by American troops. Woodbury argued that the damages may have been caused by Indians or by "mere abandonment" of the plantation. None of the deponents who testified on behalf of the Fleming claim witnessed the actual destruction of Hibernia, nor did they believe they needed to. Lewis Fleming once testified that the atrocities of the patriot invaders were "spoken of by the inhabitants of the country with as much confidence as the Battle of Bunker Hill was ... in Massachusetts."[40] Woodbury was not in the least persuaded by such arguments and ordered the case recommitted.

The Flemings were not ready to give up the fight, and no wonder. Even though the family had recently sold two of George Fleming's Spanish Land Grants, all indications are that they were on the verge of insolvency. David Palmer and Darius Ferris purchased the Langley Bryan tract in 1832 for $3000. Charles Downing bought the huge tract at the mouth of the San Sebastian River, the present-day site of Sebastian, Florida, for $6000 in June 1837, just days after the Flemings' title to the land was confirmed by the Superior Court of East Florida.[41] Apparently, even this sum of money was not enough to keep their heads above water. Subsequent to the sales, the family came out on the wrong end of a lawsuit and owed the Southern Life Insurance and Trust Company $2880.88. Lewis's brother, George Jr., was indebted to O. L. Buddington for a total of $1045.[42] Lewis had recently sent his first son, George C., to a boarding school in Massachusetts with hopes of enrolling him at Amherst College two years later. Mounting expenses placed the family in such desperate financial straits that Lewis and Sophia Fleming mortgaged all of Hibernia to Benjamin A. Putnam in the spring of 1842.[43]

With hopes of a significant payday in the form of a check from the U.S. government, they quickly arranged testimonies from John M. Bowden, who was fifty-two years old at the time and lived in Mandarin, and Jesse Long, who was fifty-six and lived in Jacksonville. Both knew George Fleming, both had been at Hibernia before and after the Patriot War, and both served the invading troops during the war. They went on foraging excursions to Fleming's Island, stealing cattle, hogs, provisions, and anything else of value. With these testimonies to bolster the claim, Lewis hired attorney Rodney Dorman, who appealed the decision to the current U.S. Secretary of Treasury, John C. Spencer.[44] Dorman argued that the Flemings were entitled to a much larger award, and that "the estate and the heirs are at this time laboring under considerable difficulty and pecuniary embarrassment," due to losses in both the Patriot War and the Seminole War. Spencer was unimpressed. Reviewing the record he was taken aback by Judge Reid's award of $3834 for lost crops, a figure that came from Lewis and Sophia's amended claim. Spencer instead chose to believe George Fleming's original claim of just $400 for crops. He reduced Judge Reid's award by the difference between the two, and now the Flemings would receive just $2845.[45] This was not even enough to settle the mortgage to Benjamin Putnam.

Almost immediately Lewis Fleming wrote General Joseph Marion Hernandez, his former commander in both the St. Augustine Militia and the Second Seminole War, to solicit his help. Hernandez, now an attorney, had at various times served as a territorial delegate to the Seventeenth Congress and a presiding officer of the Territorial House of Representatives, and later ran unsuccessfully for the U.S. Senate. Lewis explained that his father's claim of $400 for lost crops reflected only the cotton he had on hand from the harvest of 1811. It did not take into account the crop in the field in 1812, the crop that would have been planted in 1813, or the value of the orange grove. Hernandez agreed to represent the case in Washington, D.C.[46] The record of the Fleming claim does not reflect what Hernandez did on their behalf, but on July 13, 1844, newly appointed Secretary of the Treasury, George M. Bibb, restored Judge Reid's original award of $6379.[47] After nine years, three attorneys, and three changes in the office of treasury secretary, George Fleming's heirs were poised for some relief from their financial difficulties.

Several years before the claim was settled, Lewis Fleming accepted a job as manager and agent of a sawmill in Panama Mills, which was located five miles north of Jacksonville at the confluence of Trout Creek and the St. Johns River. At least three factors influenced his decision. First, the effects of the great freeze of 1835 and losses suffered during the war drastically compromised Hibernia. It would take years before planting could become as profitable as it once had been—if that were even possible—and Lewis didn't need to reside at Hibernia to resume planting. Fleming family tradition tells us that Lewis granted freedom to a trusted Negro named Pompey, and made him plantation overseer.[48] Pompey led a group of Negroes to begin planting on the family plantation in Lewis's absence, and by 1842 Hibernia once again was cultivated with cash crops. The acreage under cultivation was roughly the same as it had been in 1812: sixty acres of corn, sixty of cotton, and additional fields of provision crops.[49] Second, the job presented an opportunity for Lewis to effectively double down on sources of income by restoring Hibernia to a plantation of cash crops while at the same time reaping the profits of the mill. Third, and most important, Margaret Fleming was pregnant with her first child. Without doubt, the memory of Augustina Cortes Fleming's death in the aftermath of childbirth haunted Lewis Fleming. Living near Jacksonville put Margaret much closer to medical care.

The job at Panama Mills came from Lewis's longtime friend and Margaret's uncle, Charles F. Sibbald. In 1828 Sibbald built the first steam-powered sawmills in Florida, including one named the Panama, only to have his business shuttered due to controversies surrounding his Spanish Land Grants. In 1836 he finally prevailed in a United States Supreme Court decision granting him full title to sixteen thousand acres. Nearly two-thirds of that land surrounded Panama Mills, and the remainder was rich timberland many miles south in an area known as Cabbage Swamp. Following that judgment, Sibbald resumed operations at Panama Mills and initiated a lawsuit against the U.S. government for losses sustained during the many years it took to finally gain title to his land.[50] So confident was Sibbald of the outcome that he issued notes in Philadelphia backed by future compensation from the government, and in 1838 began construction of a new steam sawmill at Trout Creek in the area that had become known simply as "Panama Mills." He hired Lewis Fleming as manager and agent of the mill. Lewis was no novice to the timber business. As a young man he had helped his father harvest pine and oak along the St. Marys and Nassau Rivers. Lewis continued harvesting timber on family land after his father's death. He had managed work gangs in the fields and in the forests, and he had managed men during times of war. Lewis also was acquainted with Sibbald's sawmills. He frequently was present during the construction of the first steam mill in 1828.[51] While living at Panama Mills, Margaret gave birth to her first child, Charles Seton Fleming, who was named for Margaret's father, on February 9, 1839. The family called him Seton. She gave birth to her second son, Francis Phillip "Frank" Fleming, named for his great-grandfather, F. P. Fatio Sr., at Panama Mills on September 28, 1941.

Lewis Fleming managed the mill through years made difficult by the ongoing Seminole War. Sibbald had a contract with the Navy to supply nearly $300,000 worth of live oak for ship frames, and quickly fell behind on deliveries.[52] The Panama Mills area was secure but most of the live oak in the immediate area had been harvested. The best live oak forests were in Indian country, which made timber harvest a risky, potentially deadly, business. Shipments were constantly behind schedule, forcing Sibbald to appeal to the Navy for one contract extension after another. The lack of timber limited his cash flow, and Sibbald's suit against the government thus far had produced no monetary award. This, in turn, must have restricted Sibbald's ability to pay Fleming. In 1839 Lewis was unable to enroll his son, George C., at Amherst due to "pecuniary embarrassments," the common language of the day to describe the state of being short on cash. Production from 1840 through 1842 was abysmal, at just $6474.31 in shipments. Live oak production reached its highest levels under Fleming's management in the first seven months of 1843, when he shipped $27,885.29 worth of lumber. This was more than twice the amount the mill had produced since the beginning of the contract. Just when it looked as though Panama Mills was hitting its stride, the Navy lost its patience. In less than a year they cancelled the contract and Sibbald was forced to shut down operations.[53]

Lewis and Margaret Fleming left Panama Mills and lived in Jacksonville approximately six more months before returning to Hibernia for the remainder of their lives. The choice to make Hibernia home once again, even in the face of repeated losses at that place, was not difficult. Throughout his life Lewis identified himself as a planter, and he preferred making his living from the land. The family had already sold their large tracts near Palatka and the San Sebastian River, so a plantation at either of those locations was out of the question. More importantly, the family already had invested in restoring Hibernia, where Pompey continued to lead planting operations. Land had been the Fleming family's salvation in the past, and Hibernia was their only hope. Apparently life in the rough country of Fleming's Island had become too much for Sophia Fleming and her daughter Mary, though, because they chose to remain in Jacksonville.

Sophia and Mary Fleming: Last Years in Jacksonville

Mary Magdalena Juana Fleming wed Solomon F. Halliday in Jacksonville on July 6, 1840.[54] She was forty years old. Her husband, who was just twenty-nine years old, was a preacher from New Jersey. Fleming family tradition tells us that she never had children and faded into obscurity. Even with the advantages of the Internet age, that remains largely true. Census data from 1840 suggest that she ran a small boarding house in Jacksonville. She is listed as the head of a household with a total of twenty-three persons, including a mix of free men and women both black and white, as well as ten slaves.[55] The age ranges and genders suggest at least a couple of families. In 1855 Mary Fleming Halliday lived in Newnansville, Florida, where her husband was a Presbyterian preacher.[56] She died soon after that, probably in 1856, and the site of her grave remains a mystery. A year later Solomon Halliday sold the last of her share of Hibernia land to L. I. Fleming. By 1860 Mr. Halliday was still a preacher and lived alone in a hotel in Starke, Florida. In 1862 Halliday was back in Jacksonville, where he was a member of the committee of Loyal Citizens of the United States.[57] This surely did not fit well with his Fleming in-laws who had actively supported the campaign for secession from the Union.

Sophia Fatio Fleming was seventy-four years old in 1840 and lived in her own house near to her daughter, attended by her Negro servants. Foremost among these was sixty-seven-year-old Lucy, to whom Sophia had granted manumission. Sophia owned twelve slaves, four males and eight females, ranging in age from under ten to over fifty-five years old. Two years later Sophia rented a house from her daughter and husband, Mr. and Mrs. Solomon F. Halliday. This may have been the large house once occupied by the Hallidays on the southeast corner of Forsyth and Ocean Streets.[58] Sophia lived here for the remainder of her life, secure in the confines of the town close to several friends and her doctor.

Sophia's probate record provides glimpses of her last years. Dr. Abel Seymour Baldwin, who was considered among the best doctors in Florida, visited her often between April 1841 and the night of Sophia's death in 1848. During several visits he provided medical care for her slaves. For example, during separate visits he "bled" Sukey, Abby, and Dominique for fees of $1.00 to $1.50 each. [Bloodletting is among the most ancient of medical practices, and at that time was often accomplished with the assistance of leeches.] On another visit he extracted a tooth from Georgiana for a fee of $1.00. Laudanum, a bitter opium mixture administered for a variety of conditions, cost twenty-five cents per dose. His most expensive bill for medical service was for $7.00, when he was called to the house on May 1, 1848. He attended to the eighty-two-year-old Fleming matriarch for five hours, but could do nothing to prevent her death.

Settlement of Sophia's assets and debts required a great deal of work, and both of her sons were fully occupied in Hibernia. They appealed to their trusted friend, Farquhar Bethune, who agreed to administer her estate.[59] Sophia died with a variety of debts accumulated during the last years of her life. Among them was an invoice for $11.32 to T. O.

Moss for expenses related to burying a small girl, presumably a slave child. The bill included the cost of making a coffin, a burial shroud, and labor for the burial. Less interesting, but indicative of the times, is a bill from Thomas D. Jones for two pounds of butter, two pounds of lard, and four pounds of sugar, totaling $1.25. She owed her daughter and son-in-law approximately four years and two months' worth of rent totaling $462.16 2/3.

Her assets consisted of slaves and real estate, as well as various household items and a small amount of interest due on her investment in "70 money units." Mr. Bethune settled the debt she owed the Hallidays by awarding them the slave Georgiana and her child, valued at $500. Sophia still owned a large portion of the 10,762-acre tract on the south branch of the Nassau River that she and William Gibson received through her father's estate. She also owned 360 acres of Hibernia land, including the Fleming's home in the heart of Hibernia. This curious amount of land revealed the ultimate outcome of George Fleming's estate. By order of the Superior Court of Duval County in 1844, Hibernia was subdivided into four lots, one each for Sophia and her three children.[60] Each of her children received tracts of approximately 240 acres that were located to the south of Hibernia proper.

After paying Sophia's creditors, Bethune administered final distribution of the remaining assets. Her will stipulated that each of her children would receive one-third of her estate, including her land at Hibernia and the Nassau River tract. Lewis, George Jr., and Mary verbally agreed to a partition of her 360 acres that resulted in roughly equal shares of land. Mary Fleming Halliday received a 127-acre portion on the northern end of the Fleming Grant. Lewis received approximately 117 acres that included the Hibernia plantation. George Jr. received the southernmost portion, perhaps 116 acres that adjoined his own portion of the Fleming Grant.[61]

Sophia Fleming's life was a "riches to rags" story of sorts. During her lifetime she had been a citizen of England, then Spain, and then the United States. She was born into wealth and matured amid the best of society in Spanish East Florida, sharing her husband's ascendance from a textiles merchant to a prosperous businessman, militia captain, and trusted confidant of East Florida governors. Sophia suffered the loss of two infant sons before bearing healthy children who lived to maturity. Upon her husband's death she suffered "pecuniary embarrassments," unable to pay bills and forced to leave the comforts of a settled life to start anew with her children at Hibernia. When Seminoles came on the warpath, she literally ran for her life with daughter, her grandchildren, and her bloodied and seriously wounded nephew. Once again she was forced to abandon her home and start anew. Happily, it seems she found peace and comfort in her last years as a resident of Jacksonville. She died in her daughter's house attended by her physician and, almost certainly, by her trusted servant Lucy, to whom she had granted freedom.

Upon her death, Lewis traveled down river to Jacksonville and retrieved her body for burial at Hibernia. The trip back up the wide St. Johns River was severe with high waves and a rough ride due to strong headwinds. Lewis's first son, now married and a doctor at Black Creek, came to be with the family at the funeral, along with almost everyone who lived on Fleming Island and the surrounding area.[62] The sorrowful family gathered together as Sophia Fleming was laid to rest beside her husband in the family graveyard, where they share the same headstone to this day.

Sophia Fatio Fleming is buried with her husband George in the Fleming family plot at St. Margaret's Episcopal Church in Hibernia.

Scott Ritchie

Endnotes

1. "Great Florida Freeze of 1835," NOAA and The Preserve America Initiative, http://www.srh.noaa.gov/images/tbw/paig/PresAmFreeze1835.pdf. The Great Freeze of 1835 forced all orange production farther south, never again to resume on any scale in the northeast Florida area.

2. L'Engle, *A Collection of Letters*, 2:16-19.

3. *Florida Herald*, (St. Augustine), April 1, 1835, 3.

4. *Florida Herald*, April 15, 1835, 2.

5. Ibid., June 17, 1835.

6. This brief account is pieced together from *Florida Herald*, July 1, 1835 and August 6, 1835; John Lee Williams, *The Territory of Florida* (New York: A. T. Goodrich, 1837); and John Mahon, "The First Battle of the Second Seminole War, Black Point, 18 December 1835," John K. Mahon Papers, University of Florida Smathers Libraries. Hogtown was located on the west side of present-day Gainesville. The settlement originally was a village of Seminoles who raised hogs and was named by whites who traded with the Seminoles.

7. *Florida Herald*, September 10, 1835.

8. Francis P. Fleming Papers, 1694-1912, The Florida Historical Society, Lewis Fleming to R. B. Gregory, December 28, 1835.

9. Florida Department of Military Affairs, Special Archives Publication no. 69, vol. 5, Florida Militia Muster Rolls, Seminole Indian Wars, http://ufdc.ufl.edu.

10. Record Group 217, Entry 756, *State Claims Relating to the Florida Indian Wars*, National Archives, Washington, D.C., Box 10. George Fleming's horse claim was just one of fourteen submitted by Lieutenant L. B. Webster (the spelling of this name is not clear). Ten of the fourteen were denied because the horses were "impressed" into service.

11. Florida Department of Military Affairs, Special Archives Publication no. 69, vol. 3, Florida Militia Muster Rolls, Seminole Indian Wars. The Flemings' good friends, Farqhuar Bethune and R. B. Gregory, also mustered in at the same time.

12. Williams, *The Territory of Florida*, 255.

13. *Jacksonville Courier*, December 3, 1835, http://ufdc/ufl/edu. The commanders also ordered the arrest or detention of all slaves and free Negroes found at large, unless they were in the service and company of an owner or overseer. This was prompted by rumors of an insurrection by blacks for some "evil purposes."

14. Alachua County Library District Heritage Collection, Maps Collection, Part of Defensive Square #7, http://heritage.acld.lib.fl.us/1101-1150/1112.html.

15. *Jacksonville Courier*, December 31, 1835, in "Jacksonville and the Seminole War Part II," *Florida Historical Society Quarterly* 3:4 (April 1925), http://www.jstor.org/stable/30149623. George Fleming Jr. rode in the same company with Captain Hutcheson and Private Bleach, both of whom were wounded during the Battle of Black Point.

16. At that time Wacahoota was a small settlement west of Micanopy in the heart of Seminole country.

17. The fact that Warren divided his troops and sent the supply wagons south is not in Fleming's letter. This is from Mahon, "The First Battle of the Second Seminole War." I added this fact to make clear that the Seminoles did not attack Warren's full body of troops.

18. Lewis Fleming to R. B. Gregory, December 28, 1835. Fleming had no way of knowing the battle known as Dade's Massacre took place the same day that he wrote this letter.

19. *Florida Herald*, July 9, 1836, www.ufdc.ufl.edu.

20. Ellen and Corinna Brown to Mannevillette Brown, July 19, 1836, in James M. Denham and Keith L. Huneycutt, eds., *Echoes from a Distant Frontier: The Brown Sisters' Correspondence from Antebellum Florida* (Columbia: University of South Carolina Press, 2004).

21. *Enquirer*, July 29, 1836. The account in this newspaper article was copied from Captain Peck's logbook.

22. Williams, *The Territory of Florida*, 248.

23. Dena Snodgrass, *The Island of Ortega: A History* (Jacksonville, FL: Ortega School, 1981), 13.

24. Biddle, *Unreturning Tide*, 36-38. Biddle wrote that Indians came on the warpath and destroyed Hibernia after her father, Frederic Alexander Fleming, was born but before her aunt, Matilda Fleming, was born. No historic evidence supports that time frame.

25. *The Congressional Globe: New Series: Containing Sketches of the Debates and Proceedings of the First Session of the Twenty-Ninth Congress* (City of Washington: Blair and Rives, 1846), 220.

26. Fort Drane was built on the plantation of Colonel Duncan Clinch and was located about ten miles southwest of Micanopy.

27. Critics of General Call were aghast that he would order a campaign of this magnitude, yet not make arrangements for adequate provisions.

28. This account of the Battle of Wahoo Swamp is derived from John T. Sprague, *The Origin, Progress, and Conclusion of the Florida War* (New York, NY: D. Appleton, 1848), 163-66; *Independent Chronicle and Boston Patriot*, vol. 73, no. 5807, December 14, 1836, www.geneaologybank.com.

29. National Archive and Records Administration (hereafter NARA), RG 217, Entry 756, *State Claims Relating to the Florida Indian Wars*, Box 4, "Various Detachments of Militia, Abstracts of Q.M.s for forage, etc."

30. Florida Department of Military Affairs, Special Archives Publication no. 73, vol. 7, Florida Militia Muster Rolls, Seminole Indian Wars, http://www.ufdc.ufl.edu. The spelling in this muster role is "George Flemming," which was a common misspelling of the family name during the nineteenth century.

31. Dena Snodgrass, notes for Eugenia Price related to the novel *Margaret's Story*, *MWF Collection*. For an example of a website that describes Lewis Fleming's wound, see http://www.drbronsontours.com/bronsonhibernia. html.

32. E. A. Hammond, ed., "Benrose's Medical Case Notes from the Second Seminole War," *Florida Historical Quarterly* 47:4 (April 1969). See "The Case of Fleming" on p. 401.

33. Margaret Baldwin Fleming, *"An Emerald Isle"* (New York: Broadway Publishing Co., privately published, n.d.), *MWF Collection*.

34. *Evidence Taken By The Authority of the Honorable, The Secretary of the Treasury, Under A Report of the Committee of Claims, and a Resolution Concurred in by the House of Representative of the United States of America, In the Case of Indemnity of Charles F. Sibbald, of Philadelphia* (Philadelphia: John Richards, 1837). Testimony of Lewis Fleming.

35. *EFP*, 65/34, Charles Seton, et al., to Captain de Partido, December 23, 1814; *EFP*, 65/34, Francisco Ribera to Governor, December 23, 1814. Translated by Yvonne Contilo. Others at the party included Joseph M. Hernandez, Enrique Young, Juan Sharp, Carlos Sibbald, Farquhar Bethune, Robert Harrison, Samuel Betts, and Robert Blakeley.

36. St. Margaret's Episcopal Church in Hibernia originally was created as a part of the Methodist Episcopal Church, Margaret's denomination of choice.

37. To date, nothing has been discovered in historical records to provide details of their marriage beyond the fact that it took place in 1837 and before June 9 of that year. Lewis Fleming and his wife, Margaret, signed a deed of sale on that day. A copy of that deed is in the *MWF Collection*.

38. NARA, RG 217, Entry 756, State Claims Relating to the Florida Indian Wars, Box 11, "Memorial of Lewis Fleming and Others" (National Archives: Washington, D.C.). Forty-four men, including Jacksonville residents and planters, signed this Memorial during November and December in 1837. Lewis Fleming is credited as the author.

39. Cusick, *The Other War of 1812*, 305-6.

40. Fatio Jr., Patriot War Claim, Deposition of Lewis Fleming.

41. *FMP*, Fleming, George, Heirs of, Confirmed Claim for 20,000 acres on the San Sebastian River, Reported to Congress by Reg. & Rec., American State

Papers, vol. 5, pp. 398-400, rpt. 3, no. 7, 1828. Confirmed by Superior Court E. F. May 15, 1832; *FMP*, Confirmed Claim of 980 aces, "Langley Bryan," American State Papers, vol. 4, pp. 160-197, report 1, no. 45, 1824.

42. George Fleming Jr. Probate Record, Duval County, Florida, File 911.

43. Lewis and Sophia Fleming to Benjamin A. Putnam, May 16, 1842. Duval County, Florida, Deed Record E, page 14, referenced in a title abstract prepared by E. N. Holt, Abstracter, Green Cove Springs, Florida on March 27, 1913, for F. A. Fleming. *MWF Collection*. Putnam County, Florida, is named after Benjamin A. Putnam, who fought in the Seminole War, and was a lawyer, Florida legislator, and first president of the Florida Historical Society.

44. Rodney Dorman was mayor of Jacksonville before the Civil War, though the records do not indicate what years he served in this capacity.

45. Spencer also deducted $50 from a line item he interpreted as incorrect, and considered the award to be just $6327 before deducting for crops.

46. Lewis Fleming to General Hernandez, Panama, October 18, 1843, in Fleming Patriot War Claim.

47. Ibid.

48. Biddle, *Unreturning Tide*, 32.

49. Fleming Patriot War Claim, Deposition of John Bowden.

50. Sibbald's case against the U.S. government was national news in the day, with proceedings reported in newspapers from Boston to New Orleans and points in between.

51. *Evidence Taken ... In the Case of Indemnity of Charles F. Sibbald*, Deposition of Lewis Fleming.

52. House of Representatives, 32nd Congress, 2nd Session, Ex. Doc. No. 68, 44-48.

53. Sibbald's lawsuit against the United States dragged on for several more years. After much acrimonious debate in Congress, he received two separate awards totaling about $53,000. This was not nearly enough to pay his attorneys or his creditors. He was forced into bankruptcy and eventually Marshalls sold his land in Florida at auction to pay a portion of his debts.

54. Index to Duval Marriages to 1860, Clay County Archives, Clay County, Florida.

55. *1840 United States Federal Census* (Provo, UT: www.ancestry.com). Mary Fleming had two male slaves, one less than ten years old and another between ten and twenty-four years. Two female slaves were under ten years old, three were aged from ten to twenty-four, one was between twenty-five and thirty-five, and two were between fifty-five and one hundred years old.

56. Lewis Fleming to Martha [Gibson?], June 9, 1855. In L'Engle, *A Collection of Letters*, 2:13.

57. T. Frederick Davis, *History of Jacksonville and Vicinity 1513 to 1924*, A Facsimile Reproduction of the 1925 Edition (Gainesville: University of Florida Press), http://www.ufdc.ufl.edu/UF00103019/00001/3j.

58. T. Frederick Davis, *History of Early Jacksonville, Florida* (Jacksonville, H. & W. B. Drew), https://archive.org.

59. Probate Packets, Duval County, Florida, Sophia Fleming, No. 627.

60. Reference to this division is embedded within future land sales. See Clay County Deed Book F, pp. 363-66, F. P. Fleming, Commissioner to Davis Floyd, October 15, 1870; also Clay County Deed Book CC, pp. 423-30, for transactions involving the children of Lewis and Margaret Fleming and Davis Floyd, April 19, 1878.

61. Title abstract prepared at the request of F. A. Fleming by E. N. Holt, Abstracter, Green Cove Springs, Florida, March 27, 1913, *MWF Collection*.

62. Letter from Lewis Fleming to Farqhuar Bethune, May 5, 1848. This letter is among other documents related to the estate of Sophia Fleming, Probate File No. 627, Duval County, Florida, available on microfilm at the main branch of the Jacksonville Public Library. All data regarding her debts and assets at the time of her death come from this file.

Lewis and Margaret Fleming

Lewis and Margaret Fleming returned to Hibernia sometime in 1845 with their daughter Augustina, who was thirteen years old at the time; Seton, who was six years old; and little Frank, who was four. George Fleming Jr. had divorced his wife in 1839 and now lived with his daughter Mary Sophia, eighteen years old, at his own plantation across a small creek to the south of Lewis and Margaret. The family changed a great deal over the next six years. Between income from the mill, proceeds from cash crops in Hibernia, and the promise of an award from the government, George Fleming's heirs seem to have been in a less tenuous position financially; so much so in Lewis's case that he enrolled his sons in college even as his family expanded. George C. had dreams of entering the seminary, but upon advice from family members and friends he entered medical school. He graduated from the University of Pennsylvania Medical Department in 1846.[1] L. I. graduated from Amherst College in 1847.[2]

During the next four years Lewis Fleming's family experienced tremendous change. Lewis's three children with Augustina Cortes built their lives away from Fleming Island. Dr. George C. Fleming established a medical practice at Black Creek near present-day Middleburg, Florida. He married Mary O. Bennet shortly after the death of his mother in 1848. Over the years they had four children who survived to maturity. Dr. Fleming gave up the medical profession in 1851, left his wife and children to the care of extended family members, and enrolled at Princeton Theological Seminary. His second cousin, Dr. William L'Engle, wrote that George C. "had entirely too much conscience to make a successful physician" and that he would have been better off as a minister from the start.[3] Late in 1848 Augustina Fleming, then sixteen years old, married Clark Stephens and moved to his home upriver at Welaka, where they lived the rest of their long lives. Together they had five children who lived to maturity. Upon graduation from Amherst, Louis Isadore Fleming taught school for two years in Southbridge, Massachusetts, before returning to Florida to teach at Waukeenah in Jefferson County while studying law. In 1850 young Seton Fleming, just eleven years old, joined his brother there and was one of his students for three years. In the course of all these events, Margaret Seton Fleming gave birth to four more children in Hibernia: Frederic "Fred" Alexander in 1845, William "Willie" Henry in 1847, Matilda "Tissie" Caroline in 1849, and Margaret "Maggie" Seton in 1851. In the wake of such happy developments, Lewis Fleming's brother died.

George Fleming Jr. died intestate in March of 1851 with debts totaling $1895. The most significant among these was the still-outstanding $1045 legal judgment against him in favor of Ozias Buddington. His assets consisted of twelve slaves and some personal property. Deed records reveal that before his death George Jr. had sold his Hibernia land to Davis Floyd. The administrator of his estate, T. O. Holmes, sold three of his slaves, named George, Scipio, and Elsy, as well as his personal possessions, to Davis Floyd. This raised more than enough cash to satisfy his debts. His daughter, Mary Sophia Fleming, married Davis Floyd shortly after his death.[4] Mrs. Floyd was his only heir and received the balance of his estate: $305.85 in cash and nine slaves valued at $2900.[5]

Taking into account everything we know about George Fleming Jr., he may have died an unhappy man. Fleming family tradition tells us he was charming, heavy-set, and red-faced, and "there seemed to be a great sweep to his life, with everything in superlatives." His sugar mill, carpenter shop, and forge were "better equipped and operated" than any other. He had the "fastest and best" barge and the "finest slaves" on the river. But in contrast to these descriptions, "he used to complain that when he bought a barrel of whiskey, everybody thought he was going to get drunk!" This same oral tradition tells us his wife adored him, so she "probably closed her eyes while she excused his occasional straying from the fold and his sprees."[6] But a more accurate oral tradition tells us the marriage was "very unhappy."[7]

George Fleming Jr. filed for divorce in 1838. At that time in Florida only a man could file for divorce. All divorce proceedings were subject to approval by the Territorial Legislature, and only allowed for specific causes. The legislature voted in favor of the divorce, but Territorial Governor Richard K. Call vetoed the decision. This is interesting since Fleming family tradition tells us Call was well acquainted with Lewis Fleming—perhaps Call knew something of the circumstances and disapproved. George Jr. protested Call's veto. He hired Lewis's good friend, attorney R. B. Gregory, for representation and solicited supporting testimony from his sister, Mary, as well as from Orlando M. Dorman and Miss Susan A. Smith. The legislature did not keep records of the testimony so we don't know the grounds for the divorce, but possible causes included adultery, extreme cruelty, habitual indulgence of violent and ungovernable temper, habitual intemperance, or desertion for a period of three years.[8] Although we can only speculate as to which cause George Fleming Jr. charged against his wife, he ultimately prevailed and the divorce became final.[9] He never remarried and his daughter Mary Sophia lived with him for the rest of his life. In the six weeks immediately preceding his death, George Jr. purchased at least ten gallons of whiskey. The actual cause of his death is unknown, but the whiskey certainly seems suspect. George Philip Fleming was laid to rest in the family cemetery next to his father and mother. His tombstone has long since disappeared and a simple wooden cross marks his grave.

The Antebellum Hibernia Hotel

During the 1850s several real estate transactions dramatically changed the look of Fleming land ownership. Lewis Fleming sold his 245 acres at the confluence of Black Creek and the St. Johns River to Osias Buddington. This may have been how he ultimately satisfied his debt to Buddington. Mary Fleming Halliday sold her 243 acres to Davis Floyd. Three years later Floyd sold that same land to George Huston. After Mary Fleming Halliday's death, her widower, Solomon F. Halliday, sold her portion of Sophia Fleming's estate to her nephew, L. I. Fleming. Lewis and Margaret Fleming sold the family lot in Fernandina and the remaining 1600 acres on the south prong of the Nassau River Land Grant. These sales generated little cash. The Fernandina lot sold for $25 and the Nassau River Tract just $400. At one time the Fleming family had owned nearly 27,000 acres of land in Florida. By 1857 all that remained directly under Fleming control were Lewis Fleming's 117 acres, which encompassed his portion of his mother's estate at the heart of Hibernia, and L. I. Fleming's adjacent tract to the north. These land sales signaled an end to the Fleming plantation era and the birth of Hibernia as a destination for northern visitors.[10]

For over a century members of the Fleming family believed that Hibernia remained a working plantation until after the Civil War. Oral traditions tell us that the family entered the business of providing room and board following the Civil War, when Margaret Fleming made the unfortunate but financially unavoidable decision to open her home to paying guests. Perhaps Margaret did make the decision to start a boarding business, but she didn't make it alone, and it wasn't after the Civil War. As early as 1852, Margaret Fleming solicited paying guests with every intention of feeding and entertaining them at her home. The historical record is clear on this point. The editors of the *Florida Republican* added a small column to the January 1852 issue to "call the attention of persons wishing Board in a retired and rural abode ... to the advertisement of Mrs. Fleming."

> Mrs. Fleming, "Fleming's Island," near the entrance of Black Creek, Duval County, can accommodate several persons, gentlemen or ladies, with pleasant Boarding. Her house is situated near the Hibernia Post Office, immediately on the St. John's, and has regular communication with the steamboats that are now so constantly plying on the river. The distance of the location is not more than twenty miles from Jacksonville, and the site is considered highly favorable to persons in delicate health.[11]

It is not hard to understand why Lewis and Margaret chose to enter the boarding business. After returning to Hibernia in 1845 their plantation lifestyle became increasingly difficult. It seems the Flemings never had more than 120 acres cultivated with cash crops, and their labor force was small because many of their Negroes died or ran off during the Seminole War years.[12] By 1850 Lewis Fleming owned just eight slaves, five females and three males, ranging in age from one to fifty years old.[13] Only two, a man and a woman, were in the prime of life. The combination of small fields and few hands to perform the labor practically demanded another means of making a living.

Lewis and Margaret were aware that more and more visitors came to Florida each year to escape Northern winters. These people needed places to stay and the options outside of St. Augustine and Jacksonville were limited. Only a few houses located on the banks of the St. Johns River were open for paying guests, including Picolata House and Constantia. Picolata was the terminus of the rough, eighteen-mile road from St. Augustine to the eastern bank of the St. Johns River. Rates at Picolata House were $1.50 per day, $7 per week, or $25 per month. Meals were extra and cost 37.5¢ for breakfast or evening supper and 50¢ for dinner.[14] Constantia, the former plantation of Lewis Fleming's friend William Travers, was only a short boat ride upriver and in sight of Hibernia. Joseph Finegan had married Travers's widow and was now master of the plantation. He could accommodate only three single men, or one couple and two single men. The fare was $18 per month, which included laundry and other services. Finegan touted hunting in the area, as well as pleasant riding, and offered horses to his guests at no charge.[15] Picolata House was rough, Constantia was small, and opportunity presented itself.

The Flemings also knew something of what it was like to operate a boarding house because Lewis's first cousin, Louisa Fatio, was in the business. Miss Fatio began her first boarding house in St. Augustine shortly after Indians destroyed New Switzerland in 1836. She rented a location along the bay front and kept it going for more than ten years. In 1850 Louisa went to work for Sarah Petty Anderson to manage her well-established boarding house at 55 Aviles Street. Miss Fatio had had nearly fifteen years of experience running boarding houses at the time Margaret Fleming opened her home to paying guests, and there can be little doubt that the Flemings consulted her before making the decision.[16] The first few years of the Flemings' boarding business, like too many other years in their lives, are a historical void. We know nothing about what it was like to be a paying guest at Hibernia until 1855.

The First Known Guests at Hibernia, 1855

With three seasons of experience under their belts, the Flemings prepared for the 1855–56 boarding season. Margaret Fleming had given birth to her last child, Isabella Frances "Fanny" Fleming, on May 13, 1855, and it would take time to regain her strength. This compounded the chores and challenges associated with running a boarding house. A small advertisement in the *Boston Traveler* read, "Board in East Florida – To Invalids Going South. Comfortable Board can be had at Col. L. Fleming's, Hibernia." The Fleming house had limited capacity and thus could "accommodate but a small number of persons," but Fleming used that to his advantage by adding that the limited capacity enabled them to lavish attention upon their guests.[17] Fleming had a strong Northern reference to speak on behalf of their fledgling enterprise, the Honorable James H. Duncan, of Haverhill, Massachusetts. Duncan was a former state representative and senator, a U.S. congressman, and an industrious and successful businessman. Lewis hoped his reference would attract visitors from the Boston area.[18]

Before going further, take notice of "Col. L. Fleming" in the ad. Lewis served the Florida militia on two separate occasions: first in 1829 and again beginning in 1835. He was brigade inspector on the first occasion. No record has been discovered to tell us if he attained the rank of colonel at that time. The last evidence of his service during the Second Seminole War tells us he was a major. It's possible that Fleming received a promotion to colonel before the end of his service, but again, there is no record to tell us if that is the case. It is also possible that Lewis Fleming become a colonel through the old tradition of affixing that title to a respected Southern gentleman, and in the context of his advertisement it certainly sounds more distinguished than "Major Fleming." Colonel Fleming's advertisement in Boston was specifically directed to "invalids," but the first visitors that season were healthy, able-bodied young women.

Miss Julia Lord Noyes was born in Lyme, Connecticut, on September 23, 1833. At the age of twenty-two, Julia traveled with her cousin, Carrie, to winter in Florida. We are fortunate that Miss Noyes kept a journal during her travels, and that her journal has survived the years. The entries are often brief and some of them consist of thoughts from many days, but they provide us the first glimpse of Lewis and Margaret Fleming's boarding business.[19] Ironically, it seems Julia had no knowledge whatsoever of Hibernia when she embarked from her home on October 23, 1855, and she never intended to stay there. Julia and Carrie were bound for the grand new Magnolia Hotel at the former site of the Constantia plantation. Joseph Summerlin purchased that property from Joseph Finegan in 1851 and built a hotel. Almost immediately, he sold the hotel to Dr. Nathan Benedict, who was superintendent of the New York State Insane Asylum. Dr. Benedict suffered from chronic illness and, like a growing number of affluent Northerners, traveled to Florida in the winter with hopes of better health. Dr. Benedict improved the Magnolia Hotel, added medical facilities, and prepared for a grand opening in November of 1855.

Julia and Carrie began their journey south with a train ride from New York to Philadelphia, where they boarded the ship *Key Stone State*, bound for Savannah, Georgia. Young women traveling alone required a "protector," as Julia put it, and theirs was Dr. Benedict, who was in Philadelphia preparing to move his family to Florida.[20] Benedict's entire company for the trip consisted of his wife, four children, eight servants, five boarders (among them Julia and Carrie), a cow, a dog, a piano, and an "unnumbered quantity of trunks and boxes, enough to make any man look terrible!"[21]

The ship set sail from Philadelphia on Saturday, November 3, 1855. Julia and Carrie both suffered seasickness the first day and were unable to go out on deck because of rain. By noon Sunday they had recovered and the weather had improved, so they were able to go outside for fresh air. Most passengers, however, were still seasick and remained in their cabins. Monday was beautiful and they enjoyed the weather as "the sun shone on the waves so brightly." Upon arrival in Savannah early on November 6, they transferred to the Florida steamer *Seminole* and immediately set sail for Jacksonville.

The following morning they were on the ocean again, rolling with the waves and suffering another spell of seasickness before entering the St. Johns River and arriving in Jacksonville. While stopped there Dr. Benedict told them the Magnolia Hotel was "not in order," so he would take them to Hibernia. The ladies could not take their trunks and had to quickly gather personal effects before leaving Jacksonville. Still onboard the *Seminole*, they steamed upriver. At about four o'clock on the afternoon of November 7, 1855, Julia and Carrie climbed into a small landing boat and a crew rowed them the short distance to the Hibernia wharf.

At first they were happy to be there. Julia wrote these words while sitting with Carrie under the trees on the day they arrived:

> The house is built of logs but is very prettily hidden among the trees & river, the roses in bloom. Between the house & the river is a cluster of live oaks which are covered with a moss drapery which is very beautiful ... The Flemings are nice people—have been very well off but lost a good deal during the Indian war. It is so warm, we have no bonnets or shawls on, the dear little bugs run over my feet & the squirrels are hopping all over the trees, they come to a bough just over our heads & peep at us, then come in the path near our feet to form an acquaintance.

The young ladies enjoyed evening walks along the wharf to see the sunset, especially when "the glory would last sometimes an hour after the sun went down." They took rough cart rides into the pine forests. We learn that the crops at Hibernia included pomegranates, oranges, sweet potatoes, guavas, persimmons, groundnuts, chiola and laya. Their enthusiasm for Hibernia was short-lived, though, and Julia's thoughts turned sour.

Julia complained that "there was no house near & as it is an island, no roads, but cart tracks ... no neighbors, no church, no nothing." The first week in Hibernia, her cousin Carrie did not feel well and the weather stormed often. Their trunks were in Magnolia and they had little to do, not even any books to read. Julia wrote, "There is no comfort in walking about, for a kind of burr which grows everywhere, takes the first opportunity of attaching itself to your feet & the bottoms of your clothes."[22] Her annoyance is understandable. She and Carrie were two young women stuck on an isolated island and it seems they were the only guests at Hibernia the entire time.[23]

Then one fine day Colonel Fleming took them aboard his sailboat to Magnolia Hotel. There they retrieved all they wanted from their trunks and had a glorious day socializing with the many guests. Late that night they sailed back to Hibernia, guided by a beacon fire at the shoreline. Julia's brief description is enchanting:

> The St. Johns is a beautiful river, we sang all sorts of songs & came home by moonlight, a fire was lighted on the shore to show us where to land. The fire lighted the trees up, so strangely, a little black girl sat by it to keep it up, & two big dogs lay beside her, altogether it was a picturesque scene, like a gypsy encampment.[24]

After eighteen days at Hibernia, Julia and Carrie were thrilled when Dr. Benedict arrived and took them to Magnolia Hotel and its "civilized country." Later that season Julia saw Colonel Fleming at Magnolia with four young men who were staying at Hibernia. She visited the Flemings one last time in March 1856, near the end of her winter in Florida, and wrote, almost apologetically, that she was "very glad to take one last look at Hibernia. It is a pretty place & they are very kind people."[25]

During the off-season Lewis and Margaret Fleming invested in their new business. They enlarged the house to add more guest rooms, and they improved the existing guest rooms and grounds. Colonel Fleming placed an ad in the *Baltimore Sun* to inform invalids going south that "the house has been newly fitted up," and "every attention will be paid to their accommodation."[26] The first guests for the 1856–57 season arrived from New York City in late November. Mrs. Edward W. Tiers traveled south with her party of eight, which included her mother, "Uncle Ned," four children, including Charlie, and their dog, Carlo.[27] Since they were the first to arrive they had their choice of rooms. Mrs. Tiers chose a large, comfortable room that opened onto a piazza with a glorious view of the St. Johns River. Her daughters, Adeline and Emily, chose rooms next to their mother's. Even though Mrs. Tiers described the Fleming house as small, she commented that all rooms were "rather large," and that each had its own fireplace. She wrote that

Margaret Seton Fleming was "one of the best hearted women I ever met with."[28]

Though they were "on a desert island way [sic] from church and priest" in Hibernia, the Tiers party had "every thing [they] need wish for of the worlds goods," including fine game, fine fishing, excellent meals, good sugars, and even good whiskey punch "to top off with." A variety of newspapers arrived with the bi-weekly mail boat, so they were able to keep up with the happenings in New York and elsewhere. All they lacked were friends and a church. The Flemings were most attentive hosts and did "everything in their power to make us happy and comfortable," especially during the first three to four weeks when they were the only guests. Uncle Ned loved to hunt and fish, and he was good at both. He frequently contributed fresh meat for the dinner table. Charlie preferred to be busy and was skilled in all sorts of trades. He contributed all around Hibernia by helping with carpentry, upholstery, painting, gardening, and hunting. Word spread of his talents, and the proprietor at Magnolia Hotel requested that he come there to help install a billiard table. The weather was glorious and Hibernia was everything they had hoped, but the southern climate did little for their health. In fact, it made things worse.

Mrs. Tiers's mother came to Florida to convalesce, but she didn't improve much. Mrs. Tiers's three daughters arrived healthy but all got sick in Florida. Ten days after arriving, Adeline Tiers came down with "broken bone fever," so called in those days because of the excruciating muscle and joint pain. Today it is known as Dengue fever, a mosquito -borne tropical disease. She suffered terribly for thirteen days and was unable to walk without great pain. Annie Tiers had a touch of the fever but recovered after just a day or two. In February Emily Tiers suffered the broken bone fever even worse than Adeline. The illness dragged on for an alarming period of time and she could barely move at all. When she finally improved enough to travel she went to Magnolia Hotel with Charlie for several days to complete her recovery. Carlo, the dog, may have benefited most from the south. He enjoyed country life, lost weight and looked better for it, and learned to sleep outdoors. After two months in Hibernia he was "perfectly well" and passed "all his time sitting under the trees watching the squirrels."

Mrs. Tiers found the solace of a church and priest on a trip to St. Augustine. To get there they traveled by steamer two hours upriver to Picolata, and then took a rough three-and-a-half-hour stagecoach ride through pine barrens and soft sand. Were it not for the churches, Tiers declared, St. Augustine was such a "forlorn looking place" that it would be "insupportable." She much preferred Hibernia.

A visitor from Boston during this same season recommended the Fleming boarding house for health or simply to avoid the Boston snows. He wrote that Hibernia "offers advantages ... such as can rarely be found united." The river is "clear and blue" and "the climate is delightful."[29] He described pine barrens "which cover the whole country, with the exception of a narrow strip along the shore of the river." The air among the pines is "peculiarly beneficial to persons of delicate lungs." His impression of walking along the riverbank is vastly different from that of Julia Lord Noyes the previous year. He describes "a delightful walk along the bank of the river, with seats at short intervals where an invalid can rest." Anyone interested in botany or ornithology will cherish "the flowers and birds of the country [that] afford an endless source of interest and outdoor occupation." Inside, "one may be sure of comfort and neatness, and the table is said to be the best in the Southern States." Further, "ladies obliged to travel alone would find no inconvenience in so doing, and would find it a delightful house, and be sure of receiving the utmost kindness."[30]

We learn more from William James Stillman, a journalist, artist, and photographer, who stayed at Hibernia in the spring of 1857. Stillman is perhaps best known as a founding member of the Adirondack Club, a group of great minds that included James Russell Lowell and Ralph Waldo Emerson. While scouting a tract of land in the Adirondacks in search of a good spot for a clubhouse, Stillman contracted a nearly fatal case of pneumonia. His doctors ordered him off to Florida to recuperate. Stillman chose Hibernia, where he reveled in the natural abundance of Florida. He went alligator and turkey hunting with "young Fleming." This most likely was either Seton, who was now eighteen years old, or Frank, who was sixteen. He found copperheads and rattlesnakes in abundance and collected specimens for the Natural History Museum in Cambridge. The scents of the season filled the air:

> ... the groves of magnolia filling the air with new and cloying fragrance, alternating with other unaccustomed odors which made the grove resemble an orchestra of perfumes ...[31]

Stillman wrote of his host, "old Colonel Fleming was one of the traditional patriarchal planters." Indeed, Lewis Fleming likely was an archetype of the southern planter. Now sixty years old, he was molded his entire life by the plantation lifestyle. He grew up issuing orders to men under his charge, and he had the bearing of an officer who had fought in a time of war to preserve his way of life. He ran Hibernia with firm yet unusually compassionate discipline. Now, after five consecutive winter seasons, Colonel Lewis Fleming's winter boarding business was garnering a reputation as one of the finest destinations for northern visitors. Just when it seemed he could settle into his golden years with his wife and children, Fleming's world was turned upside down.

In February of 1858 Lewis's first son, George C., moved back home to Florida from his Presbyterian ministry in St. Marys, Georgia. The previous spring he developed consumption and had gotten progressively worse ever since, so much so that he had been unable to perform his duties for many months. The Reverend Fleming desperately hoped that a change of venue, and perhaps another doctor, would improve his health, so he took a room at the Magnolia Hotel. But it was not to be. He died just one week later. A fellow minister who attended his deathbed reported George Claudius Fleming's last words were, "God is love."[32] Twenty-two years earlier Lewis Fleming had buried his first wife at Hibernia, and now he had to bury his first-born son. They laid the gentle thirty-six-year-old to rest next to his uncle George and his grandfather George. As sad as this had to be, George C.'s death was not unexpected. During his prolonged illness the family had time to prepare for it emotionally. The next tragedy to befall the family came with no warning.

In early May of 1858 the last of the paying guests boarded a steamer, and the Flemings had the house to themselves once again. The guest rooms were cleaned and shuttered, ready to sit idle until the approach of the next boarding season. In the dark of night on the morning of May 17, 1858, the family awoke to the smell of smoke. Fire had broken out in one of the empty guest rooms. Flames raged and spread across the entire structure at frightening speed. The scene had to be terrifying as the family scrambled into action. They escaped with their lives, but with little more than that.[33] It soon became apparent that nothing could be done to save the structure. Lewis and Margaret must have stood in disbelief at a safe distance, watching their home and their livelihood collapse into a heap of billowing flames and black smoke. The Flemings suspected an arsonist because no one had lit so much as a candle in that wing of the house since the last guest departed. Whatever the cause, the damage was done; but the Flemings' faith in the winter boarding business remained resolute. Word of the disaster spread as effectively as the consuming flames, and, "by the kindly feeling of some persons who had boarded with them, means were procured to rebuild on a larger scale, & refurnish a house."[34]

Within a matter of weeks the *Charleston Courier* reported "Col. Lewis Fleming, at Hibernia, on St. John's River, is already in course of re-construction, and will soon rise from its ashes and adorn the same spot."[35] Lewis planned a grand mansion with enough capacity to accommodate dozens of guests. This structure was destined to survive the Civil War, become the great family home, and endure as the beloved winter escape for thousands of guests during the long northern winters for nearly ninety years. In keeping with a tradition of the times on Southern plantations, the Fleming house became known as the "Big House."

The Fleming Mansion

A writer for the *Charleston Courier* visited Hibernia prior to November of 1858 and reported that his "old and esteemed friend, Col. Fleming, ... has just completed a new and elegant house at this point." Friends and former patrons would "rejoice to know that ... the Colonel and his amiable lady are at the old spot." The fire of the past spring "was not only a great loss pecuniarily, but a severe blow." Despite that blow, Fleming almost immediately applied his "usual vigor and ambition" and built another "more extensive house" in a little more than three months. The new house would be open and ready to receive guests on November 20, 1858. Those southbound for the winter would do well to "go and see [Fleming]. His genial face and warm welcome would almost make a sick man well."[36]

The new Fleming mansion was magnificent and designed to accommodate about fifty people. The first floor was dedicated to public spaces for guests, except for Lewis and Margaret's bedroom and small office. The large dining room included a back door entrance to the kitchen runway. In keeping with the danger of fires in those days, the kitchen was an entirely separate structure. For entertainment, guests had access to a parlor, music room, library, and a smoking room, where the men gathered to play cards, smoke, and sip whiskey. A ten-foot-deep veranda wrapped the southern corner of the structure and became a popular gathering spot. A spacious ten-foot-wide hallway with stairs to the second level graced the center of the structure. Servants used a smaller stairway located in a narrow back hallway. Floors were thick tongue-and-groove native heart pine. Each room had its own brick fireplace; a total of seven on the first floor. Ceilings were over ten feet high.

The second level consisted entirely of bedrooms for family members and guests; a total of nine altogether. All but one of these rooms had its own fireplace. These were the largest of the rooms and could accommodate two or more guests. The guest room above the smoking room was especially large and easily accommodated four people. The third level contained nine smaller bedrooms constrained in size by the slope of the roof. The fourth level was primarily a storage attic, though guests lodged there from time to time. All told there were approximately 6,600 square feet of indoor space, and 1,920 square feet of covered verandas, half on the ground level and half on the second level. This did not include the expansive detached kitchen and servants' work areas, where they performed all the cooking, ironing, mending, and other chores.[37]

Crepe myrtles, live oaks, and orange trees surrounded the property. Margaret directed the creation of landscaped walkways along the river bluff. George Causey, a Philadelphia transplant, tended a flourishing garden to provide fresh produce for the Flemings and their guests. Cattle, pigs, sheep, chickens, and turkeys ranged freely on the island. These and a variety of wild game and fresh fish provided sumptuous meals. A new, wide pier stretched approximately six hundred feet into the river to reach water deep enough to tie up the steamers that transported guests and supplies to and from Hibernia. The steamboat whistle signaled the arrival of guests and supplies during the boarding season, and throughout the year meant mail and news from the world beyond Fleming's Island.

Lewis and Margaret Fleming had every reason to anticipate a bright future as they reopened in November of 1858. Little did they know that, once again, the tragedies of war would strike Hibernia. There is no doubt about the Flemings' loyalties during the Civil War. The entire family was born and raised in the Southern plantation era, and they had a history of fighting for their land and their lifestyle. Tragically, this time the family would suffer beyond anything experienced during the Patriot War or the Second Seminole War. First, hostilities would disrupt travel between the north and south, curtailing the winter boarding business and shutting off their source of income. Next, Fleming sons would join the Confederate army and march to war. One would not return. Union forces would take control of the St. Johns River valley, and the entire family would be displaced. In the midst of all this, Margaret lost her husband.

Charles Seaver captured the oldest known photographs of the Fleming mansion sometime between 1870 and 1879. *MWF Collection*

Endnotes

1. *Catalogue of the Alumni of the Medical Department of the University of Pennsylvania 1765-1877*. Published by the Society of the Alumni of the Medical Department (Philadelphia: Collins, Printer, 1877), https://www.hathitrust.org.

2. *General Catalogue of Amherst College, Including the Officers of Government and Instruction, the Alumni, and All Who Have Received Honorary Degrees, 1821-1890* (Amherst, MA: Published by the College, 1890), https://www.hathitrust.org.

3. William L'Engle to Miss Leonis L'Engle, August 25, 1851, in Gertrude Nelson L'Engle and Katherine Tracy L'Engle, eds., *Letters of William John L'Engle, M.D. and Madeleine Saunders L'Engle, his Wife 1843-1863* (Jacksonville Public Library, Jacksonville, Florida).

4. Duval County Marriages, 1851-1860, http://www.genealogytrails.com. Davis Floyd married Sophia Fleming on April 23, 1851, approximately one month after her father's death.

5. Probate Packets, Duval County, Florida, George Fleming Jr., No. 911.

6. Biddle, *Hibernia: The Unreturning Tide*, 39.

7. L'Engle, *A Collection of Letters*, 2:117.

8. John P. Duval, *Compilation of the Public Acts of the Legislative Council of the Territory of Florida, passed prior to 1840* (Tallahassee, FL: Samuel S. Sibley, Printer, 1839).

9. *Floridian and Advocate* (Tallahassee), January 30 and March 31, 1838; *News* (St. Augustine, FL), September 27, 1839. Mary Gibson Fleming returned to her home in Georgia. Two years later she married James A. LaRoche and lived with him the remainder of her life.

10. The land conveyances to Huston, Buddington, and Floyd are embedded within other deed records. For Huston and Buddington, see Clay County Deed Book F, pp. 363-66. Mr. Halliday's sale to L. I. Fleming is detailed in E. N. Holt's Title Abstract prepared for F. A. Fleming on March 27, 1913, which is a part of the *MWF Collection*. Davis Floyd's landholdings are well documented in Clay County deed books. The Fernandina and Nassau River sales are in Nassau County, Clerk of the Circuit Court, Deed Records, 1840-1890, MF Reel 02, Florida State Archives. Joseph Finegan and John D. Bellechase purchased the Nassau River tract. Finegan became a general during the Civil War and was commanding officer to F. A. Fleming in Florida, then to Seton Fleming in Virginia.

11. *Florida Republican* (Jacksonville), January 1, 1852, www.geneaology.com. The advertisement ran in multiple subsequent issues of the paper.

12. Lewis Fleming to his cousin Martha, June 9, 1855, in L'Engle, *A Collection of Letters*, 2:13; 1850 U.S. Census, Slave Schedule.

Scott Ritchie

13. 1850 United States Federal Census (Provo, UT: www.ancestry.com).

14. *Florida Herald*, January 10, 1835.

15. *News* (Jacksonville, FL), January 23, 1846.

16. Louisa Fatio was one year older than her cousin Lewis. She was the oldest daughter of F. P. Fatio by his first wife, Susan Hunter. In 1855 Louisa purchased 55 Aviles Street from Mrs. Anderson. There she lived and operated her own boarding house for twenty years until her death in 1875. Today it is known as the Ximenez-Fatio House Museum, and is owned and operated by the National Society of the Colonial Dames of America in the State of Florida. The Ximenez-Fatio House is one of St. Augustine's most authentically restored and maintained properties. It is a national treasure that is open to visitors.

17. *Boston Traveler*, December 20, 1855, 3, www.genealogybank.com.

18. George Wingate Chase, *The History of Haverhill, Massachusetts, From Its First Settlement In 1640 Through The Year 1860* (published by the author, 1861).

19. Julia Lord Noyes (Loveland), *Papers, 1855-1965*, The David M. Rubenstein Rare Book and Manuscript Library at Duke University.

20. *Florida News* (Jacksonville), October 27, 1855.

21. Noyes, Papers.

22. Ibid.

23. Miss Noyes wrote about meeting many people during her travels, but she never mentioned any other guests during her stay at Hibernia.

24. Noyes, *Papers*.

25. Julia Lord Noyes married George Loveland in 1869 at the age of thirty-six. Her husband died two years later. Mrs. Loveland lived another fourteen years and died at age fifty-four. Her journal provides a fascinating glimpse of a winter in Florida for two young women from the North in 1855–1856.

26. *Sun* (Baltimore), October 31, 1856, 4.

27. Mrs. Tiers's maiden name was Christine Nostrond. She wrote two letters at Hibernia to Bishop James Roosevelt Bayley, first bishop of Newark. The first is dated December 14, 1856, and the other is dated February 1, 1857. These letters are preserved in the archives of Notre Dame University. Abstracts of the letters are available online at http://archives.nd.edu/calendar.htm.

28. Bishop Bayley specifically asked about Margaret Seton Fleming. He was curious about her Seton ancestry because the bishop was a first cousin of Elizabeth Anne Seton, who later became the first American citizen canonized as a saint in the Catholic Church. Margaret Seton was a very distant relative of Elizabeth Seton, but apparently neither she nor Bishop Bayley was aware of that.

29. The description of a "clear and blue" St. Johns River requires an explanation. The St. Johns River is tannin-stained and generally is the color of medium-brewed black tea. Even so, it can take on a stunning blue appearance under the right conditions.

30. *Boston Evening Transcript*, October 25, 1858, 1.

31. William James Stillman, *The Autobiography of a Journalist,* vol. 1 (Cambridge, MA: Riverside Press, 1901), 284.

32. *The Dead of the Synod of Georgia: Necrology; or Memorials Of Deceased Ministers, Who Have Died During The First Twenty Years Of Its Organization* (Atlanta: Franklin Printing House, 1869), https://books.google.com/books.

33. *Daily Picayune* (New Orleans), May 26, 1858; *Florida News*, June 8, 1858.

34. Orloff M. Dorman, *Memoranda of Events That Transpired at Jacksonville, Florida,* vol. 4, Library of Congress, Manuscript Division, MMC-1884. Orloff M. Dorman was a Jacksonville attorney.

35. *Charleston Courier* (South Carolina), May 31, 1858, 2.

36. Ibid., November 2, 1858, 2.

37. Lewis Fleming's grandson, Frederic Alexander Fleming Jr., drew a floor plan of the family home that is among the *MWF Collection*. Margaret Fleming's probate record includes a room-by-room inventory that offers additional insights regarding the floor plan of the house.

The Civil War

Lewis Fleming's personal position regarding secession is unknown, but the choices of his sons, both politically and militarily, make the family position abundantly clear. L. I. gave a preview of his position on secession as a secretary of the Committee on Organization for the Whig Party Convention in July of 1852. Among the resolutions he endorsed was the "unqualified conviction" that the candidate nominated by the Whig Party for president of the United States must "above all ... support and embrace ... the Fugitive Slave Law."[1] The law was a part of the Compromise of 1850 between slave-holding states and the Northern Free Soil Party. It required everyone in free states, including elected officials and private citizens, to cooperate in returning escaped slaves to their Southern masters. Ten years later, L. I. learned that his older brother's widow, Mary Bennett Fleming, did not support secession or the Southern cause and was "anxious to go to her friends in Lincoln's dominions." L. I. immediately gave her the money she needed and seemed glad to see her go.[2]

In 1854 Seton Fleming completed his studies under his brother, L. I., in Jefferson County. He would have gone to college but his father could not afford the cost. Instead, Lewis arranged a position for him at the boot and shoe firm of Ward, Doggett & Company in Chicago, where Seton worked until February of 1857. While in Chicago, Seton learned about "the spirit of intolerance on the part of Northern politicians and fanatics for Southern institutions." Upon returning home, Seton applied to West Point but was not accepted. By now his life's ambition was to serve the military, so he enrolled in King's Mountain Military School in Yorkville, South Carolina, in 1858. Seton paid the bulk of his tuition and board with money he had saved while working in Chicago. Upon completion of his studies, Seton did not receive a military appointment. Frustrated, he eventually settled for what amounted to an internship as purser on the river steamer *St. Marys*, and did a good enough job to earn a paying position. Then Seton fell in love, though

Scott Ritchie

we do not know the name of his sweetheart, which motivated him to a higher calling. In July of 1860 he once again joined his brother, L. I. Fleming, this time to study law in Jacksonville. Now twenty-two years old, Seton was strikingly handsome and strongly built. He stood about 5 feet, 10 inches tall with clear bluish-gray eyes, brown hair, and a fair, reddish complexion befitting his Irish ancestry.[3]

Seton was a poor student of law but a passionate secessionist. He joined a group of Jacksonville men enthusiastically advocating a break from the Union. Seton "loved [the South] better than his life,"[4] and "was of no small service in ... redeeming [Duval] county from the thraldom [sic] of Northern influence—the result was that the County was carried almost unanimously for secession."[5] The rest of Florida soon followed, becoming the third state to secede from the Union. Seton's brother, Frank, shared the same zeal for secession. During his life Frank wrote, "Patriotism in 1781 became treason in 1861." He believed the Southern secessionists were the true patriots, and that the Union was led by "fanatical intolerance ... broken loose from the sheet anchor of American liberty."[6]

Two Fleming Sons Join the Confederacy

After secession Seton immediately abandoned the study of law and joined the Jacksonville Light Infantry. When he learned the unit had no intention of deploying to battle, he assisted in the formation of Company H, Second Florida Regiment, in Palatka. Several prominent Florida citizens, including Senator D. L. Yulee of Fernandina and J. M. Daniel of Jacksonville, recommended Seton to be an officer. He was elected first lieutenant serving under Captain John W. Starke, for which he was paid $90 per month. Among the enlisted men was Seton's brother, Private Frank Fleming.

Their first encampment, known as "Number Ten," was on the west bank of the St. Johns River about six miles south of Palatka. Late in May of 1861, the Second Florida Regiment boarded the steamer *Barossa*, pushed downriver to Tocoi Point, disembarked, and marched fifteen miles through the night to St. Augustine.[7] Despite the overnight march, they arrived at the city gates early the next morning in buoyant spirits.

Their few weeks in St. Augustine were a time of promise. Frank Fleming described a scene filled with anticipation of chivalric heroism and glory in battle defending the South from Northern aggressors. By day, Lieutenant Seton Fleming's military education at King's Mountain

114

was invaluable. He drilled the troops three times daily, instilling discipline and order in his collection of enthusiastic volunteers. By night, officers and enlisted men enjoyed all that St. Augustine had to offer. This was a happy time of frequent evening entertainment and moonlight walks along the seawall, and many a man delighted in a romantic interlude with a young lady of the city. The entire city showed its support for their troops.

Officers and prominent citizens like the Flemings may have enjoyed the "Ancient City," but all was not so rosy for lower-class enlisted men. Money was tight and rations were in short supply. Newspaper editors chided merchants and the wealthy to contribute to the cause: "The poor man leaves his home to defend the property of his wealthy neighbor, as well as his own family; and the man of means ought not to take advantage of the poor man's necessity."[8] Enough of the citizenry responded that all soldiers were at least able to receive a nominal daily ration of salted or fresh meat, rice or beans, and either bread, flour, or hardtack. The ration also included an ounce of coffee, a bit of vinegar, and miniscule portions of candles, soap, and salt.[9] Soldiers received their uniforms compliments of the ladies of St. Augustine, who diligently cut and sewed until every man was clothed for battle.

After about five weeks Company H received their orders to ship out. On the day of parting, Lieutenant Seton Fleming assembled his men on the plaza that still exists today in the heart of St. Augustine. In a short speech he thanked the ladies of the city for their kindness and "pledged fidelity in defense of their country's liberties."[10] Then, upon the order, the company marched along the narrow streets bordered above by cantilevered piazzas as the citizens of St. Augustine showered them with flowers.

They marched overland to Picolata, where the company once again boarded the *Barossa* and steamed downriver. The *Barossa* stopped briefly at the Hibernia pier, where Seton and Frank bid farewell to their parents and siblings. From there it was on to Jacksonville, to join nine other companies and form the Second Florida Infantry, which officially mustered in on July 13, 1861, at the makeshift "Camp Virginia" located just west of present day Interstate 95 in downtown Jacksonville.

Lewis Fleming longed to see his sons one more time before they marched to war. He planned to board a steamer to Jacksonville but was feeling ill when the time came. Instead, Lewis sent his sons extra wool socks and a bit of advice based on his personal experience during the Second Seminole War: "On a march in the morning, eat but a slight meal; never drink anything stronger than coffee, water is best; when you eat but little you will not suffer thirst. At night make your best meal and wash your feet in cold water and put on dry socks ... Morning and night, retire to yourself and offer up a prayer to your Heavenly Father ... Do your duty to your God and your country, and all will be well."[11]

On July 15, 1861, Seton and Frank Fleming boarded a train bound for Richmond, Virginia, still enjoying the giddy enthusiasm of Southern supporters along the way. The troops received many a cheerful greeting and, as in St. Augustine, were showered with flowers at several stops along the way. In Savannah, the Fleming brothers marched with their company through the city and were treated to a fine meal at the train depot. After arriving in Richmond, Seton took charge of regimental drills and exercises, training everyone from the lieutenant colonel to the enlisted men. He was appointed regiment adjutant, which increased his pay to $100 per month. Now he applied his military training as well as the clerical skills he had honed in previous jobs, performing a variety of duties for the command staff, everything from routine paperwork to updating maps of enemy positions and seeing to the proper execution of orders.

The Second Florida Infantry was assigned to Brigadier General John Magruder's command near Yorktown, Virginia, where they passed the winter drilling and preparing for a spring assault. On April 5, 1862, after many months of inactivity, they got their first taste of combat: a "quick and reckless charge" at the Battle of Yorktown to dislodge the enemy from a position too close to camp.[12] Second Florida next saw action on May 2, 1862, in the Battle of Williamsburg. In the thick of the battle on the Confederate right, Colonel George T. Ward received a mortal wound and crumpled on the field. Union forces flanked the Second, forcing them to abandon Ward's body and fall back. Lieutenant Seton Fleming led the formation of battle lines to begin another advance across the field. It was a fearless but foolhardy maneuver and a superior officer ordered Fleming to join the others in a more protected position. Union troops "kept pouring a severe fire" upon them. They lay flat on the ground to avoid getting shot as "the humming of the balls over [their] heads reminded one of the buzzing of a swarm of bees."[13] During a lull in the shooting, Seton Fleming and a party of about twelve men, including officers and enlisted men, advanced on the battlefront to recover Colonel Ward's body. Returning under fire, Fleming was shot. The Minié ball entered just above his right hip, passed through his body, and exited at the center of his back. His comrades tried to carry him back when Seton implored them, "Leave me, and let me die in peace."[14]

Private Frank Fleming sprang into action. He organized a party of volunteers to retrieve his brother, but their commander ordered them to wait for the shooting to let up. Meanwhile, Seton had recovered from the initial shock of his wound and managed to crawl back towards his regiment. He waved his sword to attract attention and was rescued from the field of battle. Frank Fleming made his way to his brother. With the help of others he carried Seton, first on a blanket then on a litter, along a badly rutted and muddy road towards Williamsburg for medical attention. They sought refuge in the middle of the night at the home of Mrs. Mary Claiborne, where a number of other wounded had gathered. There Frank had the great fortune of finding a surgeon from Georgia with whom he was acquainted. The doctor examined Seton, wrote an order for some brandy, and directed Frank to get him to a hospital as soon as possible. The next morning Frank rose early in search of help to move his brother. While on the streets of Williamsburg, Frank encountered General J. E. B. Stuart, who ordered the private to return immediately to his unit. Reluctantly, Private Fleming obeyed. Union forces quickly overran Williamsburg and made a prisoner of everyone left behind, including doctors and the wounded, leaving the Fleming family to assume the worst for many weeks.

The Yankees did not transfer Seton to the hospital, but they allowed Southern doctors to treat his wounds. They cleaned and repaired Seton's bullet holes, after which he was given to the care of Mrs. Claiborne. This kindly woman nursed him back to good health over a period of two months. Seton later told his mother that Mrs. Claiborne was "just as kind and attentive to me as though I were her own and only child."[15] Prior to leaving Williamsburg, he entrusted his prized sword, given to him by his brother, L. I., to Mrs. Claiborne.

With Seton's health restored, the Yankees transferred him to Fort Monroe, located at the southern tip of the Virginia peninsula. In July of 1862 Seton and many others were imprisoned at Fort Wool, also known as the "Rip Raps," an artificial island at the mouth of Hampton Roads near the Chesapeake Bay. Ft. Wool was perhaps two hundred yards long and only one hundred yards wide, devoid of vegetation, with little to no cover from the harsh summer sun. The prisoners subsisted on salt meat, bread, and coffee "not fit to drink."[16] Seton and others discussed plans for escape, which would require swimming several miles, but never attempted their desperate scheme. On August 5, 1862, Union and Confederate officials orchestrated a huge exchange of some two thousand prisoners. Seton received his freedom in exchange for First Lieutenant John M. Pearson of the 4th New Jersey Volunteers.[17] A few days later he was back in Richmond, eager to join the fight once again. Seton wrote to his mother and father, summarizing everything that had happened since Frank was forced to leave him behind in Williamsburg, and telling them about the deplorable conditions at Ft. Wool. Seton said, "I want at least to pay one Yankee off for what they did to me."[18] He had no way of knowing that his father would never see the letter. Lewis Fleming had passed away two days before the prisoner exchange.

Lewis Fleming died in his Hibernia home on August 3, 1862. He was stricken with a sudden congestive chill, an ill-defined malady that may have been caused by a bad case of pneumonia, a lingering case of yellow fever, or perhaps a heart attack. Family history tells us that Lewis was seized by a severe fever and died within a matter of hours. The family laid Lewis to rest immediately to the right of his first wife, Augustina, in the small family cemetery near their home. The blow to Margaret Fleming is difficult to imagine. She was now a widow, bearing the full weight of responsibility for her two sons and three young daughters during a time of war. In his will, Lewis declared that he had "already expended much according to [his] means on and for" his children by Augustina, and that "they are now grown" and could "take care of themselves." That is why he left all his property and possessions to Margaret and their children together.[19] This inheritance eventually could provide Margaret a way to support her family, but presently the winter boarding business was suspended due to war, so she had no source of income. Compounding her worry, her oldest sons were at risk in the Virginia campaign, and at the time her husband died she had no way of knowing Seton's fate in a Yankee prison.

Seton returned to his unit after his release from Fort Wool. He might have been elected major of his regiment following the Battle of Williamsburg, except his status as wounded and captured forced the withdrawal of his name from the ballot. As a result he returned to Second Florida without an officer's position. Disappointed but undaunted, he volunteered as an enlisted man and served in that capacity for about three weeks until Captain C. S. Flagg, Company G, was killed at Seven Pines. The officers and men of that company requested Seton Fleming as their temporary commander just prior to the Second Battle of Manassas. Following the battle, Seton wrote his first letter home since learning of his father's death. He briefly counseled his mother to "try and bear up under this crushing weight" because "what we have lost, father has gained, and he is now happy in heaven." The bulk of this letter is about the Second Battle of Manassas. Second Florida stood in reserve, but near enough for errant fire to wound several men. Seton Fleming witnessed "the grandest and most horrid sights." He watched as "the enemy advanced steadily ... under a storm of grape, canister, and shell ... making [them] fall by the hundreds." Yankee troops came within range of Confederate musketry and "it slaughtered them dreadfully ... It was a grand sight to see the Yankee army advance with so much pomp as they did, and then to be driven back." In the aftermath of battle, Confederate soldiers pillaged dead Yankees: "... it looked as though men had forgotten they were human beings; but we were out of provisions, and many of our men were barefooted." Seton walked away from the battle with a small cache of Yankee goods, including a supper of hard bread and the pen and paper he used to write the letter home.

Closing his letter, Seton took up the mantle of head of the family and told his mother, "Stick to the old place; do not let it go out of the family." Concern for his widowed mother compelled Seton to return to Hibernia soon after Manassas. Unfortunately, the Fleming family preserved nothing of that visit—not even a brief oral history. We can only imagine his trip up the St. Johns River, taking in the familiar sights as he drew near home. Seton would have disembarked at the end of the long pier at Hibernia. Almost certainly, that is where his mother, brothers, and sisters greeted him, tears of joy mixing with those of sorrow. He did not stay long in Florida. The officers and men of Company G formally requested the official appointment of Seton Fleming as their captain. On October 8, 1862, Brigadier General Pryor honored that request and recalled Seton to duty.[20] Within weeks, Frank Fleming was promoted, as well. He was now Quartermaster Sergeant Fleming.[21]

The Second, Fifth, and Eighth Florida Regiments joined to form the Florida Brigade, under command of Brigadier General Edward A. Perry.[22] The Florida Brigade was part of General Robert E. Lee's Army of Virginia, and served with distinction in the push north to Gettysburg and during the defensive maneuvers trailing south back to Richmond. As Captain of Company G, Second Florida Regiment, Seton served in the battles of Fredericksburg, Chancellorsville, Gettysburg, Brandy Station, The Wilderness, Cold Harbor, and lesser engagements along the way. At Fredericksburg, the Florida Brigade held a position at the left and did not engage the enemy. At Chancellorsville, the Floridians fought in the thick of it. General Perry wrote that "the firm and steadfast courage exhibited, especially by the Fifth and Second Florida, in the charge ... attracted my particular attention."[23]

At Gettysburg General Perry took ill, possibly from typhoid fever, and Colonel David Lang assumed command of the Florida Brigade. On July 1, 1863, the Floridians advanced in support on the far left of General Longstreet's line, which was near the center of the fight.

Charles Seton Fleming, *MWF Collection*

In the face of "murderous fire of grape, canister, and musketry" they charged at the double-quick. "Grape" was a cannon-fired projectile usually loaded with nine pieces of cast iron shot that when fired spread with a shotgun effect. "Canister" was a metal cylinder packed with small shot. When fired at close range it spread towards a target like a massive shotgun blast.[24] In the face of this overwhelming barrage the Floridians charged with a Rebel yell that one Union officer described as "more devilish than anything that could come from human throats."[25] Halfway across the field they swept over fortified Yankee batteries then rapidly advanced to a position in a grove of trees near the base of Cemetery Ridge. Further attempts to advance failed and Lang ordered a retreat, but not soon enough. Union forces poured into the area, flanked Lang's command, and inflicted severe loss. A total of three hundred Florida troops were killed, wounded, or missing, including Major Moore, Commander of Second Florida, who was seriously wounded and left on the field.[26] By the next morning Captain Seton Fleming was given command of the Second Florida Regiment.[27]

Even casual students of the Civil War know something about July 3, 1863, which ended in retreat and utter defeat for Lee's army. The Confederate assault reached the base of Cemetery Ridge, a position that became known as the "High Water Mark of the Confederacy," before massive Union fire forced the Rebels to either surrender or retreat. Little is written of the charge by Alabama and Florida troops that day. They were the last troops ordered forward while the great mass of the Rebel assault retreated from the field of battle. Historians generally dismiss their effort as ineffective and brief, and in the context of this terrible battle that is a fair assessment.[28] It had no bearing on the outcome of the battle, but it was a high water mark of sorts for Captain Seton Fleming at that time in his military career.

The center of the great Confederate assault, famously known as Pickett's Charge, had failed when Brigadier General Cadmus Wilcox, in command of the Alabama and Florida Brigades, received three successive orders to advance in support. The order must have come from either General Richard A. Anderson or General A. P. Hill, and it was a terrible decision. General Edward Porter Alexander, in command of Lee's artillery, saw Pickett's men in retreat, "fugitives running back" as he described them, more than ten minutes before Wilcox's command moved out. Troubled by what he had witnessed, Alexander later wrote, "As they passed us I could not help feeling real pity for the useless loss of life they were incurring, for there was nothing left for them to support."[29] The Alabamians marched forward from the

Scott Ritchie

Confederate far right of the battlefield. The Floridians were to their left and nearer the center of the field. Colonel David Lang saw that Pickett's charge had failed and that the great mass of troops were either in retreat or already safely behind Confederate lines, but he did not pause to question orders. Five Alabama regiments marched forward, followed by three Florida regiments. Captain Fleming, in command of Second Florida and nearest the center of the battlefield, was the last to move out. His left flank was totally unguarded due to the mass retreat of Pickett's command. The Florida Brigade rapidly crossed the field without confronting enemy infantry, but under relentless artillery fire the whole distance. The historian Stephen W. Sears wrote that "within minutes fifty-nine [artillery] guns had opened fire" on the combined Alabama and Florida troops.[30] When they reached the base of Cemetery Ridge, "the noise of artillery and small arms was so deafening that it was impossible to make the voice heard above the din." It was a scene of utter chaos. Troops were in disarray, scattered, taking cover among the rocks and bushes, and scrambling for their lives in the face of "certain annihilation."[31]

Colonel Wheelock Veazey, in command of the Sixteenth Vermont Regiment, couldn't believe his good fortune. He found himself less than two hundred forty yards from Second Florida's left flank but obscured from view by thick smoke from the cannonade and musket fire. He could see the Floridians "crouching behind the low bushes and rocks which afforded some shelter" from federal artillery and infantry fire falling from the ridge above. The Sixteenth Vermont struck Second Florida squarely on their flank and moved across until the Rebel line disintegrated. Veazey wrote that "the movement was so sudden and rapid that [Second Florida] could not change front to oppose [us]." The Sixteenth took more prisoners than they could count. The Floridians were so badly shaken that their captors simply told them to move behind the federal line and report themselves as prisoners. No guard was necessary as "the prisoners were quite willing to get within the shelter of our lines and away from the exposure to which they were then subjected."[32]

In the midst of this confusion, Lang issued the order to retreat, but in his own words, "not in time to save a large number of the Second Florida infantry, together with their colors, from being cut off and captured by the flanking force on the left."[33] Those who escaped, including Captain Seton Fleming and Captain William E. McCaslin, somehow found their way back to their own lines. Fleming and McCaslin thought they were beyond the reach of the Yankees as they walked side by side, discussing the horrible events of the past two days. McCaslin remarked that the good fortune of escaping death in battle one day only meant the possibility of death in the next battle. Scarcely had he spoken these words when he was hit in the head by an enemy shell and fell dead on the spot.[34] Despite such miserable defeat and horrific loss, Seton Fleming later told his brother Frank that leading Second Florida during this ill-fated charge was one of the happiest experiences of his life. Strange as this may sound, it befits Seton's demeanor. His second cousin, Captain Edward M. L'Engle, an officer with the original Second Florida, once wrote that Seton had "enthusiasm and love for the profession of arms." Captain C. Seton Fleming had finally arrived as regimental commander on a battlefield, and even in the face of defeat it was exhilarating.

Following Gettysburg, the Fleming brothers again received promotions. Seton filled the position of Assistant Adjutant General of Perry's Brigade, and Frank Fleming was promoted to First Lieutenant of the First Florida Cavalry. Seton completed Frank's discharge papers from Second Florida and bid him farewell. They never saw each other again.

In his role as assistant adjutant, Seton was instrumental in motivating Second Florida to fight until the end of the war—however long that might be. The commission of the entire regiment, now numbering just one hundred fifteen men fit to bear arms, was set to expire on July 13, 1864. Captain C. Seton Fleming helped write the resolution that bears witness to the unwavering determination of Second Florida to "never give [the southern] cause up, and that we regard as traitors, unworthy to bear the name of Southerners, all citizens (if there are any) of the Confederate States who are willing to give it up without first exerting all their influence and sacrificing their property and their lives, if need be, to maintain it." Their pledge won the praise of the *Richmond Enquirer* for "Gallant little Florida," as well as official appreciation from the Confederate Congress.[35]

In January of 1864 Seton returned to Florida under orders to "arrest absentees and procure conscripts and volunteers" for his command. All we know of this last visit home is that "those who met him at that time speak of the cheerful buoyancy of his spirits and his unshaken faith in the cause."[36] He was back with his men in Virginia sometime in February. Neither Frank nor Seton saw action again until the spring campaigns of 1864, but the Fleming family joined the war on a new front. Their younger brother, Frederic, enlisted with the Confederate army in October of 1863, and the Union would soon begin its Florida campaign and bring the war to Hibernia.

Frederic Fleming Joins the Fight

Frederic Alexander "Fred" Fleming enlisted at Camp Cooper, near present-day Yulee, Florida, on October 1, 1863, when he was eighteen years old. At the time of enlistment he served under Captain Winston Stephens, of Welaka, Florida, in Company B, Second Florida Calvary. Stephens's unit was nicknamed "The St. Johns Rangers." Fleming family tradition tells us that Fred served with the mounted soldiers, and his Compiled Service Record confirms that belief. On August 31, 1864, Fred was paid $134.40 for the use and risk of his horse in the Second Florida Cavalry. This payment came in the wake of much action between the Union and Florida forces, and it is a common entry in the service records of other men in the Second Florida Cavalry.[37] Fred's service was marked by deprivation in difficult times, glorious victory in battle, and tragedy for the extended family.

Captain Winston Stephens and Private Fred Fleming were relatives. Fred's sister, Augustina Alexandria Fleming, married Winston Stephens's brother, William Clark Taylor Stephens. Captain Stephens was every bit as zealous for the Southern cause as Captain Seton Fleming, and perhaps even more so. Lamenting the possibility of death in battle, Stephens implored his wife "to promise that no matter what befalls me that you will never marry a Yankee, no matter what his calling or position." His blood boiled against the North and he couldn't bear the thought of leaving "such a good wife for a cursed Yankee." He wanted his children "educated to hate a Yankee and glory in their Southern blood."[38]

Though we know little of Fred Fleming's specific actions during the war, Captain Stephens's letters, preserved by the Bryant-Stephens families in the book *Rose Cottage Chronicles,* provide insight into his service. After mustering into Confederate service, the St. Johns Rangers thirsted for action, but instead passed three mundane months at Camp Cooper. Much time was devoted to drilling, training, and inspections. When not on duty the soldiers idled about, reading, playing cards, singing, and hunting for fresh meat. It was an altogether boring time for two months until the Rangers received orders to march on Camp Finegan.[39] The camp was named for General Joseph Finegan, the former master of the Constantia plantation just south of Fleming Island and now the commander of Confederate troops in the Jacksonville area. The excitement of the march was short-lived, though, because it turned out to be nothing but a parade for a visiting officer. The soldiers returned to Camp Cooper under-supplied and downcast by the lack of meaningful duty.

Winter brought hard times for Private Fred Fleming and his brothers-in-arms. On January 8, 1864, a deep freeze brought two-inch thick ice in water buckets and six-inch icicles hanging off roofs—extreme conditions in Florida—and troops began to desert. Little wonder, according to Captain Stephens, because the men were granted no furloughs to visit home and had "drawn no clothing and they are nearly naked and barefoot." Even Stephens considered deserting because his troops could not "be more abject slaves than now and it appears to me it grows more and more so everyday."[40] Some deserters attempted to burn an officers' barracks before leaving. Morale was terrible, and a soldier was under arrest or facing court-martial nearly every day.

As the Rangers suffered through freezing conditions at Camp Cooper, the Union began the transport of nearly seven thousand men for their Florida campaign. They intended to take control of Florida, recruit Negro troops and officers, organize a regiment of white Florida troops, and cut off all supplies that flowed north to aid Rebel armies. In the face of a far superior enemy some three hundred fifty Rebels, including the St. Johns Rangers, consolidated at Camp Finegan, which was located west of downtown Jacksonville along present-day Lenox Avenue about one-half mile west of Normandy Boulevard.[41] A contingent of the Union army known as the "Light Brigade," under command of Colonel Guy Vernor Henry, led an assault on Camp Finegan on the evening of February 8, 1864, and captured an artillery battery behind Confederate lines. Facing certain defeat, Lt. Colonel McCormick ordered the Rebels to leave Camp Finegan under cover of darkness and march to Camp Beauregard near Ocean Pond.[42] Union forces pressed their advantage, moving deeper into enemy territory and cutting off escape routes. Three days later Captain Winston Stephens reported, "We have so far been able to elude the enemy, though we have at times been surrounded and from the appearances we thought our prospect was fair for a northern prison." Some Rangers were captured, reducing their company to just forty-five men, including Private Fred Fleming.[43]

During the next eight or nine days Union forces fell back north of the St. Marys River to create a defensive position and concentrate troops for an attack on the Rebel stronghold at Lake City. All the while General Finegan gathered Confederate troops near Olustee Station, about thirteen miles from Lake City, where they constructed fieldworks and prepared for the enemy attack. On February 20, 1864, twelve Union regiments, including three regiments of U.S. Colored Troops, marched on Lake City. Among them were the remnants of the 54th Massachusetts, decimated at Fort Wagner, South Carolina, and immortalized in the 1989 movie "Glory." Colonel Guy V. Henry was in command of the Union's mounted forces. The Yankees came within three miles of General Finegan's position when he ordered the Second Florida Cavalry, supported by troops from Georgia, "to advance and skirmish with the enemy and draw them to our works." Captain Stephens and his mounted troops rode to the front, engaged the enemy, and then fell back, firing all the while. Scattered skirmishes quickly developed into a full-blown battle, and for a while the Union seemed to have the advantage. The Confederate troops rallied, though, and the Yankees pulled back. Stephens's men gave chase on the Confederate right, where they commenced a course of action that was "grand and exciting." Stephens "felt like he could wade through [his] weight in wild cats." The St. Johns Rangers overtook the enemy, dismounted, and "went on with a wild yell and the Yanks and negroes [sic] gave way." Then the Rangers hustled back to their horses, remounted, and galloped close to the enemy. Again they dismounted and attacked on foot until the enemy withdrew. They repeated this pattern of foot charges followed by advance on horseback until the fight ended. With the enemy thoroughly routed, the Rangers returned to camp after a long day and a night in the saddle, without rest for man or horse, and feasted on captured Yankee fare that Stephens called "first rate." The St. Johns Rangers won the day on their portion of the Olustee battlefield without a single man among them wounded.[44]

In his official report of what became known as the Battle of Olustee, Colonel Caraway Smith, Commander of the Florida Cavalry Brigade, wrote:

> It is due to the companies of Captains Stephens and Maxwell, of the Second Florida Cavalry, to state that the conduct of the men and officers, while acting as the rear guard of the cavalry as we were falling back before the enemy, was highly satisfactory. They behaved with the coolness and deliberation of veterans.[45]

The Battle of Olustee was the largest Civil War battle fought in Florida. Under General Joseph Finegan's command, Southern troops thrashed the Yankees and put a halt to their advance across Florida. Private Fred Fleming was present with Company B the entire time. Though we don't know his particular actions during the day, he was there among the 202 men of the Second Florida Cavalry. The Yankees retreated towards Jacksonville, but the fight was not over for Captain Stephens's men.

The St. Johns Rangers were pushed to the limit as they followed in the Yankees' wake, and neither man nor horse had much food. The horses were "mere skeletons." The men wore filthy clothing and hadn't bathed in weeks. Stephens wrote that he was "well but nearly worn out as any man you ever saw and so black I am ashamed." On March 1, 1864, Colonel Guy Henry sent a reconnoitering party to scout the Rebels' position near Twelve Mile Station west of Jacksonville.[46] Stephens's company rode on picket duty protecting the Confederate perimeter. They engaged the scouting party then took off in pursuit "fighting step by step." The Yankees reassembled at a position near Cedar Creek, in the heart of the present-day Westside area of Jacksonville. Colonel Henry sent reinforcements and moved forward to personally take command of the situation. Henry's men lay in wait for the mounted Rebels coming their way. Stephens led a charge on the Yankee position and the enemy shot him dead from the back of his white horse. The Rangers dismounted, pressed the assault on foot, and eventually forced the Yankees to retreat towards Jacksonville.[47] This engagement became known as the Skirmish at Cedar Creek. Eight men were killed, seven Rebels and one Yankee, and more than thirty were wounded, mostly Rebels. Stephens was killed in a still heavily wooded area on the west side of Jacksonville near the creek along Lenox Avenue, between Lane Avenue and Old Middleburg Road.[48] His death reverberated throughout the extended family. Augustina Fleming Stephens wrote her widowed sister-in-law, Octavia Stephens, to say "I think and think about you and cry until my brain seems to be on fire."[49] The news of Stephens's death was deeply troubling to the Flemings, not just for the loss of a dear family member but also because the Union officer in command, Colonel Guy Vernor Henry, was their cousin.

About a month later, Colonel Henry and the 40th Massachusetts were back in Virginia, where they joined General Ulysses S. Grant's Army of the Potomac in an aggressive offensive known as the Overland Campaign against Robert E. Lee's Army of Northern Virginia. After fighting an enemy that included the Second Florida Cavalry and Private Fred Fleming, Colonel Henry now would face an enemy that included the Florida Infantry Brigade and Captain Seton Fleming.

The opening salvos of this campaign rang out during the Battle of the Wilderness on May 5, 1864. Historian Gordon C. Rhea wrote a definitive account of the battle in which he summarized the actions of the Florida Brigade. The Floridians began their march to battle at two o'clock in the morning on May 6 and arrived near the front at eight o'clock. In a tentative maneuver, the Floridians "began snaking through the foliage," along with General Wilcox's Alabamians, scouting for the enemy. The Floridians were on point when Union Brigadier General Robert B. Potter's division poured into the field. Just as they had at Gettysburg, Union troops hit the Floridians "squarely in the flank" with devastating force.[50] The Floridians and Alabamians managed to rally and temporarily drove back the Yankees, but were forced to retreat once more. Captain Seton Fleming's small Company G supported the action from a short distance. Even though they were not actively engaged in the fight, Seton was hit twice by enemy fire and knocked to the ground both times. The wounds were painful but not severe. He refused to leave the fight and stayed in command, even directing his men forward while he was unable to stand.[51]

Margaret Fleming likely took little comfort in Seton's letter home following the battle. He told of "slaughtering [the enemy] by thousands" and how he was dropped "twice by glance-shots—once in the right breast and once in the stomach," but that he was "quite well again."[52] Seton was wounded in battle for the second time during the war, and his mother received this news in the wake of Captain Winston Stephens's death. She must have been weak with worry. Just days later, Seton sent his last known letter to his mother. He wrote that they "may fight another great battle here any day" and that he hoped to write again soon to give "an account of another victory for our army."[53] There was, indeed, a great victory coming for the South in the battle, but not for the Fleming family in Hibernia. Seventeen days after Seton wrote that letter, Margaret Fleming's life was turned upside down.

The Yankees Take Hibernia

Colonel Guy Vernor Henry figures prominently in a Fleming family oral history of events that took place in Hibernia on June 9, 1864. The story was recorded by Margaret Fleming's granddaughter and is so well known to Jacksonville area history buffs that it bears repeating here:

> Now the gunboat was coming up the river—now it was anchoring, now the landing party was rowing to the wharf. Hibernia awaited the enemy: Margaret, with her three girl children, stood silently in the hall, silently waiting for the intruders. Who was this officer in the enemy uniform walking the length of the long piazza followed by a group of men?

Margaret gazed in amazement! A foe—but he was a relative and a trusted friend—Colonel Guy V. Henry! The denouement was complete. Here was a man and an enemy, wearing the uniform of the United States, sent by his government to "destroy the houses along the St. Johns River."

Colonel Henry paced back and forth across the piazza, greatly conflicted by his predicament. Could he carry out the order to destroy Hibernia, where "he had been an honored guest in happier days?" He would not:

> [Henry] would misread the orders; he would interpret them as 'Destroy the horses' in this one particular case. He would not burn the house as he had burned the others.[54]

This story is dear to the hearts of many. For many years the congregation of St. Margaret's Episcopal Church in Hibernia brought Colonel Henry's actions to life during their "Annual Tour & Tea." Nearly the entire congregation participated in the event, which took place along the full length of the narrow sand road that dead-ends just beyond the Church. Hundreds of visitors joined walking tour groups each year and were treated to historical reenactments, lectures, music, art shows, food, and more. The reenactment of Colonel Guy Henry informing Margaret Fleming that he would spare Hibernia was a particular favorite of the congregation and the tourists, but the facts of the story are entirely different and lead to a tragic twist. Here is what really happened.

Margaret Fleming described herself as "a quiet and peaceable citizen" when a Union gunboat steamed up the St. Johns River in February of 1864. The commander assured all residents of Hibernia and the surrounding area that they could remain safely in their homes under U.S. protection. The gunboat remained at anchor near Hibernia for nearly four months, but Margaret had reasons to feel threatened rather than protected.

Margaret's fate was set when Brigadier General William Birney, in command of Union forces in Jacksonville, received a report that loads of torpedoes were on Fleming Island. This news demanded immediate action because just two months earlier five soldiers from the Second Florida Battalion had set torpedoes in the St. Johns River. Each of these tar-coated wooden kegs was packed with seventy pounds of cannon powder. On the evening of April 1, 1864, the U.S. cargo ship *Maple Leaf* struck those torpedoes. The explosion killed four African

American crewmembers and the *Maple Leaf* settled on the bottom of the shallow river, her smokestack protruding above the waterline. Though not an important military target, the entire ship and cargo were a total loss, including the equipment of three Union regiments and two brigade headquarters.[55] That is why General Birney sent nearly two hundred men with orders to "scour completely the island," capture any Rebels, and send all those disloyal to the United States to the west behind Confederate lines.[56] Margaret Fleming may have been a peaceable citizen, but she most certainly was not loyal to the United States. Moreover, Birney had specific intelligence that Margaret was furnishing information to the enemy.[57] At least one source assumes that Margaret was not guilty, but facts suggest otherwise.[58] Just weeks before, Colonel Henry's men had gunned down her stepdaughter's brother-in-law, Winston Stephens. Her son, Private Fred Fleming, rode with the St. Johns Rangers and was presently at risk of death by Yankee hands. Seton Fleming was in the thick of the war in Virginia, and Frank Fleming was serving Confederate forces in Georgia, where Union General William Tecumseh Sherman was massing troops for his Atlanta campaign. Her stepson, L. I. Fleming, provided legal services in Lake City for the Confederate cause and was a known conduit through whom Floridians could provide information about the Yankees.[59] If Margaret became aware of anything at all about the Yankees that might help keep her sons safe, she surely would have passed it along.

On June 9, 1864, Union forces under command of Colonel Slidell stormed Fleming Island. The troops divided into several parties, one under command of Captain Clark. His company confronted fifty-six-year-old John Brantley, the Flemings' friend and neighbor, at his home two miles north of Hibernia. Clark ordered Brantley and his family to leave. If they did not, the Union gunboat would shell the house with the family in it. Clark assured Brantley that if he left peacefully nothing would be disturbed. Just moments later, Clark ordered a soldier to shoot Brantley's horse dead in its stall.[60]

The raiding party continued overland to Hibernia, where only Margaret, her sister Matilda Seton, her three daughters, the old gardener George Causey, and a few Negroes remained. The Yankees took all the hams from the smokehouse and pillaged the house of anything that struck their fancy, including everything from silver to stockings, handkerchiefs, and even paper and pins. All the while Captain Clark distracted Mrs. Fleming and assured her that "not a thing should be disturbed." Margaret discovered the thefts and confronted Clark, who told her pillaging was against orders and he would look into it. Compounding the shock, Margaret discovered that the Yankees had killed all their horses, one quite brutally. A Union soldier had slit the throat of an old plow horse standing in its stable.

George Causey fared no better. An officer detained Causey in one room, asking him questions and holding his attention. At the same time Union soldiers entered Causey's room, broke open his trunk, and stole all of his money, valuables, and clothing.[61]

That evening, Clark ordered Margaret, her sister Matilda Seton, and her three daughters to leave the place on foot, "to find food, shelter, and raiment where she might" (as Margaret put it years later) and forbade George Causey from helping them.[62] They left Hibernia accompanied by one little Negro girl, spent most of the night in the woods, and walked nearly eight miles before finding any help.[63] Shortly thereafter Union soldiers steamed upriver to Hibernia aboard the *Hattie*. They carried much of Margaret Fleming's furniture to the end of the pier, loaded it aboard the *Hattie,* and took it to headquarters in Jacksonville. The furniture was divided among the officers in command.[64]

Eventually Margaret, her daughters, and her sister made their way to Lake City where they could seek help from L. I. Fleming, who worked there as an attorney. Fleming family tradition tells us that Margaret stayed in Lake City for the duration of the war, where she became the "matron of the hospital ... giving some help and comfort in a world gone bleak."[65] While it may be true that Margaret Seton Fleming assisted at a hospital in Lake City for a short time, it is apparent she had other priorities. Margaret was nearly destitute and had to find a way to support herself and her daughters. For the remainder of the war she put her skill set to work and ran a small boarding house in Monticello, Florida.[66]

Returning to the family legend about the Yankees taking Hibernia, it is true that Guy Vernor Henry was related to Margaret Seton Fleming. Her first cousin, William Seton Henry, was his father. Guy Henry was born March 3, 1839, and was just one month younger than Margaret's eldest son, Seton. He began military service immediately after completing West Point, just days after the first shots rang out at Fort Sumter to begin the Civil War. Commissioned as a first lieutenant, he quickly rose through the military hierarchy.[67] Colonel Henry took command of Company S, 40th Infantry Regiment Massachusetts, in November of 1863. He arrived in Florida with his "Light Brigade" in February of 1864 and shipped back north for the Virginia campaigns in late March, thus making it impossible for him to save Hibernia from

Scott Ritchie

destruction in June.[68] Perhaps Guy Henry did, in fact, visit his father's cousin during his deployment to Florida. It's certainly plausible, and he may even have assured Margaret Fleming that no harm would come to her or to her home. If he did, his words obviously did nothing to save Hibernia; but that is not the end of the story. At the very moment Union forces cast Margaret out of her home, no one in the Fleming family knew about events that had transpired in Virginia five days earlier.

The Battle of Cold Harbor

Just a few days prior to Margaret's eviction and sad trek from Hibernia, both her eldest son, Captain Seton Fleming, CSA, and his second cousin, Colonel Guy Henry, USA, served their countries during one of the most horrific engagements of the Civil War: The Battle of Cold Harbor. Colonel Henry served General Ulysses S. Grant under General Meade's forces in the Army of the James as commander of the 3rd Brigade. Captain Fleming and the much-decimated Second Regiment, Florida Infantry, received orders to join General Joseph Finegan's Florida Brigade. Finegan and his men had recently arrived from Florida to join the Army of Virginia. His men were newly minted soldiers and took the usual ribbing from their battle-hardened comrades. David L. Geers, a Florida veteran, commented that they "were all smoked from the lightwood knots and had not washed or worn it off ... most of them with bed quilts instead of blankets."[69] Captain James E. Phillips, of 12th Virginia, said they were "very young ... not healthy & strong" and that "they was a pitiful, sorrowful looking crowd."[70]

During the opening salvos on June 1, 1864, Colonel Henry's 40th Massachusetts charged Major General George Pickett's entrenched Confederate forces, fell back under withering fire, charged a second time, and again were sent running by murderous repelling fire. Henry, remembered as "an intrepid young West Pointer of magnetic presence and merciless discipline," rode back and forth, driving his men throughout each charge. Then, according to one of his captains:

> ... with a cool smile of defiance, [Henry] leaped his horse over the enemy's works, and as the dying steed lay struggling on the parapet, its rider coolly standing in his stirrups emptied his revolver in the very faces of the awestruck foe.[71]

Incredibly, Henry wasn't even wounded, though his remarkable daring did nothing to help the day. The Rebels repulsed Union forces up and down the line, with but one exception a little more than a mile south of Henry's position. There the Yankees pushed forward against Major General John C. Breckenridge's position and nearly took that ground. At the end of the day, General Robert E. Lee ordered his only two reserve units to change their position to support Breckenridge: Finegan's Floridians and the 2nd Maryland Battalion.

Amid the horror of the Battle of Cold Harbor, June 3, 1864, stands alone.[72] It was also a fateful day for the Flemings of Fleming Island. The coordinated Union assault began with signal shots and faint bugle calls at four-thirty in the morning. Union forces gained almost no ground and suffered staggering losses. Guy Henry's troops had pulled back slightly after their useless charges on June 1 and now supported a disastrous effort to take Lee's left. Union troops charged Alabama sharpshooters and suffered the most destructive fire one officer had ever witnessed. The Yankee losses were horrendous at this line of battle, prompting Confederate General Evander Law to say, "It was not war, it was murder."[73]

In contrast, Yankees were overwhelming Brigadier General John C. Breckenridge's breastworks to the south. Breckenridge, a former vice president of the United States under James Buchanan, could not hold out long. As the Yankees pulsed forward, Finegan's Floridians and the Marylanders were roused from their sleep and ordered into action. They rallied in such haste that they carried neither water nor gear, only their munitions. En route they crossed paths with the Virginians who were "running over [the Floridians] like a bunch of Texas steers, stampeded the worst sort" in a frantic retreat. Around five o'clock in the morning, Captain Seton Fleming's command and the other Floridians charged headlong into the fight. They "poured two volleys into the advancing droves of Yankees then jumped the breastworks and charged them."[74] A Confederate war correspondent on the scene wrote that the Floridians "came upon [the Yankees] like a whirlwind."[75] The combined charge of Floridians and Marylanders sent the Yankees running, but not for long. Many of them found cover behind stumps, in picket holes, or in hastily dug shooting holes, some of them as close as thirty-five yards from the Confederate breastworks.

Suddenly the retreating Yankees turned the tables. Cold Harbor historian, Ernest B. Furgurson, wrote, "The Yankees there, crouched on the field among their wounded and dead comrades, were in a vengeful mood."[76] They held scattered positions and were under good cover. They flanked the Rebels on two sides, and they looked up a rise of about thirty degrees to the Rebel breastworks. Captain Fleming and his comrades crouched or laid on the ground safely below the breastworks, but in order to see the enemy below they had to rise from behind their protective mound. One Yankee eyewitness reported, "... to aim at our men a Rebel must raise his head so far above the earthworks" and "not a head or the least portion of a man's person can be exposed but what a dozen guns are instantly fired by our men."[77] Confederate troops could not leave or approach Fleming's part of the line without risk of being shot. Orders and communication were passed by word of mouth from man to man, or by written messages placed in a cap box that was passed from hand to hand.

For the next five hours the Yankees and Rebels traded jabs, with the Yankees getting the best of it by far. At such close proximity they could easily hear each other, so the Yankees hollered out, trying to trick Rebels to raise their heads. They succeeded many times, wounding or killing numerous Confederate soldiers. The Yankees riddled the Stars and Bars with bullets then dared their enemy to raise another "rag." The best the Rebels could do in return was to tease the Yankees by holding their hats upon their ramrods then hoisting them above the breastworks to draw harmless shots.

Around ten o'clock in the morning, General Finegan, commanding from the rear, received a message that the situation hadn't gotten any better. He ordered Major Pickens Bird to form a skirmish line comprised of every fifth man in his company and charge the enemy. When Bird issued the command to charge, many of his men would not go, but Captain Robert D. Harrison jumped upon the breastwork, waved his sword to urge the men forward, and was immediately cut down by enemy fire. Major Bird moved forward "in broad daylight over an open, unobstructed field and in full view of the enemy from the start." His skirmishers followed at the double-quick as the enemy "poured death-dealing missles [sic]" upon them. Major Bird moved forward hardly thirty paces before he was hit. Captain James Tucker ran to Bird and fell wounded. Lieutenant Ben Lane scrambled over the breastworks, hoisted Bird's body, and received a mortal wound in the process.

Major Bird's charge was an unmitigated disaster and Captain Seton Fleming witnessed the deadly outcome. Several hours later, he received the exact same order from General Finegan. Captain James F. Tucker witnessed Seton Fleming's fatal charge and later described the last few moments:

I shall never forget how he looked as he came into the traverse where I lay, so as to have a more central position. He crouched under the breastworks like a tiger before its spring. He was silent but thoughtful. He knew that from the moment they left the shelter of our breastworks he and his men would be exposed to a concentrated and deadly fire which neither they nor their friends could return; nor could a diversion be made in their favor. He had witnessed the charge of Maj. Bird and his detail, and his practiced eye told him this second effort to dislodge the enemy must prove as futile as the first ... As he leaned there against the breastworks he took off his watch and handed it to some one near him with some directions inaudible to me. Several times he looked at me, but spoke not a word. The occasion was too serious ... The crucial moment had come. At the agreed signal Capt. Fleming and his brave band of heroic soldiers scaled the entrenchments and disappeared from my view ... There was no touch of the elbow to give confidence and encouragement, no wild and exultant "Rebel yell," as with a massed brigade or division making a charge ... [78]

Seton Fleming's brief, potentially brilliant, life ended at age twenty-six. He somehow managed to run one hundred feet or so from the Floridians' breastwork before he was cut down. So intense was the Union fire that his comrades were forced to leave his body on the field as they retreated for cover. Fighting raged for three more hot and humid days until a general cease-fire allowed both sides to recover their wounded and dead. Alabama troops found Seton's body in a disturbing state of decay. They carried him behind Confederate lines and buried him among a grove of trees.[79] Years later his brother, Frank Fleming, had his body disinterred and moved to Hollywood Cemetery in Richmond, Virginia. His frock coat, sash, and canteen are among the collections at the American Civil War Museum in that city.[80]

So ends the story of Colonel Guy Vernor Henry and the Flemings of Hibernia. Henry was involved in three deadly fights that included his Fleming second cousins as enemies. In the first, he retreated in defeat with the St. Johns Rangers on his heels harassing all the way. In the second, he issued the orders that were directly responsible for the death of Augustina Fleming's brother-in-law. At Cold Harbor he was a mile away from Seton Fleming's death, but among the enemy nonetheless. Many years after the Battle of Cold Harbor, Henry was awarded the Congressional Medal of Honor for his heroic charge across enemy lines.[81] He did not save Hibernia from destruction during the

Civil War, but he did win our country's highest military honor while leading Union troops during a horrific battle that took the life of his second cousin.

Nearly a month passed before Margaret Fleming knew for certain that her son was dead. Dr. Richard P. Daniel, surgeon of 8th Florida, sent a letter to L. I. Fleming in Lake City to inform him of the tragedy. L. I. conveyed the sad news in a letter to Lieutenant Frank Fleming, then serving in Northern Georgia:

> ...we ought to have been prepared to hear of [Seton's] fall at any moment, yet the sad intelligence of his death gave me a shock that almost unmanned me. I felt that he would survive the war, and that when peace came, he would reap the reward of his gallantry and patient endurance of the hardships in the field ...

Frank simply would not accept the news. After all, Seton had been wounded and taken prisoner once before. It could have happened again. Frank wrote to Captain J. H. Johnston, who still served Second Florida in Virginia, and asked about the rumor of Seton's death. Late in July, Johnston confirmed the heart-breaking truth of the matter.[82]

We can only imagine the depth of Margaret Fleming's grief. Her stepdaughter, Augustina Fleming Stephens, wrote that Margaret was "almost crazy" with grief, and little wonder that she was.[83] In two years she had lost her husband, her home, and her eldest son, and her other sons were still at risk in the war. As soon as he could, Frank Fleming traveled two hundred long, lonely miles south to Monticello to mourn with his family and to counsel his mother.[84] Whatever comfort he could offer was short-lived. Frank returned north to rejoin his regiment near Atlanta, where Union forces, led by General William Tecumseh Sherman, massed to take the city.

Civil War Service of Frank, L. I., and Willie Fleming

On the way back to his unit, Frank checked into the Confederate hospital at Barnesville, Georgia. He suffered two nasty illnesses during the war: erysipelas and chronic diarrhea. Erysipelas is an acute skin infection usually caused by streptococcus bacteria. Doctors had treated an outbreak on Frank's face just two months earlier. The skin infection may have been under control but, like many other Confederate soldiers during the war, Fleming was continually dehydrated and weakened by diarrhea. He recuperated at the hospital for a few days then joined the

First Florida Cavalry, which was a part of General John Bell Hood's Army of Tennessee engaged in the defense of Atlanta.

Lieutenant Fleming and his men entered the action when General Hood dispatched two corps under command of Lieutenant General William Hardee to confront Yankee troops as they approached Confederate supply lines. The Rebels had no idea that nearly the whole of Sherman's Army was coming their way. On August 31, 1864, Hardee's troops attacked the Yankees just west of Jonesboro, about eighteen miles south of Atlanta. Lieutenant Fleming and his men charged through "a terrific fire of artillery and small arms" in an attempt to take a heavily fortified Union entrenchment, but were forced to retreat. Fleming was still weak due to his chronic illness, and his strength gave out. A sergeant recognized his struggle and assisted him in the escape. The next morning Frank's first concern was for his mother. A thick fire of Yankee artillery sailed over his position as he hastily scrawled a letter to assure her that he was safe.[85] The conflict he had just survived became known as the Battle of Jonesboro and opened the way for General Sherman to take Atlanta and continue his march to the sea.

Little more is known of the Fleming brothers during the Civil War. Frank was back in Florida on sick leave in the spring of 1865 when the Yankees made one last attempt to take Tallahassee, the only Confederate capital that had not fallen during the war. On March 6, 1865, a hastily assembled force of home guard militia, infantry, reserves, and volunteers that included teenagers from the Florida Military and Collegiate Institute met the Union offensive at Natural Bridge about fifteen miles southeast of Tallahassee. Lieutenant Fleming led one company of volunteers. As they had at the Battle of Olustee, the Floridians repelled the Yankees, who retreated to the Gulf.[86] The war effectively ended one month later, on April 9, 1865, when General Robert E. Lee surrendered at Appomattox.

Fred Fleming's entire service was with the St. Johns Rangers, Company B, Second Florida Cavalry. By 1865 Captain H. A. Gray had taken the place of Winston Stephens as company commander, and Winston's brother, Swepston Stephens, served as his second lieutenant. That spring Private Fred Fleming rode alone to scout a remote area of West Florida astride his trusted horse, Roderic. Fleming had raised Roderic from a colt and rode him the entire war. Both horse and rider were lean but strong from their many months on the campaigns. Private Fleming came into an open, swampy area of palmettos and scrub trees. He was picking his way through shallow water when

Roderic suddenly slipped in the mud and fell, pinning Fleming's leg beneath his weight. Roderic's frantic kicking entangled his legs in some roots below the water's surface, and Fred lay trapped under his horse in black mud. Hours passed, his pain and thirst intensified, and he grew desperate. He considered killing his horse and trying to hack his way out from under the dead weight, but reconsidered when he saw buzzards gathering above. Fortunately, a wagon appeared in the distance. Fred hollered and waved his arms. A farmer who was searching for a lost cow came to his aid with an ax and chopped the roots to free the horse. Bruised but not seriously injured, horse and rider returned to their unit. [87]

The story of Fleming Civil War service is incomplete without mention of William Henry "Willie" Fleming, the youngest of the four brothers, and Louis Isadore Fleming, the older brother they all greatly admired. Family oral tradition tells us that when Willie was a teenager he aided local guerillas along the St. Johns River as they harassed Union ships. There are rumors that he had some part in the sinking of the *Maple Leaf*. Even though no documentary evidence supports that claim, it is possible that he played some minor part. Perhaps that explains why, in years to come, the doorknob to the smoking room of the great Fleming home came from the wreck of the *Maple Leaf*. Seventeen-year-old Willie Fleming officially began his brief military service for the Confederacy when he enlisted at Camp Lay on July 7, 1864, less than a month after his mother was evicted from Hibernia. He served under command of Major McGrady in Captain Wiley Barwick's company, First Reserve of Florida. Willie was five feet, four inches tall at the time, with red hair, grey eyes, and a fair complexion. By his own report he once had a near brush with death when a bullet clipped his hair. His greatest injury of the war was chronic dysentery, a severe intestinal disorder that plagued him for the rest of his life.[88]

At the start of the Civil War, thirty-three-year-old Louis Isadore Fleming was the district attorney for the eastern circuit of Florida. He retreated to Lake City when the Yankees took control of Jacksonville and served as a volunteer aid de camp to Brigadier General Joseph Finegan, the Flemings' former neighbor along the St. Johns River who later traveled north with the Florida Brigade and issued the order that led to Seton Fleming's death. Among other services, L. I. defended the actions of a major who had commandeered supplies from a private citizen. Finegan asked General P. G. T. Beauregard to appoint L. I. as an assistant attorney general with the rank of captain. Beauregard approved the position but not the rank. In November of 1863 L. I.

replaced Lieutenant T. E. Brown as judge advocate of the general court martial. He served in that capacity for a total of thirty-two days at a salary of eight dollars per day. Fleming family oral tradition tells us that L. I. was awarded the rank of major while he was judge advocate, but his service record does not corroborate that claim.[89]

On May 10, 1865, Willie and Frank Fleming surrendered as prisoners of war at Tallahassee. They were paroled five days later at Madison, Florida, and set free. Ten days after that, Fred Fleming and all of the Second Florida Cavalry surrendered at Waldo, Florida. Like most Confederate soldiers from Florida, they signed oaths of allegiance to the United States then were paroled and set free a few days later.

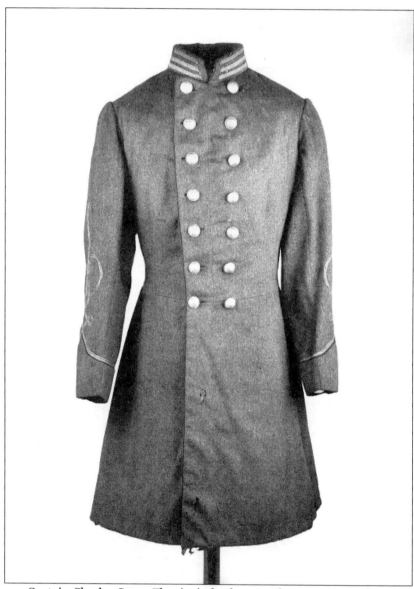

Captain Charles Seton Fleming's frock coat. *Photo courtesy of the American Civil War Museum, Richmond, Virginia*

Endnotes

1. *Florida Republican* (Jacksonville), July 29, 1852.

2. L. I. Fleming to his second cousin, Captain Edward M. L'Engle, July 3, 1862, in L'Engle, *A Collection of Letters*, 2.

3. Francis P. Fleming, *Memoir of Capt. C. Seton Fleming, of the Second Florida Infantry, C.S.A.* (Jacksonville: Times-Union Publishing House, 1881), 18-24.

4. Ibid.

5. Chs. Seton Fleming Compiled Service Record, *Compiled Service Records of Confederate Soldiers Who Served in Organizations from the State of Florida*, NARA, RG 360, M251, https://www.fold3.com/. The vote in favor of secession was by county delegates, not by popular vote.

6. Fleming, *Memoirs*, 31.

7. *St. Augustine Examiner*, June 8, 1861, 2. The *Barossa*, Captain E. R. Ives, ran regular routes from Jacksonville to Palatka, Enterprise, Mellonville, and intermediate landings, including Hibernia.

8. Ibid.

9. Ibid.

10. Fleming, *Memoirs*, 27.

11. Lewis Fleming to "My dear Seton and Frank," July 10, 1861, in L'Engle, *A Collection of Letters*, 2.

12. Shane Micah Turner, "Rearguard of the Confederacy: The Second Florida Infantry Regiment" (masters thesis, Florida State University, 2005), 1459, http://diginole.lib.fsu.edu/etd/1459.

13. *Fleming Family Letters*, Collection M02-3, University of North Florida, Jacksonville, Florida. F. P. Fleming to Miss Eliza, June 6, 1862.

14. Fleming, *Memoirs*, 36.

15. C. Seton Fleming to Margaret and Lewis Fleming, August 9, 1862, in Fleming, *Memoirs*, 47-48.

16. Ibid.

17. United States War Department, *The War Of the Rebellion: A Compilation of the Official Records of the Union and Confederate Armies* (Washington, D.C.: GPO, 1880–1901), series 2, vol. 4, serial 117, 442.

18. C. S. Fleming to his mother and father, August 9, 1862, in Fleming, *Memoirs*.

19. Copy of Lewis Fleming's will, *MWF Collection*.

20. Chs. Seton Fleming Compiled Service Record.

Scott Ritchie

21. F. P. Fleming Compiled Service Record, *Compiled Service Records of Confederate Soldiers Who Served in Organizations from the State of Florida*, NARA, RG 360, M251, https://www.fold3.com/.

22. Edward Aylesworth Perry became the 14th governor of Florida.

23. General Perry to Major Thomas S. Mills, May 9, 1863, in Fleming, *Memoirs*, 72-76.

24. Ellen Kanervo, "The Foundry's Connection to the Civil War," n.d., http://clarksvillefoundry.com/about-us/civil-war/.

25. Hugh Bicheno, *Gettysburg* (London: Cassell, 2001), 136.

26. *War Of The Rebellion*, Colonel David Lang to HQ, July 29, 1863: Lang's official report of action at Gettysburg, series 1, vol. 27, part 2, 631-633.

27. Chs. Seton Fleming Compiled Service Record.

28. David J. Eicher, *The Longest Night: A Military History of the Civil War* (New York: Simon & Schuster, 2001), 547-48; Stephen W. Sears, *Gettysburg* (Boston: Houghton Mifflin, 2003), 451-54.

29. Gary W. Gallagher, ed., *Fighting for the Confederacy: The Personal Recollections of General Edward Porter Alexander* (Chapel Hill: University of North Carolina Press, 1989), 263-65.

30. Sears, *Gettysburg*, 454.

31. *War Of The Rebellion*, Colonel David Lang to HQ.

32. Richard Rollins, ed., *Pickett's Charge: Eyewitness Accounts* (Redondo Beach, CA: Rank and File Publications, 1994). Account of Colonel Wheelock Veazey, in command of 16th Vermont, 192-95.

33. *War Of The Rebellion*, Colonel David Lang to HQ.

34. Fleming, *Memoirs*, 79-80; William E. McCaslin Compiled Service Record, *Compiled Service Records of Confederate Soldiers Who Served in Organizations from the State of Florida*, NARA, RG 360, M251, https://www.fold3.com/.

35. Fleming, *Memoirs*, 92.

36. Ibid., 93.

37. Fred A. Fleming Compiled Service Record, *Compiled Service Records of Confederate Soldiers Who Served in Organizations from the State of Florida*, NARA, RG 360, M251, https://www.fold3.com/.

38. Arch Frederic Blakey et al., eds., *Rose Cottage Chronicles: Civil War Letters of the Bryant-Stephens Families of North Florida* (Gainesville: University Press of Florida, 1998), Winston Stephens to Octavia Stephens, January 26, 1864, 310.

39. Camp Finegan, named for Joseph Finegan, was located on the west side of Jacksonville not far from the intersection of present day I-10 and I-295.

40. Blakey, *Rose Cottage Chronicles*, Winston Stephens to Octavia Stephens, January 4-11, 1864, 301-05.

41. William M. Jones, "A Report on the Site of Camp Finegan," *Florida Historical Quarterly* 39:4, (1961).

42. *War Of The Rebellion*, series 1, vol. 35, part 1 (Olustee). Major General Q. A. Gillmore to Major General H. W. Halleck, February 9, 1864, 281, and Brigadier General Joseph Finegan to Brigadier General Thomas Jordan, February 26, 1864, 330-33.

43. Blakey, *Rose Cottage Chronicles*, Winston Stephens to Octavia Stephens, February 11, 1864; Fred A. Fleming Compiled Service Record.

44. Blakey, *Rose Cottage Chronicles*, Winston Stephens to Octavia Stephens, February 21, 1864, 318-21; *War Of The Rebellion*, series 1, vol. 35, part 1 (Olustee), Brigadier General Joseph Finegan to Brigadier General Thomas Jordan..

45. *War Of The Rebellion*, series 1, vol. 35, part 1 (Olustee), Colonel Caraway Smith to Captain W. Call, February 24, 1864, 353.

46. Twelve Mile Station was at present-day Whitehouse, Florida.

47. *War Of The Rebellion*, series 1, vol. 35, part 1 (Olustee), Reports of Colonel Guy V. Henry and First Lieutenant R. M. Hall, 364-65.

48. Historical Marker Society of America, http://www.hmdb.org.

49. Blakey, *Rose Cottage Chronicles*, Augustine Fleming Stephens to Octavia Stephens, March 21, 1864, 330.

50. Gordon C. Rhea, *The Battle Of The Wilderness, May 5-6, 1864* (Baton Rouge: Louisiana State University Press, 1994), 385.

51. Fleming, *Memoirs*, 94.

52. Ibid., C. Seton Fleming to Margaret Fleming, May 14, 1864, 94.

53. Ibid., C. Seton Fleming to Margaret Fleming, May 23, 1864, 96.

54. Biddle, *Hibernia: The Unreturning Tide*, 52-53.

55. Thomas M. Fleming, "The *Maple Leaf* Adventure: A Florida Civil War Shipwreck Reveals Civilian and Soldier Life in the Mid-19th Century," http://www.militaryhistoryonline.com/civilwar/articles/mapleleaf.aspx. Dr. Keith Holland of Jacksonville, Florida, led a remarkable salvage effort of the *Maple Leaf*. His team recovered an irreplaceable treasure of Civil War cultural material. Some of that collection can be viewed at the Mandarin Museum near Jacksonville.

56. Francis P. Fleming Collection, University of Florida Smathers Libraries, General Birney to Colonel James Shaw, June 7, 1864.

57. Ibid., E. C. Woodruff, August 1, 1865.

58. Florida Irish Heritage Center, "Florida's 'Gone With The Wind,'" https://floridairishheritagecenter.wordpress.com/2011/04/15/floridas-gone-with-the-wind/.

59. *War Of The Rebellion*, series 1, vol. 35, part 2 (Olustee), S. to L. I. Fleming, 446-47..

60. *Daily Constitutionalist* (Augusta, GA), July 2, 1864.

61. Orloff M. Dorman, *Memoranda of Events That Transpired at Jacksonville, Florida*, Library of Congress, Manuscript Division, MMC-1884.

62. Interestingly, Margaret's grandmother (for whom she was named) was ejected from her home during wartime. During the Revolutionary War, Andrew and Margaret Seton lived in Brooklyn and remained loyal to England. In 1776 a group of armed Patriots ransacked their home, set it ablaze, and drove Margaret's grandmother and children out in the snowy cold.

63. *Daily Constitutionalist*, July 2, 1864; Francis P. Fleming Collection, papers associated with Margaret Fleming's petition for reparations under the Southern Claims Commission. These include Margaret's personal statement, as well as depositions from George Causey and neighbors.

64. Dorman, *Memoranda*.

65. Biddle, *Unreturning Tide*, 54.

66. Dorman, *Memoranda*. Mr. Dorman recorded the fact that Margaret Fleming ran a small boarding house until the end of the war. The location is revealed in F. P. Fleming's letters to his mother and Aunt Matilda in Fleming, *Memoirs*, Appendix I.

67. For readily available information about Guy V. Henry, see http://www.arlingtoncemetery.net/ghenry.htm. Guy V. Henry's personal papers are archived at the U.S. Army Military History Institute in Carlisle, PA.

68. Guy V. Henry Compiled Civil War Service Record.

69. Ernest B. Furgurson, *Not War But Murder: Cold Harbor 1864* (New York: Vintage Books, 2000), 138.

70. Ibid.

71. Captain W. S. Hubbell, "Chapter XV: The Battle Of Cold Harbor," in W. S. Hubbell et al., eds., *The Story of the Twenty-First Regiment, Connecticut Volunteer Infantry, During the Civil War, 1861-1865* (Middletown, Cooperating Teacher: Press of the Stewart Printing Co., 1900), 233, https://books.google.com/books.

72. Furgurson, *Not War But Murder*. The Battle of Cold Harbor dragged on for nearly two weeks; however, most of the fighting took place June 3. Furgurson's book is about that day alone.

73. Ibid., 150.

74. Furgurson, *Not War But Murder*, 147.

75. *Daily Constitutionalist*, June 7, 1864.

76. Ibid., 170.

77. "The Battle of Friday. Further Particulars of Gibbons' and Barlow's Divisions—List of Casualties," *New York Times*, June 8, 1864.

78. James F. Tucker in S. A. Cunningham, ed., *Supplement to July Veteran, 1904*, Index, Confederate Veteran, Vol. XI (Nashville, TN, 1903), 363-65, http://archive.org/stream/confederateveter11conf#page/n5/mode/2up. Tucker provides the details and associated quotes regarding the hours and moments before Seton Fleming's death.

79. Fleming, *Memoirs*, 101.

80. "The Confederate Capital: Richmond, as ever, the Heart of the Confederacy," *Weekly News and Courier* (Charleston, SC), March 24, 1897.

81. Congressional Medal of Honor Society, www.cmohs.org.

82. Fleming, *Memoirs*, 101-03.

83. Blakey, *Rose Cottage Chronicles*, 344.

84. Fleming, *Memoirs*, Appendix I. Frank's letters to his Aunt Matilda on August 21 and September 15, 1864, contain information that reveals his visit to Monticello.

85. Fleming, *Memoirs*, Appendix I, Frank Fleming to Mother, September 1, 1864.

86. The Battle of Natural Bridge preserved Tallahassee as the only Confederate capital east of the Mississippi River not captured by the Union. Florida Military and Collegiate Institute later became Florida State University.

87. Many years later Frederic Fleming told this story to his daughter, Margaret Seton Fleming, who preserved it. There is a copy in the *MWF Collection*.

88. William Fleming Compiled Service Record, *Compiled Service Records of Confederate Soldiers Who Served in Organizations from the State of Florida*, NARA, RG 360, M251, https://www.fold3.com/.; Civil War Pension Claim no. 4487, William Henry Fleming, October 10, 1907. Copy in the *MWF Collection*.

89. Louis J. Fleming Complied Service Record, *Compiled Service Records of Confederate General and Staff Officers, and Nonregimental Enlisted Men*, NARA, RG 109, M331, https://www.fold3.com. Louis I. Fleming's middle initial was frequently mistaken for a J.

Post-War Hibernia

Fleming family tradition tells us that Fred Fleming was the first to return to Hibernia after the war, where he found their grand home occupied by Union deserters. In fact the house and property had been converted to a horse hospital and were occupied by Union officers and soldiers, along with some of their wives and families, under command of Captain Russell. Margaret Fleming returned to Jacksonville and petitioned General Israel Vogdes, Commander of Forces in East Florida, for the return of her property. This initiated a rapid chain of written communiqués, beginning with A. W. Cole at Union headquarters in Jacksonville. Ultimately, Margaret was at the mercy of General William Birney, who had ordered the raid on Fleming Island that resulted in her eviction. Jacksonville secessionists loathed the Yankees in general and Birney in particular. A local attorney wrote that the Yankees "surpass the fiends of Hell in wickedness & cowardice. And that Birney (Wm is his given name) was one of their primest, base cowardly fiends."[1] It must have been difficult, to say the least, for Margaret to appeal to this man for what was rightfully hers.

Cole informed General Birney that Captain Russell, Quartermaster-in-Charge, had possession of Hibernia and was ready to return it to Mrs. Fleming. Birney referred that information to E. C. Woodruff, Captain and Provost, who reiterated that Margaret was ejected from her home for providing information to the enemy. Even so, Woodruff recommended the return of her property on the condition that the Union forces retain their option to exercise authority at Hibernia as necessary. With these memos in hand, Birney issued the order that Mrs. Fleming could retake possession of her home, but that Quartermaster Russell could keep his horses on Fleming Island until further notice.[2] Margaret also received permission to reclaim her furniture in Jacksonville. Several Union commanders had shipped north, though, and likely had taken some of her furniture with them. Margaret probably felt some satisfaction upon recouping her property, but in the words of one Southerner who felt that Margaret had been unfairly singled out for particularly vile treatment, "A more fit, appropriate redress would be the head of Birney thrown to the dogs at her feet."[3]

Margaret returned to her home in November of 1865. She must have been heartbroken by what she found less than a year and a half after being evicted. The Yankees had burned the fences and most of the pier. Doors, windows, and floors were defaced and broken. Whatever furniture the Yankees had not taken was all destroyed. Most tragically for historians, every scrap of paper had been stolen or destroyed, including a large collection of family papers. Yankees had killed her horses on the day she was evicted, and now all other livestock, stores, and crops were lost or destroyed. George Causey's garden had gone completely to weeds. Margaret later estimated the damage at $2,000 or $3,000 for the buildings, pier, and fences; $1,500 for the loss of livestock, stores, and crops; and $1,600 for furniture; as well as an additional $2,000 the Union army should pay her for the use of her property during the occupation. Surrounded by the ruins of their once-beautiful home and business, the Fleming family once again had to rebuild. George Fleming's heirs rallied after his death and created a working plantation that sustained the family. Lewis and George Jr. led the reconstruction of the family plantation after the Second Seminole War. Lewis and Margaret had built their grand home immediately after the devastating fire of 1858. For the fourth time, the family set about the task of rebuilding Hibernia. The Big House was bruised and battered, but it was intact. The first order of business was to make the "Old Place," which had become the family name for their Hibernia home, fit for boarders as quickly as possible, because without paying guests, the family had no source of income. In order to receive guests, the wharf also had to be in working condition. These projects were expensive at a time when Margaret apparently had little money. Jacksonville historian Dena Snodgrass devoted a great deal of research trying to identify Margaret's financial backers, but the source of funding remains a mystery today. One way or another she managed to complete essential repairs in short order. In January of 1866 Margaret placed this small ad in a Jacksonville newspaper:

NOTICE: Mrs. Flemming [sic] Gives Notice, that she has re-opened her House at Hibernia 25 miles above Jacksonville and can accommodate a limited number of boarders. The wharf has been repaired so that steamboats can land without difficulty.[4]

There is no record of any paying guest at Hibernia that winter. Even if we assume some did come, Margaret's ability to accommodate only a limited number of boarders implies that her income was modest at best. Yet somehow Hibernia was fully repaired and ready to resume normal operations the next year, much to the delight of northern visitors. One guest passed two weeks during the 1866–67 boarding season at "the celebrated boarding house kept by the widow of the late Col. Fleming" and it was "perhaps the most desirable place of residence on the St. Johns River."[5] There followed a period of ten years during which Hibernia garnered a reputation as one of the finest guesthouses in Florida. Margaret Fleming was the hostess and her son, Frederic, faithfully served as host. Her three daughters and her youngest son all assisted with the operation.

Frank and Louis Isadore Fleming were no longer directly involved with the family business after the Civil War. Before the war, L. I. had already chosen a path that took him away from Hibernia. Now he joined with Colonel James Jaquelin "J.J." Daniel to create the law firm of Fleming & Daniel in Jacksonville.[6] L. I. and Colonel Daniel were brothers-in-law: L. I. married his own second cousin, Mary Evelyn L'Engle, in 1854; Colonel Daniel married her sister, Emily Isabel L'Engle, in 1860.[7] After some soul-searching, Frank Fleming also chose the legal profession. Frank initially declared he would never live in Jacksonville again because "the place is filled up with Yankees—it will be a worse Yankee hole than ever." Like many other ex-Confederates, he contemplated a move to Brazil,[8] but ultimately rejected that idea. Instead, he followed in Seton Fleming's footsteps and took up the study of law with his older brother. Frank earned a position as a member of Fleming & Daniel and was admitted to the Florida Bar on May 12, 1868. Three years later he married Floride Lydia Pearson, the orphaned daughter of former Florida Supreme Court Justice Bird Pearson and Elizabeth Croft Pearson. Louis Isadore and Frank Fleming lived in Jacksonville for the rest of their lives, but remained deeply connected to their extended family.

In 1868 a visitor remarked that Margaret had two milk cows at Hibernia that produced enough for coffee, tea, and "drinking straight up," which was a rarity at guesthouses along the river.[9] In 1869 travel writer Daniel Brinton described Hibernia as a hotel with room to accommodate thirty-five guests. The fare was $2.50 per day or $15.00 per week, all-inclusive, and potential guests needed to write and request a reservation. Jeffries Wyman, a former member of William James Stillman's Adirondack Club and professor of anatomy at Harvard University, visited Hibernia from 1870 through 1874. Mr. Wyman used Hibernia as a jumping-off point for his anthropological and naturalistic studies of Florida. Early in 1871 Mr. Wyman hired Pompey, an African American and most likely a resident of Hibernia, to be his guide and hired hand as he traveled through the wilds of the St. Johns River valley.[10] At night Pompey entertained their small group with his fiddle playing. Wyman described a comical old rooster who traveled aboard a steamer that docked at the Hibernia wharf and other locations along the St. Johns River. At each stop the rooster disembarked along with the passengers, strutted down the wharf to go ashore, and went about his business of scratching and pecking. When the pilot blew the whistle to signal his departure, the rooster hustled back along the wharf and jumped aboard on his own accord.[11]

At the opening of the 1875–76 boarding season, Margaret announced the addition of a new guest cottage adjacent to the Fleming House. "The Cottage," as it was initially called, had eight bedrooms that significantly expanded guest capacity, and had extra space in the attic that also could be used to accommodate guests. Orange trees, crepe myrtles, fig trees, oleanders, and a productive grapery surrounded the two Hibernia residences. Guests from Boston, New York, Philadelphia, and western states enjoyed food and activities that were "all that can be desired." In addition to fresh oranges and grapes, the "venerable gardener," George Causey, expertly tended rotating crops of peas, tomatoes, radishes, lettuce, celery, cauliflower, cabbages, potatoes, beets, carrots, and strawberries. For meat, large flocks of turkeys roamed the property. Sheep and hogs grazed freely beyond the fences. Beef, venison, and fish arrived regularly on steamers, enhanced by weekly deliveries of oysters from the nearby coastal waters. Rowboats from Black Creek pulled up to the long wharf with supplies of eggs and poultry.

Guests also contributed to the table. They enjoyed catching or shooting the rabbits that scuttled about Hibernia. Fishing in the wide St. Johns was great sport; anglers caught any of the species that cruised through with the seasons, including bass, redfish, black drum, croaker, bream, and catfish. By far the greatest attraction for the hunter was quail. The longleaf pine forests, long since gone from Fleming Island, provided prime habitat for bobwhite quail. One guest brought his own pointers south for the winter and averaged sixteen birds per outing during the 1875–76 season. The favorite pastime for most visitors, though, was the "pleasant [walk] along the river under the boughs of live oaks festooned with creeping plants and the yellow

This scene of the "myrtle walk" leading to the Big House is among the earliest known photographs of Hibernia. It is from Charles Seaver's Southern Series and was taken sometime between 1870 and 1880. There is speculation that some of the women may be Fleming family members. However, that is only a guess. *MWF Collection*

Jessamine [sic]." Many guests rowed or sailed in the river. The mail boat pulled up to the wharf daily, usually before noon, and was "the important epoch of the day." Letters sent from Boston usually arrived in four days' time. Those from New York took just three days. Guests rounded out their days by gathering on the verandas for conversation, reading in the parlor, strolling along the wharf to watch the sunsets, or singing around the piano in the evenings.[12]

During this same season Margaret began an effort to obtain compensation for damage done to Hibernia by Union troops during the Civil War. The United States established the Southern Claims Commission just for this purpose. Margaret enlisted the aid of her

Another photo by Charles Seaver shows the gate at a popular creek crossing south of the Big House. There is speculation among Fleming family members that Margaret and Lewis Fleming's daughters are in this scene. *Photo courtesy of Clay County Archives.*

friend, U.S. Congressman Henry Blair of New Hampshire, who apparently was a winter guest at Hibernia. Interestingly, Blair operated a boarding house of his own for summer guests near Portsmouth, New Hampshire. In correspondence that indicates a warm, personal relationship, Blair invited Mrs. Fleming to join him in New Hampshire for the summer, and promised to "seek the aid of some gentlemen" to settle her claim against the United States.[13] Margaret collected sworn depositions to support her case. Blair enlisted the assistance of attorney E. H. Derby and presented those depositions to C. L. Robinson, Special Commissioner for the Southern Claims Commission, with hopes of taking her case to the United States Congress.

Blair had some influence, but not enough. In truth, Margaret had little or no chance of success with the Southern Claims Commission, and some might say she had incredible chutzpah for even trying. There were two criteria for filing a claim: (1) the petitioner must have been loyal to the United States, and (2) supplies or property must have been officially taken by, or furnished to, the United States. Margaret failed on both counts. Official correspondence from Union officers identified her as complicit with the enemy. Even if she could somehow have disproved that accusation, the United States at that time had a history of denying claims for damages suffered during war. The courts likely would have determined that she abandoned her property, and that the Union returned it immediately after she claimed it. The only way she could have prevailed would have been through political influence, and she could not muster enough of that.

Almost immediately after her failed bid for reparations, Margaret literally mortgaged the farm, as the old saying goes. On May 6, 1876, she borrowed $1,500 from Jacksonville physician Emil F. Sabal, and promised to repay the full amount plus 12 percent annual interest within one year. As collateral Dr. Sabal received title to Hibernia, now consisting of approximately one hundred acres, the Big House, the Cottage, all the furniture, and all associated outbuildings—in short, everything she owned. What could possibly have forced Margaret Fleming to do such a thing? There can be but one explanation: If she hadn't, she would have lost the place anyway. She must have owed a debt and the only choice was to pay cash immediately or forfeit Hibernia. It's possible that she was indebted to Dr. Sabal, but that seems unlikely since he executed the mortgage without mentioning anything about prior debts. Perhaps the debt explains how Margaret could afford to rebuild Hibernia after the Civil War, but that is just a guess. We do know that Dr. Sabal and members of the Fleming family were well acquainted, and everyone involved with the mortgage probably held great hopes that the 1876–77 boarding season would be sufficiently profitable. It must have been, because Margaret paid her mortgage in full just before the deadline.

During these years Margaret Fleming nurtured her cherished dream of establishing an Episcopal church at Hibernia. As early as 1858, and probably even before that, visiting clergy held services in the parlor of the Big House. One of the first was the Right Reverend Alonzo Potter, Bishop of Pennsylvania.[14] Lewis Fleming was born a Catholic but, because of Margaret's religious preference, Bishop Potter confirmed him into the Episcopal Church. Bishop Potter also baptized little Isabella Fleming in 1858. Several other missionary preachers held services in the Fleming's parlor throughout the next seventeen years.

The Reverend C. W. Knauff of Connecticut held services up and down the St. Johns River in 1875, and he was involved with the construction of the long-awaited church building.[15] Christian Black, to whom Margaret had recently sold five acres of riverfront land just south of the Big House, completed the framing and the roof in the fall of 1875.[16] The family's financial challenges of 1876–77 limited progress, but boarders and visiting clergy contributed to the cause so construction proceeded at a slow place. In the fall of 1877, when Margaret was sixty-four years old, her dream of a church at Hibernia was nearly fulfilled when she made the worst decision of her life.

That fall yellow fever broke out in Jacksonville. At the time people generally had no knowledge of the cause of the disease, must less its treatment. Almost everyone in the Frank and Lydia Fleming residence at the corner of Newman and Ashley Streets contracted the disease. Both parents, their two youngest children, Margaret and Peyre, and three servants took ill in early November. Three of these cases included the dreaded "black vomit," which was caused by internal bleeding in the mouth, eyes, and gastrointestinal tract. Margaret Fleming sent her oldest daughter, Maggie, to help nurse the family back to health. We know little about Margaret "Maggie" Fleming. Family tradition tells us her hair was a burnished gold. Her only surviving letter indicates that she liked Hibernia best when the boarders had all gone home, and that she loved to walk in the woods and pick flowers.[17] On Sunday, November 25, Maggie took sick herself. Five-year-old Margaret and six-week-old Peyre remained critically ill, so caretakers immediately transferred Maggie to the home of her brother, L. I., on the south side of Monroe Street between Market and Liberty Streets. The next day Frank and Lydia watched their daughter, Margaret, die. Four days later, tiny Peyre breathed his last. Three blocks away, family members and friends "carefully and tenderly" nursed Maggie Fleming, but nothing could quell the repeated, violent bursts of black vomit. Maggie died the same day as Peyre, November 30, 1877, when she was just twenty-five years old. Frank and Lydia Fleming buried their babies side by side at the Old City Cemetery in Jacksonville. The family chartered a steamer to bring Maggie's body back upriver to Hibernia, where she was laid to rest in the family cemetery.[18]

The Fleming family understandably has preserved few oral traditions regarding this heartbreaking episode. Frank and Lydia Fleming recovered from the disease but obviously suffered terribly. Margaret Fleming's granddaughter tells us all we need to know about the impact on the family matriarch:

Margaret never recovered from this blow. She felt responsible and she blamed herself for her daughter's death. Her interest and energy evaporated overnight. She lost the will to live.[19]

Winter boarders during the 1877–78 season witnessed Margaret Fleming in the depths of despair. She scarcely left the house again, and spent a great deal of time in her private room on the ground floor of the Big House. There, warmed by her fireplace, she had a mahogany bedstead, a writing desk with a small oil lamp, a bureau, a few chairs, and a well-worn ottoman. The only ornament seems to have been a "fancy clock." Her health failed rapidly. During her life Margaret had the moxie to rebuild Hibernia once after a devastating fire, and again in the aftermath of the Civil War, despite the deaths of her husband and oldest son. She had the strength and the business savvy to make Hibernia a successful business enterprise and a beloved winter escape, and she saved the family home more than once in the face of financial ruin. For nearly sixteen years as a widow she had done all she could to "stick to the Old Place," as Seton had asked after Lewis Fleming's death, but she could not summon the will to overcome Maggie's horrible death. Margaret Seton Fleming died in her home on April 4, 1878. She was sixty-five years old. Ironically, Margaret's funeral was the first official service held in the Episcopal Chapel at Hibernia. The family laid her to rest next to her husband.

In her will, Margaret stipulated that Frederic should receive the Big House and the Cottage, including all furniture, outbuildings, and personal property. The only exception to this was a short list of personal items she specifically set aside for individual members of the family. Margaret expressed "great trust and confidence" in Frederic, and her dying wish was that he would "at all times offer and provide for his unmarried sisters and his brother William a home under the shelter of the old roof."[20] The family worked in concert to honor her wishes. The first order of business was to eliminate title issues encumbering Hibernia land. Sophia and George Fleming's children, Lewis, George, and Mary, had all agreed on a division of their mother's approximately 360 acres, but that agreement was never legally recorded. With the help of legal expertise from L. I. and Frank Fleming, the issue was largely cleared up in a matter of days.[21] Soon after Margaret's death, every relative who owned any part of Sophia Fleming's former lands signed quitclaim deeds to establish clear title to their respective portions. A year later the children of Augustina Fleming Stephens and George Claudius Fleming signed deeds relinquishing any claim they might have to Hibernia land. Then Margaret's children cooperatively divided her 111 acres. That division set the boundaries for some of the properties on Old Church Road in Hibernia to this day.

For the first seven years following Margaret's death, Fred and his sister, Matilda, were host and hostess at Hibernia. Then in the spring of 1885, Fred was thunderstruck by a "vivacious and energetic" young woman with "red-gold curly hair" and a voluptuous figure. Frederic first saw Margaret Prior "Margot" Baldwin laughing on the upper deck of an incoming steamer at the end of the Hibernia wharf.[22] Miss Baldwin was a native of New Jersey whose family had moved to Federal Point about fifteen miles upriver from Hibernia. Frederic was almost forty years old. Margot was twenty-two or twenty-three but claimed to be a teenager. Family tradition tells us he proposed after three days. Six months later, on November 19, 1885, the morning "dawned bright and beautiful" as Fred, a few family members, and intimate friends steamed aboard the *Mary Draper* to the wharf at Federal Point. The brief wedding ceremony in St. Paul's Episcopal Church began at nine-thirty in the morning, followed by an elaborate breakfast at the Baldwin home. Guests showered the newlyweds with toasts of sparkling wine and beautiful presents, after which the enthusiastic party bid them farewell at the wharf. Mr. and Mrs. Fred Fleming boarded the *Mary Draper*, privately chartered for the occasion, and steamed to West Tocoi where they embarked by train for a honeymoon in New England.[23] Upon their return, Hibernia could have but one hostess, so Matilda Fleming moved out of the Big House and into a small cottage of her own.

Frederic Alexander Fleming became the longtime patriarch and the central figure in Hibernia on Fleming Island while his older brother, Frank, earned his place in Florida history.

Many years after Margaret Fleming's death, her son Frederic sits on the steps of St. Margaret's Episcopal Church. The family burial plots are behind the church. *LCA Collection*

Scott Ritchie

Endnotes

1. Orloff M. Dorman, *Memoranda of Events That Transpired at Jacksonville, Florida,* Library of Congress, Manuscript Division, MMC-1884.

2. Dena Snodgrass Collection, University of Florida Smathers Libraries. Copies of all this correspondence are in the collection.

3. Dorman, *Memoranda.*

4. *Florida Times-Union,* (Jacksonville), February 3, 1866.

5. *Newport Mercury* (Rhode Island), July 6, 1867, www.genealogy.com.

6. Captain J. J. Daniel served with the Second Florida Infantry during the Civil War. The law firm changed names over the years but operated continuously until 1997. Fleming descendants and in-laws worked at the firm nearly the entire time.

7. Mary and Emily L'Engle were granddaughters of Sophia Fatio Fleming's brother, Francis P. Fatio Jr.

8. Fleming, *Memoirs,* Appendix I, Frank Fleming to Aunt Tilly, May 16, 1865.

9. *Newport Mercury,* February 22, 1868.

10. There is no historic evidence to tell us if this is the same man who was overseer at Hibernia while Lewis and Margaret Fleming lived at Panama Mills.

11. George E. Gifford Jr., ed., *Dear Jeffie: Being the letters from Jeffries Wyman, first director of the Peabody Museum, to his son, Jeffries Wyman, Jr.* (Cambridge, MA: Peabody Museum Press, 1978).

12. *Boston Daily Advertiser,* February 16, 1876.

13. H. W. Blair to Margaret Fleming, March 16, 1876. Copy in *MWF Collection.*

14. M. A. DeWolfe Howe, *Memoirs Of The Life and Services Of The Rt. Rev. Alonzo Potter, D.D., LL.D., Bishop of the Protestant Episcopal Church In The Diocese of Pennsylvania* (Philadelphia: J. B. Lippincott, 1871), https://books.google.com/books. Alonso Potter's wife was a sister of Dr. Nathan Benedict, who ran the Magnolia Hotel near present-day Green Cove Springs. Mrs. Potter's health was frail and she stayed at Magnolia between 1855 and 1856.

15. The Reverend Knauff and his wife, Martha Ryland Knauff, are buried in the cemetery at St. Margaret's Episcopal Church in Hibernia.

16. Notes written by the Reverend Washington B. Erben. These notes were based primarily on information received from the Fleming family. A copy is in the *MWF Collection,* along with Christian Black's bill of sale for the timbers to build the church at Hibernia; Clay County Deed Book F, Margaret Fleming and others to Christian Black, May 26, 1875, 192-96.

17. Maggie Fleming to her niece, Minnie, March 14, 1874. Copy in *MWF Collection.*

18. R. P. Daniel, "Report on Yellow Fever in Jacksonville, Fla. in 1877," in *Proceedings of the Florida Medical Association, Session of 1878* (Jacksonville, FL), 46. A typewritten transcript of this report, done by Dena Snodgrass, is in the *MWF Collection*.

19. Biddle, *Hibernia: The Unreturning Tide*, 76.

20. Last Will and Testament of Margaret Seton Fleming, File Case No. 71-393, Clay County Archives, Clay County, Florida. An original copy of the will is in the *MWF Collection*.

21. Clay County, Florida, Deed Book H, 423-30; Deed Book I, 84-85 and 91-93.

22. Biddle, *Hibernia: The Unreturning Tide*, 83.

23. *Palatka Daily News*, undated newspaper clipping in the scrapbook of Dorothy Fleming, the youngest daughter of Frederic and Margot Fleming. The scrapbook contains a second, unattributed, newspaper article that provides additional details of the wedding day. *Lurana Crowley Austin Collection* (hereafter *LCA* Collection).

Francis Philip "Frank" Fleming:
Politics and Yellow Fever

Frank made his "political debut" (these are his own words) at Green Cove Springs in 1868 when he tried to rally support for Democratic presidential candidate Horatio Seymour against Republican Ulysses S. Grant.[1] He served several years as a member of the State Democratic Executive Committee and was an outspoken critic of northern "carpetbaggers" and southern "scalawags" who supported Reconstruction Republicans. Frank Fleming spoke frequently and passionately on behalf of Florida gubernatorial candidate George Drew in 1876. Drew ultimately won the election to replace Republican incumbent Marcellus Stearns and reclaim the governor's office for Democrats. Twelve years later, Frank Fleming embarked on a remarkable journey as a candidate for governor of Florida.

In early April of 1888 Frank Fleming was a member of the Duval Conservative Democratic Party Executive Committee. This is when his name first appears in public records as a possible candidate in the upcoming gubernatorial election, but he isn't singled out. One Jacksonville citizen wrote that Frank, L. I. Fleming, and Colonel J. J. Daniel would all be excellent candidates because "better or purer men never lived."[2] Perhaps the three law partners put their heads together with committee members and decided Frank was the best choice among them. A month later the *St. Johns Weekly* announced that Frank was generally favored throughout that county as their candidate. A few days after that the Clay County Democratic Convention met at Middleburg and elected its delegates for the upcoming state convention in St. Augustine. The members elected Frank's younger brother, Fred, as delegate for Precinct 3, but since the county could send just five delegates to the state convention, he became an alternate. Clay County Democrats voted overwhelmingly in favor of Frank Fleming's candidacy and became the first in the state to officially endorse their "favorite son."[3]

By mid-May, as the fever to go to the Democratic Convention in St. Augustine was building throughout the state, only two counties had formally declared a favorite son and few expressed any preference. Clay County was for Fleming and Marion County was for General Robert Bullock.[4] Putnam County was evenly split between Fleming and their own local favorite, Captain Robert W. Davis.[5] Less than a week before the state convention, Duval Democrats had not officially declared a candidate, but Fleming clearly was their choice. The *Times-Union* came out in favor of Fleming, writing, "It is the sterling worth and unostentatious ability of the man that give him such a hold on the confidence and admiration of the people of Florida."[6]

On May 28 delegates poured into St. Augustine from throughout the state. About 150 had arrived the day before on the evening train, and they kept coming throughout the day. This was the off-season when most hotels and boarding houses cut back or curtailed operations, but now all were filled with politicos in anticipation of the convention at the Opera House the following day.[7] Fleming was an early favorite in north Florida, but he had many challengers. One reporter wrote, "... candidates are as thick as leaves in autumn ... the race for Governor is complicated and beyond comprehension." One gets a sense of the backroom dealings and machinations from the editors of the *Times-Union,* who reported that less than ten percent of the delegates had any instructions regarding whom they should support and "not one delegate in a dozen knows what his constituents want." Those assembled included some who would "knife Fleming," but still admit his "unsullied character and unquestioned ability," because of his friendship with current governor Perry. Others "would destroy" Bullock because of his friendship with former governor Drew.[8]

Fleming's group lodged at Hasseltine House (sometimes called Hasseltine Cottage) immediately adjacent to the Opera House on St. George Street. At ten o'clock on the morning of September 29, Fleming and his caucus met at Cleveland House farther down the street. At that same hour the State Democratic Executive Committee tended to business in the Opera House. At eleven o'clock visitors filed into the Opera House, and a half-hour later delegates from "the highways, byways, caucuses, and meetings" filled the spacious hall. Fleming's ardent supporters walked with him from Cleveland House along St. George Street to the convention. They strolled past a fruit market, a laundry, a confectionery, private homes, and a few vacant lots. Crossing Hypolita Street, they passed a cigar store, a vendor of "fancy goods," and a curio shop. They saw the stately Magnolia Hotel on their right, where many delegates and party officials had secured rooms, and reached the entrance to the Opera House, directly across the street from the Colored Methodist Episcopal Church.[9] The ground floor of the Opera House contained retail businesses—clothing, drugs, news & cigars, and a restaurant.[10] Ascending the stairs to the convention, Fleming entered a positively electric setting humming with voices, animated gestures, scuffling chairs and feet, and waving fans. There were at least 365 delegates and party officials. Spectators filled every available seat, nook, or cranny allotted to them. Thirty-five reporters from newspapers throughout the state and around the south filled the orchestra pit. The weather was mild for that time of year in St. Augustine, still in the 70s, but the packed house and customary humidity created a heated environment. Precisely at noon Chairman Samuel Pasco called the convention to order. Party business filled the opening day for the most part, but occasionally delegates spoke out in support of their favorite son. Judge James C. Vertrees of Palatka championed Fleming.[11] When he wanted to be heard the judge shouted, "Hello, Central!" to command attention. The meeting adjourned at ten o'clock, but political operatives and delegates carried on behind the scenes. They filled the wee hours of the night with mysterious conversations, and "rumors of deals were rife."[12]

The convention reconvened at 9:10 the following morning. R. H. Hall succinctly nominated General Bullock for governor, saying, "It requires no beautiful rhetoric" to present such an esteemed candidate. Next, R. F. Taylor of Alachua County nominated Frank Fleming. In his five-minute speech Taylor praised Fleming as "a Floridian to the manor born" who had dedicated himself to the success of the Democratic Party in every election since 1868. Duncan U. Fletcher of Duval County rose to second the nomination.[13] His "clear, silvery voice" offered a "musical and persuasive" endorsement of Fleming, saying, "He lives in Florida. His feelings, sentiments, and connections were born of her soil." In all, six candidates received nominations and the balloting began. Through the first four ballots Fleming, Bullock, Judge J. G. Speer, and Captain Robert W. Davis emerged as the leaders.[14] The convention adjourned at midnight without a winner and the backroom dealings commenced. Some argued that the South Florida delegations must choose Davis, Bullock, or Speer, then throw all their support behind that man. Others believed the apparent stalemate was engineered to create a deadlock and bring former governor William D. Bloxham forward to rescue the party. Fleming's supporters lobbied energetically, and at one o'clock they were more enthusiastic than ever.[15]

The deadlock consumed much of the next day. Robert Davis withdrew after the twenty-third ballot. Party officials called a recess after the twenty-fifth ballot and instructed delegates to consult and agree on a candidate. Judge Speer withdrew and the race narrowed to just Fleming and Bullock. Balloting continued. The lead shifted from Fleming, to Bullock, to Fleming, and back again to Bullock without a clear winner. On the thirty-second ballot the frenzied delegates tossed votes to men who hadn't been nominated; then J. B. Beggs of Orange County rose to renominate Robert Davis.[16] There followed a display of grandstanding with delegates voicing their unfailing and never-ending support of Davis, Fleming, or Bullock. During the thirty-third ballot, George W. Barden of Clay County rose to declare his support for Davis despite the fact that his delegation had pledged all of its five votes to Fleming.[17] The Clay delegates engaged in a heated squabble before Mr. Wolf from Escambia County moved that all five Clay votes should go to Fleming. The motion did not carry, and on the thirty-fourth ballot Mr. Barden again rose to vote for Davis. Once again a delegate from Escambia, this time Mr. O'Connor, protested in support of Fleming, only to be hastily rebuked by Mr. Clark of Polk County. After one more ballot failed to identify a winner, the convention adjourned until eight o'clock. The delegates immediately resumed voting upon their return. B. F. Kirk of Hernando County took the platform and nominated yet another candidate, current lieutenant governor Milton H. Mabry. A crowd of supporters jumped to their feet shouting, "Davis!" and mayhem ensued until Chairman Pasco restored order. Kirk's own delegation insisted Davis was their choice, so he withdrew the nomination. On the next ballot Fleming once again took a slight lead, and then the tide turned. Former State Senator Stephen R. Mallory Jr. rose to announce nineteen votes in favor of Fleming. Immediately, Fleming's supporters jumped to their feet "as one man cheering, shouting, and hurling hats, fans, and handkerchiefs into the air ... It was the first sign of victory." Fleming's lead increased dramatically on the next two ballots. Finally, on the fortieth ballot, Fleming received 246½ votes, surpassing by a half vote the two-thirds majority required to secure the nomination. Colonel A. W. Cockrell, an attorney with the Duval delegation, stood on a chair and "raised an old-time Rebel yell" while others joined him. Before the convention formally nominated Fleming for governor, General Bullock called for party unity and unanimous support of the Democratic Party's chosen candidate.[18]

Frank Fleming and General Bullock returned to Jacksonville together aboard the Jacksonville, St. Augustine & Halifax River Railroad. The Metropolitan Light Infantry Band struck up a spiritual rendition of

"Dixie" as the train rolled into the depot at six o'clock on the evening of June 1. Fleming and Bullock disembarked together and "prolonged and loud cheering rent the air." The depot was south of the St. Johns River so the party took a ferry over to the city. The band and infantry company led a procession up Bay Street and into the park. Frank took the podium and thanked the Duval delegates. He commended the faithful performance of their duties at the convention and "pledged himself to use his best efforts and talents to secure an overwhelming success" for Democrats in the campaign ahead. Little did he know how terribly difficult that campaign would be.[19]

During the ensuing weeks, Frank contracted an illness. In late June he vacationed at Pablo Beach with his family to recuperate and prepare for the campaign.[20] In early July he resigned his commission as commander of the Metropolitan Light Infantry, and soon thereafter took his family to pass the remainder of the summer in the cool of the mountains with his wife's relatives in Greenville, South Carolina.

By mid-July Jacksonville residents were on edge because of rumors of yellow fever in Tampa. The *Times-Union* assured its readers that it was a mild case and "not the slightest alarm exists."[21] During the next two weeks health officials diligently enforced sanitation measures to keep the city "germ free." Despite their best efforts, doctors confirmed that Richard D. McCormick, visiting from Tampa, had yellow fever. Even in the face of a confirmed case, health officials, who were still ignorant of how yellow fever was transmitted, assured the public that "there is no danger whatsoever of an epidemic, no matter if any number of cases of infectious disease should be brought here."[22]

Frank returned to Jacksonville on August 7 refreshed, healthy, and ready to begin the campaign, but told his wife and children to stay in Greenville. Given his personal heart-breaking experiences with "Yellow Jack" eleven years earlier, Frank would not risk exposing his family to the fever. The decision to leave his family in South Carolina while he canvassed the state may well have saved their lives and his campaign. There they were safe from the worst yellow fever epidemic in the history of Jacksonville.

On August 9 Dr. Kenworthy, City Health Officer, declared a ban on watermelon sales and took measures to ensure that all unripe or imperfect fruit would be destroyed. On August 10 the headline of the *Times-Union* read, "The Quarantine Made Against Jacksonville Today." Four cases of yellow fever were confirmed on one city block. U.S. Surgeon General John B. Hamilton reported that no one should

Scott Ritchie

go to an infected area of Jacksonville if they could keep away from it. City residents did not wait for the official statement saying that yellow fever was "assuming an epidemic form." Dozens of families fled the city before the declaration of quarantine, and that was just the beginning of a mass exodus. Frank Fleming managed to escape on the train bound for Monticello, where he was quarantined for twenty days.[23]

While Frank waited out his quarantine in Monticello, L. I. and Mary L'Engle Fleming remained in Jacksonville. Fear mounted in the city but Mary clung to the hope that "the danger that threatened [was] averted." She was terribly lonely, though, because so many friends and family had abandoned the city before the quarantines. Fred and Margot Fleming, apparently undaunted by the presence of yellow fever, were in Jacksonville on August 11 and dined at L. I.'s home. They invited his entire household, including servants, to come stay in the Cottage at Hibernia until the epidemic passed. Mary Fleming seemed disappointed when she wrote, "Louis thinks it best for us to remain quietly at home."[24] In fact, L. I. did more than remain home quietly during the epidemic. He joined his brothers-in-law, J. J. Daniel and Henry L'Engle, in the formation of the Jacksonville Auxiliary Sanitation Association (JASA), whose more than two hundred members managed the daily, often grisly, tasks brought on by the full-blown and deadly epidemic.

Health officials released Frank Fleming from his quarantine and he hit the campaign trail on August 30, first in Blountsville and then on to Quincy, Wakulla, Crawfordville, and Tallahassee. During these first stops Frank established three themes that he would repeat throughout the statewide canvass: (1) Republican carpetbaggers were bent on taking advantage of honest Floridians, (2) Republican policies damaged the State, and (3) African Americans needed to cross party lines and join Democrats for the good of Florida.

At Blountsville (known today as Blountstown) he spoke "straight from the shoulder" as he accused Republicans of making the rich richer by taxing every consumer in America through tariffs on all manner of goods "from his hat to his boots." Frank used this story at the Quincy courthouse to describe carpetbagger "bummers" as deceitful snakes:

On a frigid day an honest farmer found a frozen viper, took it home, and warmed it back to life. The viper stung his wife, children, and mother-in-law and then started after the farmer's "yaller dog." The farmer could stand it no longer so he grabbed a club and quickly killed the snake saying, "You vile

166

wretch! After robbing me of everything else, you even seek the life of my favorite dog, do you? I'll let you know I can't stand everything.[25]

He next attacked the Republican Party Platform as a confused, indistinguishable collection of odds and ends that reminded him of a young man who fell in love with a cat:

> In answer to his prayers the cat was transformed into a beautiful girl. In time, they were married and went on their honeymoon. At a hotel they sat for dinner and a mouse ran across the floor. The bride, true to her nature, gave chase, caught the mouse, and ate it raw.

> "Hold!" cried the mortified and indignant bridegroom. "For heaven's sake, woman, what do you mean?"

> "Mean?" replied the bride. "I know this: When dining on a mouse I know what I am eating, but when it comes to boarding house hash, blast my eyes if I don't have to guess at what the stuff is made of, and trust to luck."[26]

Fleming called the Republican Platform a political hash, and then tried to connect the cat story to that of the "yaller dog." This was an age of unscripted, extemporaneous speech-making, and the deeper he went, the more he realized it just wasn't working. Fleming admitted as much to the crowd of nearly three hundred and, looking embarrassed, he closed by saying, "We'll try, however, and save our yaller dog." Fleming then "sat down, mopping his brow amid uproarious applause." Later Fleming confided, "It's strange, isn't it? It's strange what freaks the mind will sometimes indulge, especially at the moment we most need to harness it down."[27]

The African American population in Florida was almost entirely Republican, and Fleming hoped to bring some of them over to the Democratic Party. His strategy seemed to be based partly on a desire to reduce racial tension and divide, but also on his belief that Negroes were going to have to live under Democratic rule so they might as well get used to it. In speeches at Quincy and Wakulla, Frank appealed directly to the large audience of Negroes among the crowd saying that when white men prosper, black men must also prosper. Fleming acknowledged racial divisions, then said, "I do not want to see the colored people on one side and the white people on the other ... I don't want [Negroes] to say 'I can't vote for Captain Fleming because he is a

Democrat.' I want them to come with us, if only to show that they have no bad feeling towards us, as we have none towards them." But he also insisted it was "entirely hopeless" to align against white Democrats, saying, "Come with us, if you will, by all means; but no matter whether you do or do not we are going to elect the [Democratic] ticket."[28]

At the start of the campaign Frank learned that his sister-in-law, Mary L'Engle Fleming, her son, Edward, and their servant, Easter, had contracted yellow fever. All three recovered, though Mary Fleming's case was severe enough that the family "felt great anxiety about her."[29] As a matter of course, L. I. Fleming's entire household was quarantined for seven days after they recovered. By August 31 L. I. wrote that all of them were quite well and "at liberty to go where we please."[30] Really, though, there was no place to go. Those who remained in the city could not leave and the death toll began to climb. By day, business in Jacksonville had come to a complete standstill. Everything was quarantined, including mail and groceries. In their ignorance of the disease, the JASA led hundreds of men to apply any conceivable method to disinfect the city. They burned huge fires of tar and pine to purify the air with billowing black smoke. They applied lime and disinfectants to structures and trees. They sprayed the streets with bichloride of mercury. The Wilson Battery repeatedly fired large cannons based on a theory that concussive explosions could destroy yellow fever "microbes" in the air. The only certain effect of the cannon fire was shattered glass. At night, people believed their best safety was to remain indoors. Historian T. Frederick Davis reported that after sundown "there settled over the city an uncanny stillness, broken only by the occasional rattle of death carts or the muffled voices of those whose duty called them out after dark."[31]

Matilda Fleming described the effects of the fever and the quarantine in Hibernia. The steward of the steamer *Manatee* came down with yellow fever so the entire ship was quarantined. In fact, for a time practically all steamers were shut down along the St. Johns River. Without the ships, mail delivery ceased. Fred Fleming sent someone to Green Cove Springs every day to look for mail. Grocery deliveries ceased as well, but in Hibernia the Flemings knew how to be self-sufficient. Between the gardens, the livestock, the forests, and the river they could fend for themselves, even when a few paying guests somehow managed to show up in early September. Margot Fleming's brother-in-law, Herbert Anderson, came down with yellow fever, but fortunately he recovered quickly. No one else in Hibernia showed any sign of the dreaded disease.[32]

Out on the campaign trail in September, Frank Fleming kept apace of news through correspondence with multiple family members.[33] After a large meeting in Live Oak he traveled to Jasper, but many other campaign stops were cancelled when cases of yellow fever broke out in other parts of the state. J. J. Daniel was deeply concerned about his law partner's health and urged family members that Frank should "not expose himself unnecessarily [because] he is not strong."[33] Frank generally spoke for more than an hour at each campaign stop and, despite the rigors of the canvass, his voice never failed him and his health remained robust. Tragically, this was not the case for his relatives in Jacksonville. The "fearful scourge" struck his brother, L. I., his nephew, L. I. Jr., and his brother-in-law, Henry L'Engle. A yellow flag fluttered at the gates of the Fleming and L'Engle homes to indicate quarantine, and guards wearing yellow badges paced outside around the clock to forbid anyone except doctors from entering or leaving their residences. All three men failed rapidly. On September 12 a death cart arrived and took away the body of twenty-one-year-old L. I. Fleming Jr. Even as they hauled him away, Mary L'Engle Fleming watched her husband suffer the same deadly symptoms. Two days later L. I. Sr. died at one o'clock in the afternoon. Almost inconceivably, Mary's brother, Henry, died a half-hour later. In a span of just two days she had lost her son, her husband, and her brother. The Right Rev. Edwin G. Weed, third bishop of the Episcopal Diocese of Florida, held funeral services in the Fleming home. There is no firsthand account to describe that scene. Immediately afterward, the bishop led the widow and a solemn group to the L'Engle residence. A family member recalled the poignant sight of fifty-one-year-old Mary L'Engle Fleming, "the bereaved wife, mother, and sister, flung silently across the foot of her brother's coffin with the robed Bishop at the head."[34] Mary's trials continued even after these tragic deaths. L. I. had died insolvent. In the ensuing months she was forced to sell land on Fleming Island and auction off personal possessions, including furniture, paintings, and books, to pay his creditors.

Frank Fleming knew that his relatives had yellow fever, so he was already on edge, and a few days later he learned about their deaths. As he descended the platform after a speech in Lake City, someone handed over a telegram informing him of the tragic losses.[35] Though not entirely unexpected, it was a shock, nonetheless. Now the circumstances of the campaign seemed to match Frank's downcast mood. Repeated rainstorms flooded the waterways and the roadways were a muddy mess. All other speakers for the Democratic Party had abandoned the campaign until the weather improved. Frank's only

Scott Ritchie

traveling companion was the reporter for the *Times-Union*, Colonel C. E. Merrill. He must have felt a powerful longing to be with his family, but Frank continued his campaign secure in the knowledge that his wife and children were safe in the mountains of South Carolina, and knowing that his speeches took him ever closer to Hibernia and his brothers and sisters. Before he got there, Frank kept a campaign appointment that proved just how determined he was no matter the weather, the quarantines, or the personal loss.

While in Fort White on September 19, Frank and Colonel Merrill discussed traveling by wagon to keep his appointment in Judson, thirty-five miles to the south.[36]

> "Is the road practicable?" asked Frank. The reply was, "The roads are full of water—the Sante Fe is out of its banks, and quarantine officials block the country everywhere." Frank replied, "That's nothing. I shall fill every appointment on the list, if no greater obstacles than those you mention interfere."

A group of Columbia County men harnessed wagons, four of them joined the trip, and they set off. Five miles out of town they faced the swollen Sante Fe River "roaring out of its banks" with quarantine officials blocking the road. Frank persuaded the quarantine officers to let them pass. The impressed ferryman agreed to risk the crossing provided they carried only one buggy or one mule at a time. It took considerable coaxing to load the animals. The men hauled each wagon aboard by hand. Floodwaters surged over the flat deck as the barefoot ferryman negotiated one crossing after another. Two hours later the men reharnessed the mules and set off along the waterlogged road to Judson. Given the river, the roads, and the quarantine, no one in Judson expected them to make the trip, so they had cancelled their plans for a grand meeting. Judge Ira Carter volunteered his large warehouse for an impromptu gathering where about seventy or eighty men and woman listened to Frank's speech. He opened by expressing disappointment that the locals "didn't know what sort of man the St. Augustine Convention had nominated," otherwise they would have known he would "get there in spite of fever, fire, and flood." On their return trip that night the Santa Fe River was two feet higher. They repeated the crossing once again, this time in the dark with the river ominously illuminated by huge lightwood fires on each side.[37]

Frank and Colonel Merrill continued through floodwaters and quarantine officers to campaign appointments at Providence and Lake Butler, and then on to Starke. In three days' time they covered 150 miles by wagon, crossed five or six rivers in ferries, and haggled their way past upwards of forty quarantine officials, and Frank delivered four speeches, each more than an hour long. His brother, Fred, met him in Starke to take him home to Hibernia. Fred expected five men in Frank's party so he had hired Emile Aubert and his large wagon to carry them all. They set off in comfort at three in the afternoon determined to reach Hibernia before midnight. After a brief supper in Middleburg, they crossed on the Doctor's Lake ferry by moonlight to Fleming Island and followed the sand road four more miles to Hibernia, back in the family fold. Together the Flemings mourned the loss of too many loved ones so suddenly. For Frank the death of L. I.—his brother, his mentor, his law partner—had to be painfully acute. Surely it did him good to share that sorrow with his siblings.

The family was planning to attend Frank's upcoming speech in Green Cove Springs on September 24, but a political enemy may have sabotaged that appointment. Someone circulated a petition asking the Clay County Health Board to forbid Frank Fleming from entering the city because he possibly had been exposed to yellow fever microbes during his travels. By now there had been well over 2,000 cases and nearly 250 deaths in Jacksonville due to Yellow Jack, and it was easy enough to stir up a scare. Some called it nothing more than political gamesmanship because other travelers were not denied access to Green Cove Springs—Frank was singled out. Some said it was the work of George M. Barden, who had attempted to undermine Clay County support for Fleming late in the balloting during the Democratic Convention in St. Augustine. Following the convention Mr. Barden lost his own bid for nomination as clerk of the circuit court, which makes this look like political tit for tat.[38]

Fred Fleming was now chairman of the Clay County Democratic Party Executive Committee. He sprang into action. Fred traveled upriver to Green Cove Springs on Sunday, September 23, and invited everyone in the city and throughout the county for a campaign meeting at Hibernia the following day. At the same time all the Fleming women, including Fred's wife, Margot, his sisters, Matilda and Isabel, his sister-in-law, Die Baldwin, and Caroline Seton managed all the preparations for a large impromptu gathering. As storms threatened in the morning, residents from the surrounding area began to assemble at the Fleming home. By noon the steamer *Manatee* arrived at the wharf carrying a large number of men and women, including many candidates for county office and one quarantine officer. C. E. Merrill wrote sarcastically that the "unterrifed democracy" of Clay County had arrived. As rain poured down, over one hundred men and women packed under cover of the L-shaped piazza on the Big House. Fred Fleming stood on a hastily constructed platform at the corner of the piazza and offered an opening welcome. He explained that "an old fashioned barbeque and Democratic love-fest" were planned in Green Cove Springs, but "circumstances beyond the control of the Executive Committee" prevented that. Frank took the platform, alternately facing one group then the other, while delivering a long speech frequently punctuated by applause. Afterwards everyone walked the short distance across the lawn to the porch of the Cottage where the Fleming women had supervised the preparation of a veritable feast, including barbequed pigs, roast turkeys, breads, pastries, desserts, and other treats. When the meal and the visiting were over, the river travelers boarded the *Manatee* for the thirty-minute ride back to Green Cove Springs. They invited C. E. Merrill and Frank Fleming to join them. A crowd met the party as they landed. No one objected to Frank's being there, which prompted one supporter to say, "It looks like the authorities were determined not to quarantine against Captain Fleming, but only against his speech."[39]

As the unrelenting yellow fever epidemic continued, more and more health officials cancelled campaign appointments. Frank learned that he was denied access to his next stops in Palatka and St. Augustine. He arranged transport on the Jacksonville, Tampa & Key West Railroad in hopes of a meeting in DeLand and other points south, then traveled back to Hibernia for one more visit with his family before going south. This may have been the most vulnerable moment of Frank's gubernatorial campaign. Foul weather continued. The remaining campaign appointments were uncertain at best. He was still the only Democratic candidate or speaker out on the trail. It would have been easy to withdraw from the campaign, temporarily at least, and spend more time in the comfort of his family. He seemed to be encouraging himself as much as he was his young son in a letter after leaving Hibernia: "We had a severe storm and rain yesterday and last night. Today it is still blowing but with more sunshine. The gloomy weather and trouble I have getting about the State to fill my appointments is enough to discourage most people but the greater the difficulties we have to contend with in life the greater effort we should make to surmount them. And the more we should draw upon whatever vision, force of energy, and pluck we may have to overcome them."[40]

Frank and Colonel Merrill were denied access to DeLand but continued onward to appointments in Seville, Rockledge, and

Titusville. During his travels south Frank Fleming received the news that J. J. Daniel had died on October 1. He was the two-hundred-sixty-fifth victim of yellow fever in Jacksonville. No correspondence survives to help us understand the candidate's emotional state upon receiving this news. During the past two weeks alone doctors had identified more than 1,600 new cases, and 112 more people had succumbed to the disease. The epidemic showed no signs of abating. Who else might he lose before it ended? Circuit Judge George H. Hanson said of Frank, "From the opening hour of the campaign he has been assailed by such trials as has never confronted a candidate in this State ... and his physical and mental sufferings, the sad bereavements which have darkened his home, have enlisted everywhere heartfelt sympathy for his gallantry and heroic efforts."[41] We can only imagine how he must have struggled to once again "draw upon whatever vision, force of energy, and pluck" he could muster. Fortunately, Frank and Colonel Merrill no longer had to go it alone. A full speaking docket joined them for an appointment at Kissimmee on October 3, and a changing roster of speakers accompanied them for the remainder of the campaign.

The morning after his speech in Ft. Myers, Fleming and his three companions, E. J. Triay, senatorial candidate G. N. Hendry, and Colonel Merrill, rode a taxi boat to Punta Rasa at the mouth of the Calooshatchee River. There they boarded the *Ada*, a small sloop about thirty feet long and perhaps thirteen feet wide. Captain Fulton McGuire and the ship's cook, Dode, loaded three days' supplies, two barrels of water, and a huge block of ice.[42] The captain got underway at four o'clock that afternoon intending to sail through the night and cover the 130 miles to Key West by the next afternoon. Mr. Triay and Mr. Hendry were repeatedly seasick in the monotonous swells on the nearly windless sea. Frank's party slept in a small cabin with just two bunks, so two men had to get what rest they could on the floor as the sloop bobbed on a light breeze. They awoke in the morning out of sight of land with very little wind and a sweltering, intense sun throughout the day. Frank got "pretty thoroughly sunburned ... my nose became about the color of a boiled crab."[43] By Sunday evening the wind freshened and they sailed through the night once again. Monday morning the four men were convinced the captain was incompetent because they were still on the open Gulf with no wind and no land in sight. Frank looked in his Episcopal prayer book but couldn't find a prayer for wind. Captain Maguire scuttled up and down the mast over and over looking for land. Eventually he spotted some small islands that he recognized and adjusted course for Key West. The wind came up and the four men cheered their captain. Frank led a brief Episcopal service of thanks, but also credited the lucky four-leaf clover in his pocket. Riding a stiff breeze they arrived at nine o'clock in the evening. They were so late that a search boat had cruised the waters to look for them along the route, but they were too far off course to spot.[44]

The canvass meeting in Key West on Tuesday, October 16, was an elaborate affair. Fleming estimated there were well over two thousand people in attendance when he spoke "in the open air at the intersection of two streets." (Perhaps it was not a coincidence that one of them was Fleming Street.) After his speech Frank joined a "grand procession headed by a brass band with torch lights," followed by a dazzling display of rockets and Roman candles.[45] Then he was off to a wine and waltz cotillion at the City Guard Armory that lasted until three o'clock in the morning. In the midst of such enthusiasm, Frank received news from his brother Fred that there were several cases of yellow fever in Green Cove Springs. He feared this would dash plans to meet his wife and children in Hibernia after the campaign. Frank advised Lydia to investigate train fare to both Black Creek Station west of Fleming Island, and to Monticello as an alternative.[46]

Frank didn't risk another errant voyage aboard the *Ada* to make his way out of Key West. Instead, he took the steamer *Hutchison* to one of its regular stops on the way to New Orleans, and then boarded a train for his final canvass meetings back up the peninsula. After stops in Dade City, Brooksville, and Mannfield, Frank and six companions packed into a four-seater buggy for the trip over to Floral City. They headed a procession of carriages, buggies, and horsemen that stretched for nearly a mile behind them. On the outskirts of town the principal of the school, Mrs. O. S. Young, stood in wait with her large choir of boys, girls, and ladies. Frank's buggy pulled up in front of the choir, and those following formed up to his left and right in a semi-circle around the singers. Mrs. Young led a heartwarming concert, including a song with this chorus:

> *Then hurrah for Cleveland,*
> *Hurrah for Fleming too!*
> *We'll rally round the stars and stripes,*
> *The red, the white and blue,*
> *We'll shout for Fleming day and night,*
> *And sound the loud alarm,*
> *Hurrah for Cleveland, Fleming too,*
> *And revenue reform!*

Frank complimented the choir and spoke of Florida as "the mother of his earliest and tenderest affections," and then pledged his support of public schools. He insisted on a personal introduction to each singer and kissed the hand of every girl who came forward to meet him.[47]

Frank continued up the state, including stops at Sumterville, Leesburg, and Tavares. Ocala hosted a grand Democratic Love-Fest nearly as large as the meeting in Key West. The campaign was now drawing to an end. Fred Fleming sent the welcome news that Green Cove Springs was free of yellow fever, so Frank advised Lydia to take the train to Florida as soon as she could after the election. He would meet her in Hibernia after the returns. There, Frank told his wife, he could "pass his time more profitably while waiting before we can return to Jacksonville."[48]

Frank had just two more campaign stops, but to reach them he had to travel approximately 450 miles. His determination had not faltered the entire campaign and he still would not cancel a single appointment if he thought he could make it. His group set off by train for Pensacola. They negotiated and pulled political connections to pass through a strict quarantine line at the Suwannee River. In Tallahassee stunned health officials couldn't believe they had made it past the Suwannee and forbid them from leaving their railcar for the comfort of a hotel that night. They made their way to the canvass meeting in Pensacola on November 2, then traveled east to Defuniak Springs for Frank's final speech the following day. Colonel Merrill was Frank's constant companion throughout the entire campaign. He estimated that they traveled a total of 2,774 miles, crisscrossing the state for 55 days: 1,819 miles by train, 464 miles by water, and 491 miles by wagon, buggy, hack, or horse.[49] Frank delivered forty-eight speeches. Throughout it all, various county, city, or town health officials enforced, or failed to enforce, an ever-changing hodgepodge of quarantine restrictions. Somehow Frank and Colonel Merrill managed to find their way through most of them. One health inspector said that Frank had "given the quarantine officials of Florida more trouble than all the balance of the State put together."[50]

Frank estimated that he would carry the election by a margin of six or seven thousand votes. After the final tally of the November 6 elections, he received sixty percent of the vote, and the margin of victory over Republican candidate V. J. Shipman was 13,770 votes. Francis Philip Fleming's landslide victory made him the second native-born Floridian to serve as governor for the State of Florida.

Scott Ritchie

Securely back in the family fold at Hibernia, Frank had no choice but to wait out the quarantine in Jacksonville. He began working on what would become his finest achievement as governor of Florida—the swift establishment of a State Board of Health. There can be no doubt that his experiences with yellow fever among his family, his friends, and out on the campaign trail influenced Frank to act quickly. The number of cases continued to climb until a hard freeze on November 26 brought an end to the proliferation of disease-transmitting mosquitoes. The last death on December 5 ended the Jacksonville epidemic of 4,704 cases and 427 deaths from yellow fever. Health officials lifted the quarantine on December 15 and Frank returned to Jacksonville in late December. In an abundance of caution, though, he had his wife and children stay in Hibernia until later in January. The panic was over, for now at least, but Florida winters are short. Though the cause of yellow fever remained a mystery, people were well aware of the correlation between warm weather and the disease. Governor Elect Fleming wanted the state to be prepared for the worst before the summer.

His first action after inauguration was to order an extra session of the 1889 Florida Legislature to begin on February 5, which was two months before the regular session. In his opening address to the assembly Fleming laid out the legal foundation granting him the authority to call for the extra session, noting that the state constitution required the establishment of a State Board of Health but to date the Legislature had not acted on that mandate. He chided that "the failure of the Legislature" resulted in "an entire want of harmony or uniformity of action" to battle the disease in 1888. Fleming continued, "Some counties quarantined only against infected places ... others against vast sections of the State, making no discrimination between infected and non-infected localities; and still others against the world outside their county limits ... Grief and affliction overwhelmed many of our people. Business was seriously interrupted throughout the State, and in places utterly prostrated or destroyed."[51] The 1889 Legislature did not shirk its responsibility. After several days of back-and-forth haggling between the House and Senate regarding amendments, the bill passed on February 19. The next day Governor Fleming formally notified Patrick Houstoun, President of the Senate, that he had signed into law Statute No. 1, Chapter 3839, An act to create and establish a State Board of Health.[52] Twenty years later the State Board of Health praised the "far seeing wisdom of Governor Fleming" for bringing continuity to health law in Florida. Today the Florida Department of Health continues to support Florida residents at over 250 locations around the state.

Governor Fleming's opening address to the extra session also included a call to recognize citizens who had battled disease during the yellow fever epidemic. He believed that "the labors of heroic men and women ... facing pestilence and death in the late epidemic [presented] the noblest phase of human character." Fleming urged the Legislature to "let their names be added to those of the bright galaxy of heroes which adorn the history of our State." Joint Resolution No. 1 from the extra session stated that "Colonel L. I. Fleming, Colonel J. J. Daniel, and Hon. Henry L'Engle ... died the death of heroes, patriots and Christian gentlemen, while bravely standing at their posts of duty, fighting courageously the battle of humanity."[53] With due respect to their service as members of the Jacksonville Auxiliary Sanitary Association and to the ultimate price they paid for staying in Jacksonville to fight the epidemic, it seems nepotistic on the part of the governor that these three were the only private citizens in Florida so recognized by the Legislature for heroism. Governor Fleming limited accolades to his relatives, whereas the JASA saw fit to honor four of its members: Charles G. Elliot, James M. Fairlie, Colonel Daniel, and Henry L'Engle.[54]

During his four years in office Governor Fleming championed many causes beneficial to the state, but he also is ignobly remembered for an historic embarrassment. He wrongfully removed James Dean, a Harvard-educated lawyer and an African American, from his position as Monroe County judge. Dean won the job during the 1888 elections. Even though he was clearly the most qualified candidate, much of the white population didn't like a "colored man" holding the position. Their initial objection was not because of the judgeship, per se, but because he had the authority to issue marriage licenses. Reportedly many white couples either abstained from marriage after he took office or went to the mainland to get their license from a white judge. Dean became a perceived embarrassment to influential white Republicans, who now were associated with an unpopular black elected official, and they looked for an opportunity to remove him from office. That moment came when a fair-skinned man of Cuban descent, who said he was a mulatto, requested a marriage license. The man's bride-to-be was a dark-skinned mulatto. Interracial marriage was illegal at that time so Judge Dean had a responsibility to confirm the ethnicity of the bride and groom. The judge asked all the routine questions, confirmed that this was a legal marriage, and issued the license.

Political enemies claimed the man was white, not mulatto, and that Judge Dean knew it. They presented charges against the judge to

Francis Philip Fleming soon after being sworn in as the fifteenth governor of Florida. *Courtesy of State Archives of Florida*

Governor Fleming and demanded his removal from office for violating the law. Fleming undoubtedly heard rebuttal to the charges from Judge Dean's supporters, and he initially took no action on the matter. The most influential Republicans in Monroe County pressed the matter, so Governor Fleming formally presented the charges to Judge Dean and allowed him the opportunity to defend himself. According to historians Canter Brown Jr. and Larry Rivers, this is where the judge erred. In his response, Judge Dean wrote, "... it is a notorious fact ... that nearly nine-tenths of the Cubans here are mulatto ... large numbers of these mulatto Cubans pass for white. In fact, they are not."

Now influential white Cubans joined the chorus for Dean's removal. They decried his "reckless slander, uttered without foundation" as an attempt to shield himself from his own official misconduct. Frank Fleming bowed to pressure and perhaps saw an opportunity to garner political favor. He dismissed the judge and appointed Angel de Lono, the native-born Cuban who had opposed Dean in the 1888 election. In one action of the pen, Governor Fleming won the approval of white Democrats, Republicans, and Cubans of both political parties.[55] James Dean may have been the first African American elected as judge in Florida after Reconstruction, and history makes it clear that Governor Fleming's decision was unsupported by evidence. More than one hundred years later Florida Governor Jeb Bush posthumously reinstated Judge James Dean to office.[56]

Following his term as governor, Frank refused enticements to return to political life but continued to serve the state and his community. He worked tirelessly to honor Confederate Civil War veterans. He served as Florida division commander of the United Confederate Veterans and dedicated efforts to secure pensions for surviving veterans or their widows. He was a warden of his church and a chancellor of the Episcopal Diocese of Florida. Frank Fleming was a valuable member of the Florida Historical Society in the early twentieth century. He wrote its first constitution, served as vice president, then as president from 1905–1908. He helped organize the creation of the *Florida Historical Quarterly*, was a frequent contributor to that publication, and served as its editor until his death. His book, *A Memoir of Captain C. S. Fleming*, is a valuable resource for anyone interested in the Second Florida Infantry during the Civil War. Fleming applied his energy and commitment to many other civic, professional, and educational organizations during his life.

After he left public office Frank and his sons, Charles Seton[57] and Frank Jr., renamed the law firm Fleming & Fleming. They worked together until his death from a long and painful illness on December 20, 1908. He was sixty-seven years old. Today he rests beside his beloved wife and children in Jacksonville's Old City Cemetery. Francis Philip Fleming's law practice and political activism took him away from Hibernia after the Civil War, but his love and abiding commitment to his family and "The Old Place" never faltered.

The story of the Flemings of Fleming Island must also include a note about the lives of Frank and Fred's siblings. Their younger sisters both married hotel guests. Matilda wed Murdoch McRae and lived with him for a short time until his death. Isabella married Edward Sudlow, an Englishman with a minor title who was British vice consul in Jacksonville.[58] She, too, was widowed and eventually lived with her sister in Jacksonville. William never married and lived in Hibernia his entire life. Family tradition tells us that William was an eccentric, and that he may have had some sort of cognitive disability. He lived in his own house at Hibernia, and one oral history recounts harmless, erratic behavior. Matilda, William, and Isabella obviously are important to the Fleming family, but fade from the historical record of events on Fleming Island. Matilda and William both died in 1922. Isabella Fleming Sudlow outlived all Fleming family members who were born before the Civil War. She died in Jacksonville in 1934. All three are buried in the family cemetery at Hibernia.

Augustina "Tina" Fleming lived her entire adult life in Welaka, Florida, with her husband, William Clark Taylor Stephens. Together they had five children who lived to adulthood. Over the years she frequently visited her family members in Jacksonville and Hibernia. One relative recalled her "rusty greying red hair – her specks pushed way down on her nose." The family knew her as a charming companion with a ready wit. She once described a long-winded guest as "a bore with a quart of conversation and a thimbleful of brains."[59] Augustina Fleming Clark died in 1900 and is buried beside her husband in Oakwood Cemetery in Welaka.

Francis Philip Fleming later in life. He is wearing his uniform as
Florida division commander of the United Confederate Veterans.
Courtesy of Kenneth Keefe

Endnotes

1. *Francis P. Fleming Collection*, MS 243, University of Florida Smathers Libraries, Frank Fleming to Edward L'Engle, August 21, 1868.

2. *Florida Times-Union* (Jacksonville), April 2, 1888.

3. Ibid., May 11, 1888.

4. A North Carolina native, Bullock came to Florida when he was sixteen years old. Five years later he was elected circuit clerk of Marion County. He served as a captain with the Florida militia for eighteen months, protecting remote settlements from Indians, then later took up the study and practice of law. He served the Confederacy with distinction during the Civil War, rising from the rank of lieutenant colonel to brigadier general. Along the way he participated in numerous battles. He was taken prisoner and held at Johnston's Island in Lake Erie until freed through a prisoner exchange. Back in the campaigns once again, Bullock was severely wounded in the Battle of Utoy Creek. His injuries prevented further service in the field. After the war Bullock resumed his law practice along with an active life in public service and politics. He was every bit as qualified for governor as Fleming—if not more so.

5. Robert W. Davis was born in Lee County, Georgia. He joined Confederate forces when he was just fourteen years old. After the war he studied law and was admitted to the bar at age twenty. In 1888 he was a relative newcomer to Florida, having moved there in 1879. In 1884 Clay County residents elected him as their representative in the state legislature. The next year he was elected Speaker of the House.

6. *Time-Union*, May 13, 1888.

7. Also known as the Genovar Opera House. In 1889 Frederic Douglas spoke here to St. Augustine residents about the struggles by African Americans to achieve civil rights. An historic marker on St. George Street commemorates this occasion and indicates the location of the Opera House, which burned to the ground in 1914.

8. *Time-Union*, May 28, 1888.

9. Originally constructed in 1847 by B. E. Carr. By 1888 the Magnolia Hotel could accommodate 250 guests. The hotel was destroyed by fire in 1926.

10. St. Augustine, St. Johns County, Florida, Sanborn Map Company, 1888, *University of Florida Digital Collections*, http://ufdc.ufl.edu/.

11. James Vertrees was a native of Kentucky. He served the Confederacy in the Missouri campaign during the Civil War then returned home to Gallatin, Kentucky. Vertress moved to Palatka, Florida, in 1884, where he worked for the county and became active in local politics.

12. *Times-Union*, May 31, 1888.

13. Duncan Upshaw Fletcher was born in Georgia, studied law at Vanderbilt University, and set up practice in Jacksonville. In 1887 Fletcher became active in local politics. During his life he served in the Florida House of Representatives, was mayor of Jacksonville, and was elected to four consecutive terms to represent Florida as a U.S. Senator. He helped create the Jacksonville Bar Association and served as its first president.

14. Born in South Carolina, James G. Speer arrived in Orange County, Florida, around 1854. During his life Speer served in the Florida Legislature and the Florida Senate. Judge Speer is one of the many individuals rumored to have given Orlando, Florida, its name.

15. *Times-Union*, May 31, 1888.

16. James D. Beggs, a Florida native, began his career as a lawyer in Madison County, but the bulk of his professional life was in Orange County. He was a member of the firm Beggs & Palmer in Orange County, a state's attorney, president of the Orlando Bank and Trusts Company, and judge of the Orange County criminal court.

17. In 1850 George W. Barden was a carpenter in Green Cove Springs. He was Clay County judge in 1900.

18. *Times-Union*, June 1, 1888.

19. Ibid., June 2, 1888.

20. In 1907 Pablo Beach was renamed and since then has been known as Jacksonville Beach.

21. *Times-Union*, July 17-18, 1888.

22. Ibid., July 26, 1888.

23. *FPF Papers*, University of Florida, MS 243, Frank Fleming to Frank Jr., August 11, 1888.

24. Ibid., Mary L. Fleming to Lydia Fleming, August 16, 1888.

25. *Times-Union*, September 6, 1888.

26. Ibid.

27. Ibid.

28. Ibid., September 8, 1888.

29. *FPF Papers*, J. J. Daniel to Lydia Fleming, August 29, 1888.

30. Ibid., L. I. Fleming to Lydia Fleming, August 31, 1888.

31. T. Frederick Davis, *History of Early Jacksonville*, 182.

32. *FPF Papers*, Matilda Fleming to Seton Fleming, September 5, 1888.

33. Ibid., J. J. Daniel to Lydia Fleming, August 29, 1888.

34. L'Engle, *A Collection of Letters*, 2:152.

35. *Times-Union*, September 20, 1888.

36. Judson no longer exists. Frank Fleming had campaign stops in at least two other towns that have long since vanished: Providence and Mannfield. All three towns can be found on detailed 1888 maps of Florida. The former site of Mannfield is now a part of the Withlacoochee State Forest.

37. *Times-Union*, September 23, 1888.

38. Ibid., September 29, 1888.

39. Ibid.

40. *FPF Papers,* Frank Fleming to son, September 25, 1888.

41. *Times-Union*, October 10, 1888.

42. Fulton McGuire (sometimes spelled Maguire) was born around 1840 in Key West. McGuire, a mulatto, was a free man when he enlisted with the U.S. Colored troops in February 1863. He initially served with Company F, 2nd Regiment South Carolina Infantry of the 34th U.S. Colored Infantry. Fulton was promoted to sergeant and transferred to Company G in June 1863. He mustered out at Jacksonville on February 28, 1866. Among the 34th Regiment's many postings for service were duties in Jacksonville, Palatka, and Picolata. His service record indicates that he had light skin, black eyes and hair, and was 5' 11" tall.

43. *FPF Papers*, Frank Fleming to Frank Jr., October 17, 1888.

44. Ibid.; *Times-Union*, October 21, 1888.

45. *FPF Papers*, Frank Fleming to Frank Jr., October 17, 1888.

46. Ibid.

47. *Times-Union,* October 30, 1888.

48. *FPF Papers,* Frank Fleming to Seton Fleming, October 28, 1888.

49. *Times-Union*, November 8, 1888.

50. Ibid., November 6, 1888.

51. Senate Journal, A Journal of the Proceedings of the Senate of the Extra Session of the Legislature of the State of Florida (Tallahassee: N. M. Bowen, Printer, 1889), https://www.hathitrust.org.

52. *The Acts and Resolutions Adopted By the Legislature of Florida at its Extra Session, Under The Constitution of A.D. 1885* (Tallahassee: N. M. Bowen, Printer, 1889), https://books.google.com/books.

53. Ibid. Dr. Joseph Y. Porter of Key West, who subsequently was appointed the first Public Health Officer for the new State Board of Health, also received state recognition for his "untiring and skillful efforts" during 1888.

54. Charles S. Adams, ed., "Report of the Jacksonville Auxiliary Sanitation Association of Jacksonville, Florida. Covering the work of the Association during the Yellow Fever Epidemic, 1888," (Jacksonville: *Times-Union Print,* 1889), https://www.hathitrust.org.

55. Canter Brown Jr., and Larry E. Rivers, "The Pioneer African American Jurist Who Almost Became a Bishop: Florida's Judge James Dean, 1858-1914," *Florida Historical Quarterly* 45:1, (2008).

56. Brendan Farrington, *Associated Press,* 2002, http://www.cbsnews.com/news/a-measure-of-justice/.

57. Frank Fleming named his second son Charles Seton (b. 1876) in honor of his beloved brother who died at the Battle of Cold Harbor. All references to Seton Fleming in Chapter 7 refer to Frank Fleming's son.

58. Isabel "Fanny" Fleming and Edward Sudlow Jr. were married April 30, 1890. Murdock McCrae and Matilda Fleming wed on September 9, 1891. *Clay County, Florida, Marriage Records.*

59. L'Engle, *A Collection of Letters,* 2:71.

The Era of Fred and Margot Fleming at Hibernia

Frederic and Margot Fleming were host and hostess of Hibernia for thirty-two years. During their time together they transformed Hibernia from a winter boarding house into a complete "winter resort." Their business and their family grew together. Margot Fleming gave birth to four children: Margaret Seton (October 26, 1887), Mary Augusta (August 20, 1889), Frederic Alexander Jr. (February 7, 1893), and Dorothy Baldwin (November 9, 1899). Margot loved to play lawn tennis, so Frederic constructed a grass court under the trees near the river. The tennis lawn doubled as a croquet court and guests took full advantage of both games. Margot loved to swim, so Frederic built a bathhouse and a swimming pool that he surrounded by a high fence. An artesian well poured a constant flow of seventy-two-degree water from deep within the Florida aquifer, so the pool remained cool in the

The tennis court was in front of the Big Cottage. Holly Cottage is barely visible in the background. *LCA Collection*

summer and warm in the winter. The overflow meandered through a short serpentine trough then down an underground pipe to the river. The pool delighted the family and their guests, and the privacy of the fence enabled a long-standing tradition of midnight skinny-dipping. This pool is among the oldest in Florida. Today it is part of a private residence and is still fully operational.

These were the halcyon days of Hibernia—a time of peace without threat of attack by Indians or insurgent forces, and a time during which northerners flocked to the winter boarding houses and hotels along the St. Johns River. This also was an era during which some of those winter guests purchased land in Hibernia and built private residences. Three guests from Philadelphia made lasting contributions to the "Hibernia Winter Resort."

The Fleming family found a most generous and endearing friend sometime around 1880. Miss Fanny Brown was the daughter of William and Deborah Norris Brown, part of an old and respected Philadelphia family. She remained a spinster her entire life. Thanks to a trust established by her father, she lived a life of leisure. When she wasn't traveling or in Hibernia, she resided with her sisters, Mrs. Samuel Brown Glover in Philadelphia, or Mrs. Debra Brown Coleman in Lebanon, Pennsylvania. Interestingly, Mrs. Coleman and her husband, George Dawson Coleman, were intimate friends of former president Ulysses S. Grant.[1] Fanny could have chosen to live just about anywhere, but she chose Hibernia for her winter home.

On November 25, 1882, Fanny purchased approximately five acres of land along the St. Johns River from Christian and Mary Black. The Blacks had purchased this tract from Margaret Fleming in 1875 for $400. Seven years later Miss Brown paid a whopping $4,500, a ten-fold profit for the Blacks. Miss Brown constructed a private three-story residence that she called "The Myrtles," and lived in Hibernia throughout much of the winter for the next thirty years.

Miss Brown purchased many more tracts of former Fleming land over the years, enough to build a golf club for the enjoyment of her friends and the guests at Hibernia. The Hibernia Golf Club consisted of nine holes and was located just south of the Big House on land that once belonged to George Fleming Jr. It became know as "The Links." The Links had many clear views of the St. Johns River and surrounded The Myrtles on three sides. Remnants of the Hibernia Golf Club are easily seen today. The streets of a small residential development called Hibernia Links roughly follow the original fairways. Before the development of Hibernia Links, members of the sixth generation of the Fleming family learned to drive a car around the abandoned golf course. Driving along those roads today, it is hard to imagine whacking a golf ball down open fairways, and even harder to imagine the once-expansive river views. Thick woods, immense magnolias, live oaks, pines, laurel oaks, and comfortable homes have replaced sand traps, putting greens, and open vistas.

The Hibernia Golf Club opened prior to the turn of the twentieth century, most likely during the 1899–1900 season, which was the

Guests had clear views of the St. Johns River while golfing at "the links." *RA Collection*

inaugural year of the annual Hibernia Golf Tournament. From the very beginning, The Links hosted one of the most notable woman players in the country, part-time Hibernia resident Francis "Pansy" Griscom, daughter of Mr. and Mrs. Clemont Acton Griscom. Miss Griscom won the U.S.G.A. women's national championship at Shinnecock Hills County Club on Sept 2, 1900, when she was twenty-one years old. Discussing her daughter's achievement, Mrs. Griscom remarked, "Last winter [Frances] had some excellent practice at Hibernia in Florida. That's about the only really dry place in Florida. It is on a bluff on the St. Johns River, and the nine hole course is a good one."[2] Clement Acton Griscom and his wife, Frances Canby Biddle Griscom, began wintering in Hibernia as early as the 1890s. Mr. Griscom was a wealthy shipping magnate who teamed with financier J. P. Morgan to create International Mercantile Marine. The company's holdings eventually included the White Star Line and the ship *Titanic*. In 1897 the Griscoms purchased approximately five riverfront acres from Isabel Fleming Sudlow and constructed a shingle-style cottage just a stone's throw from the edge of the river and a short walk north of the Big House and the Cottage. Little did the Griscoms know that their private cottage would eventually become a part of the Hibernia Winter Resort know as "Holly Cottage," and would survive longer than any other dwelling at Hibernia.

Hibernia at the Dawn of the 20th Century

Descendants of Frederic and Margot Fleming have preserved a marvelous collection of personal and official documents from the late nineteenth and early twentieth centuries. Perhaps even more valuable than the documents, though, are three tape-recorded oral histories that tell us a great deal about life in Hibernia at the turn of the century and beyond.[3] These resources are a virtual treasure-trove that enables us to imagine a typical day during the boarding season. They even tell us a little about the lives of children in Hibernia. In good weather each day usually began the same way.

As was his habit, Fred Fleming rose before sunrise to release his turkeys from their pen. In pleasant weather he then strolled up to his seat on the wide veranda overlooking the river. Throughout the years various servants came from the kitchen carrying his cup of tea or coffee. One of those was Ellen "Ellie" Norton, known affectionately as Aunt Ellen to the Fleming children. Mrs. Norton worked for the Fleming family much of her life until her death on May 21, 1925. Frederic sat quietly, often by himself, taking in the scents of the season—the sweet aroma of tea olive, orange blossoms, and Cherokee roses in bloom; the pungent odor of the rich river mud. He heard the livestock and wildlife stir, cattle lowing, his turkeys scratching through the low ground cover in search of early morning grubs and worms, raccoons scuffling about on the water's edge, birds chirping high in the live oaks, the cries of wood ducks as they took flight. On clear mornings he reveled at the shimmering ribbons of sunlight cast across the expanse of the St. Johns River. Mr. Fleming was a Southern man through and through. He started the morning at an unhurried pace and carried that temperament throughout the day.

Margot Fleming, on the other hand, was a New Jersey girl, raised in a fast-paced culture and usually on the move. Mrs. Fleming carried a large set of keys as she hustled about, deliberately jingling them when rounding corners and entering rooms. This is how she signaled the staff that she was approaching to give everyone a chance to look sharp and on the job. She met the head cook, Katie Frazer "S'Katy" Murray, in the kitchen at five o'clock every morning to unlock the pantry and plan the meals for the day. The family and the staff had a comical relationship with that pantry. Former staff member Margaret Frazier once said that whenever a servant went unwatched into the pantry, "You always got enough to have some for yourself." The Fleming family was well aware of this and didn't think of it as stealing. It was just different, something you might not understand if you didn't grow up in that culture. Even so, a cup of sugar here and there added up, so Mrs. Fleming kept the pantry locked and managed the key as much as possible.

Margot was always involved in planning meals, but never in the actual cooking. Her daughter, Dorothy, never knew her to cook anything at all. Instead, S'Katy was head cook for all meals, and to understand what she did one must keep in mind the times. There was no electricity, no gas oven or cooktop, and no plumbing for many years at Hibernia. S'Katy commanded a large wood-burning cookstove that stretched across one wall of the detached kitchen, perhaps ten feet in

Hibernia Employees. *LCA Collection*

Katie "S'Katy" Murray, the master chef at Hibernia for many years.
LCA Collection

length. S'Katy ruled that kitchen and was often disagreeable to those
who worked under her. She was the undisputed master of her domain.
During boarding season she cooked breakfast, dinner, and evening
supper over that hot, smoky stove for the Flemings, their guests, and
staff seven days a week. She rarely took a vacation or a day off, and only

occasionally left her post for a funeral or some other equally pressing matter. S'Katy lived in a small house behind the Big House, raised a daughter there, and collected stray dogs, cats, and birds. At one time she had perhaps fourteen cats at her house, to which Margot Fleming said, "No more!"

S'Katy had a special relationship with Dorothy, the youngest of the Fleming children, whom she called "Miss Pet." Every morning around eleven Dorothy wandered into the kitchen where S'Katy served her a drink. Dorothy's favorite was orange juice topped with whipped egg white. Once, while sipping her juice, Dorothy asked S'Katy what she was cooking. S'Katy replied, "Oh, I don't know Miss Pet. Just making my bug juice."

Guests and other family members rose at their leisure. Some took advantage of the early morning darkness to skinny-dip in the pool behind the privacy of the high fence. When she was about six years old, Mary Augusta Biddle, Frederic Fleming's granddaughter, known in the family as "Dusty," often walked to the pool before sunrise for her private swim. Her route passed under the window of journalist and author Samuel Hopkins Adams. Adams began his day well before sunrise, and young Dusty remembers the sounds of his typewriter in the early dawn.[4] Other guests took morning walks, gathered on the verandas to watch the sunrise, or otherwise passed the time until breakfast at eight-thirty sharp.

Good food was one key to success in the St. Johns River valley boarding house business, and numerous sources attest to the outstanding table fare at Hibernia. Each meal was an elaborate affair choreographed by Margot Fleming and executed by numerous African American servants who prepped, cooked, served, and cleaned up after the entire production. Like all meals, breakfast was served in the dining room. There were six large tables, five for guests and one for the Fleming family. Altogether, they could squeeze in up to sixty-five people at one sitting. One of the waitresses, often Mary Miller during her many years at the hotel, rang a cowbell to signal that breakfast was served. Guests filed in chatting among themselves and the dining room filled with sounds of footsteps on the heart pine floors and chairs scraping back from the tables. Six wait staff members in uniform, one for each table, bustled to and fro from the detached kitchen to serve guests individually. The Fleming family dined privately at their table unless they invited special friends to join them. Unlike the guests, the Flemings did not tip their waitress. As a result, the staff members were reluctant to wait their table. It was a sumptuous morning feast each

The Fleming family gathered on the veranda of the Big House late in the ninteenth century. The two girls in front are Margaret Seton Fleming and her sister, Augusta. The three adults seated on the porch steps are (left to right) Margot's sister, Die Baldwin, Margot Fleming, and an unidentified man. Frederic Fleming Jr. is seated to Margot's right. Seated in chairs (left to right) are: an unidentified woman (possibly Matilda Fleming), Fred Fleming, Reggie Woolston, and Margot's parents, Augustus Baldwin and Mary Adelaide Prior Baldwin. Standing are S'Katy Murray and an unidentified man. *MWF Collection*

and every day, consisting of some or all of the following: eggs cooked to order, hominy, oatmeal, bacon, pancakes, toast, muffins, biscuits, orange and grapefruit juices, coffee, tea, and milk. In season there were blackberries aplenty. On Sundays Mrs. Fleming added a special treat of fresh handmade fish cakes.

After breakfast the guests would assemble on the verandas, play golf, croquet, or tennis, or engage in other outdoor activities. Some would retire to their rooms or public spaces within the Big House. The library was stocked with many books. Newspapers and magazines arrived regularly with the mail delivery on the river steamer *May Garner*. The parlor included a piano and a comfortable place to sit and chat.

Sportsmen fished in the St. Johns River or went quail hunting. It was still prime quail habitat in those days, with vast longleaf pine forests and sandy soils in the dry portions of the island. Some guests brought their own bird dogs. Margaret Frazier recalled tired dogs sleeping on the floor by the fireplace in the Holly Cottage after a long day of hunting. They must have been very good dogs, indeed, because the ladies put their fur coats down as beds for the happy hunters.[5] Other outdoor activities included leisurely strolls, canoeing and sailing, excursions up Black Creek, and horseback riding. The beautiful walk along the riverbank provided guests numerous vistas with places to sit and enjoy the natural beauty. A crow's nest high in the arms of a live oak tree on the riverbank was a popular spot. Guests in suits and dresses climbed the steps to while the time away. This was really an adults' tree house, offering a high vantage point with a unique view. Craftsmen used natural tree branches to construct Adirondack-style enhancements along the walkway, including a cozy gazebo, a footbridge over a small ravine near Holly Cottage, and a sort of boardwalk that looped out over the river then back to the shore.

While the guests began their post-breakfast activities, the staff ate in the kitchen at a long table that sat ten or more. Except for leftovers, they didn't get the same food as the guests. They ate well, though, including plenty of stews, soups, and beef. Staff members loved S'Katy's cooking as much as the guests did. After breakfast the staff flew into action, taking care of every chore required around the Fleming property, which the staff called simply "The Yard." Whenever members of the African American community in Hibernia left their homes to go to The Yard, friends and neighbors knew what that meant—they were off to some part of the Fleming place to do their job. The waitresses cleaned, dried, and put the dishes and utensils away. S'Katy and her cook staff cleaned the kitchen and cooking area. Young boys cleaned the pots and pans. Meanwhile, other staff members began the tedious housekeeping chores. When the Hibernia Winter Resort was at full capacity, which happened often during these years, there were many rooms to clean each day. Servants made beds, swept floors, trimmed wicks on candles and lanterns, delivered laundry, cleared ashes from fireplaces and reset fresh wood for the evening, cleaned washbowls, and filled water pitchers. The washbowl and pitcher served many purposes, from freshening one's face, to cleaning teeth, and even to washing hair. Swedish artist Bror Anders Wikström strolled outside the Big House late one Saturday night and spied a young woman hanging her head out a window while her companion poured water over her soapy hair.[6]

Scott Ritchie

Bror Anders Wikström's sketch of a scene he observed walking the
grounds of Hibernia one evening in 1886. *MWF Collection*

 With so much to do, it's unlikely the staff was able to finish all these
chores before it was time to prepare for dinner, which was the large
meal of the day, served promptly at one-thirty. Preparation in the
kitchen began almost as soon as cleanup from breakfast was complete.
For many years Moses Knight, the chief gardener at Hibernia, came
into the kitchen mid-morning with his wheelbarrow full of just-
harvested fresh produce. Depending on the time of the year, he
delivered peas, beans, okra, berries, potatoes, and a variety of other
vegetables. Meats included beef and pork roasts, chickens roasted or
fried, a variety of seafood, and turkey every Sunday. The turkeys were
from Fred Fleming's own flock. They roamed freely about the grounds
and each Sunday their number was reduced, much to the delight of
the hungry guests. The Flemings' own cows provided much of the milk
and cream, and their chickens provided eggs and meat. Every dinner
included rice and potatoes, three or four vegetables, at least one meat

entrée, a baked good such as bread, rolls, cornbread, or biscuits, and dessert. The guests did not dress formally for the afternoon dinner. When a waitress rang the cowbell they took assigned seats in golf attire or whatever they had been wearing for their morning activities. Immediately the wait staff began serving the most sumptuous meal of the day.

Food not grown, harvested, or hunted in Hibernia came in on the river steamer *May Garner* or an oyster boat that regularly pulled up to the long wharf, or from a delivery wagon that made rounds to Hibernia every week. Margot Fleming placed orders with a supplier in Jacksonville who sent the requested foodstuffs and products to Hibernia on board the *May Garner*. The master of the oyster boat delivered a fresh catch consisting alternately of oysters, clams, redfish, sea bass, mullet in the fall, bass, or any of the remarkable variety of seafood available in the brackish waters of the St. Johns River and the ocean beyond. One of the more impressive deliveries arrived on a horse-drawn truck two or three times a week—one hundred pounds of ice. During the nineteenth and early twentieth centuries, suppliers regularly shipped ice from New England to Charleston, South Carolina, then on to Florida with minimal loss of product. Even more remarkable is the fact that these suppliers shipped ice as far as Calcutta, India.[7] The key to success was to tightly pack the ice in thick layers of insulating sawdust. Upon delivery, the ice quickly was transferred to the Flemings' icehouse where it was covered with more sawdust. In addition to cooling drinks, the ice was used weekly as part of a traditional Sunday treat—peanuts and hand-cranked ice cream served in the dining room. Margaret Frazier recalled this as a special time. She said that "big ol' Johnny Miller or whoever they could catch" often cranked the churn. The gardener, Moses Knight, sometimes came back to The Yard on his day off just to crank the ice cream. He would top off the mixture with lots of salt and crank away until the cream and chocolate, vanilla, or strawberry flavors transformed into frozen goodness. Margaret Frazier and Dorothy Austin both had fond memories of the times Moses or Johnny Miller handed them the dasher, which was a paddle inside the ice cream bucket that turned round and round as the ice cream solidified. It was impossible to remove it without some of the ice cream still attached, soon to be licked off by eager children.

After the midday dinner, guests engaged in any of the great variety of activities available, but golf was king in Hibernia and the young women who played so well attracted much attention. During the 1900–01 season Mrs. Caleb Fox, Miss Eunice Terry, and Miss Sophia

Starr joined Miss Frances Griscom at Hibernia.[8] Mrs. Fox was runner-up women's U.S.G.A champion in 1899 and Miss Terry competed at a high level, winning several prominent club championships. Miss Starr was Philadelphia champion in 1901.[9] These young women, all spirited individuals as well as excellent golfers, refused to take the game too seriously and enjoyed pranks. After a bad round on the links, Miss Griscom and her friends sometimes buried their clubs, complete with a funeral procession and the young ladies singing anything from a Negro spiritual to Wagnerian opera strains. Another prank at Hibernia, intended as a frolic, instead caused panic. Miss Helen Biddle, among the fourth generation of her family to enjoy Hibernia and a national golfer in her own right, was forbidden by her family to swim in the river. She and her sister decided to go for a swim anyway by taking out a canoe and purposely tipping it over. They splashed into the deep water far from shore. Immediately twenty or more people rushed to the banks of the river to help. A servant jumped in a boat, hurriedly rowing their way as he urged them to stay above water. They were never in any danger—both could swim—and the shamefaced girls waited many years before telling the truth of the matter.[10]

The Flemings had their own horses, and guests could go riding through the pine forests. On one occasion, though, two young women made a splash with hired horses from a nearby stable. After qualifying for the finals in a golf tournament at Magnolia Springs, Miss Frances Griscom and her friend, Miss Cassatt of Philadelphia, hired horses and rode back to Hibernia. Galloping around the grounds, they led their horses through the shallow waters on the banks of the St. Johns River, out to deeper water where they remained astride their swimming horses, to the delight of those watching from shore.[11]

Following the annual Hibernia Golf Club Tournament in 1906, Fred Fleming hosted a "most successful and enjoyable gymkhana" on the resort grounds. Events included a 100-yard dash for boys and girls, the high jump and broad jump, and a spoon and egg race. The great event of the day was a "fox hunt," with a friend of guest Lord Sykes playing the role of "fox." The fox was given a few minutes' head start before the handler, Mr. Herbert E. Anderson, who was Mrs. Fleming's brother-in-law, released the "hounds." After a spirited two-mile run the fleetest of the hounds, Frederic Fleming Jr. and his sister Augusta, caught the fox.[12]

As in years past, the highlight of any day was the arrival of the steamboat laden with travelers, supplies, and mail for everyone in Hibernia. The sound of the steam whistle brought guests, family members, servants, and neighbors, both black and white, to the long wharf in front of the Big House. This was the social event of the day. Guests greeted old friends and said goodbye to those departing. Neighbors socialized and exchanged news. Servants bustled about, unloading baggage and supplies onto a rail cart, and then loading more baggage back onto the boat. The ship's captain delivered the mailbag to postmaster Fred Fleming in his small post office at the end of the wharf, and Fred exchanged a bag of outgoing mail. A small crowd gathered, eagerly hopeful for a delivery, as Mr. Fleming sorted the letters and packages. When he was ready, Fred opened a small door and began calling names to personally distribute the mail, which was the only means of communication with the world beyond.

When the afternoon drew towards an end, guests returned to their rooms for a nap or simply to freshen up. Eventually everyone came out smartly dressed for the evening supper at six-thirty. Despite the fact that guests dressed more formally for this meal, it was much smaller and less elaborate than the midday dinner. Typical offerings included casseroles, soufflés, tomato dishes, and breads. There were fewer organized activities after supper. On warm evenings some guests strolled to the end of the wharf to take in the last of the sunset. Men frequently gathered in the smoking room, where some drank strong spirits with their cigars, pipes, and cigarettes. Other guests met in the parlor, on the porches, or in the music room. Margot Fleming was an accomplished piano player and frequently led groups in song, especially on Sunday evenings when they sang hymns. There were many favorites and they rarely sang more than three verses so that Mrs. Fleming was able to honor all requests.

While the paying guests enjoyed their evenings, the staff ate a quick meal then began to wrap up the long day of work. Some cleaned the dining room, kitchen, or other areas. Others tended the guest rooms and made sure that all the lanterns and fireplaces were ready for the evening. As the hours passed everyone gradually drifted to their rooms, warmed in the glow of their fires on chilly winter nights.

Three distinct groups of children roamed freely in and around Hibernia: the Fleming children, the children of the winter guests, and the children of the African Americans who worked for the Flemings. Two of those children, Dorothy Fleming and Margaret Frazier, spoke about their youth many years later. They both were born in Hibernia, and both had fond memories of their childhood there, but they actually lived in different worlds.

Dorothy Fleming awoke early in her comfortable room on the second floor of the Big House. Whenever she dressed during the day, Dorothy would toss her used garments aside. In her own words, "You just threw them in the corner and later it came back cleaned and pressed and ready for you." She never made her bed or cleaned her room. Servants took care of that. Dorothy made her way down the wide central staircase into the dining room to join her siblings and parents for breakfast. After breakfast Dorothy walked over to the schoolhouse located across from St. Margaret's Episcopal Church. This was a small frame structure, formerly a private winter residence of a guest, set aside solely for the purpose of educating the Fleming children and the children of winter guests. For many years a cousin named Sophie taught their daily lessons, which lasted until noon. Then Dorothy and the other children strolled back to the Big House for the main meal of the day.

Margaret Frazier was born March 1, 1894. Her grandmother, Ellen "Ellie" Norton, raised her in Hibernia, though little Margaret sometimes stayed with her mother in St. Augustine. Ellen Norton's mother, Bea, was a slave near Welaka, Florida. Margaret Frazier didn't know her enslaved great-grandmother's surname, but she did know that Ellen Norton's father was the white plantation master who owned Bea. Ellen married twice before leaving central Florida for Clay County. Lightning killed her first husband while he was plowing a field, but not before she gave birth to a child, Rebecca. Her second husband, George Norton, was born a slave somewhere near Charleston, South Carolina. He escaped bondage and made his way to central Florida. In Margaret Frazier's words, "... they couldn't catch him. He would run. He stayed in the woods [so] no one would damage him." George Norton married Ellen somewhere near Welaka. Their friend, Pompey Jenkins, had left Welaka years earlier and found his way to a better life in Hibernia. George and Ellie Norton followed in his footsteps, first to Green Cove Springs and then downriver to Hibernia. Both the Jenkins and Norton families eventually purchased their own land from L. I. Fleming.[13] During her youth Margaret traveled "to and fro," spending time with her mother in St Augustine and with her grandmother in Hibernia, but she always considered Hibernia her home.

When she was in Hibernia, Margaret awoke early in her grandmother's small frame house. Sometimes the water supply was low, and Margaret remembered the well where her grandmother drew water. She called it "the stink hole." Anyone who has had the dubious experience of drawing water from a sulfurous well in North Florida understands this perfectly appropriate name. The rancid rotten-egg smell of sulfur water is unmistakable. Margaret attended a small Negro schoolhouse that was located near the intersection of present-day Hibernia Road and U.S. Highway 17. Each morning her grandmother prepared Margaret's lunch pail, which was a small metal bucket with a handle, loading it with peas, rice, and cornbread. Margaret worked on her morning lessons until lunchtime when the children took recess outside and ate their cold, simple meals.

After lunch Dorothy Fleming was free to do whatever she chose. As a very young child she spent hours in her playhouse near the kitchen. As she matured Dorothy took up golf with great passion. Dorothy was an accomplished player in her day, making her mark in the annual Hibernia Golf Tournament and later in life as an amateur in Connecticut. She also enjoyed canoeing, especially late in the afternoon. Dorothy loved to paddle along the shallow flats of the St. Johns River, alone in the boat with her thoughts.

Margaret Frazier recalled afternoons in the woods with her sister, Daisy, catching gopher tortoises and picking wild violets. When they had enough flowers, the girls left the woods and walked along the sugar-sand road to The Yard, carrying their flowers with them. Many guests gathered on the porches of the Big House and the Cottage in the afternoons, whiling away time before the evening supper. Margaret and Daisy walked up with their bouquets of fresh violets, knowing that the guests would be happy to buy them. Sometimes they paid twenty-five cents; sometimes more, sometimes less. Then the girls turned out on the sparse grass-covered ground and danced for the crowd. Guests clapped rhythm as Margaret and Daisy danced jigs and their own special dance, the Buzzard Lope, a slow, gangling imitation of buzzards as they walk and hop about on the ground. After that the girls would climb the steps to the porch, thank the guests for the money, and go on home.

Dorothy Fleming affectionately remembered "Aunt Ellen" Norton tending to the family's needs. Margaret Frazier remembered waiting for her grandmother Ellie to return home in the evenings, hopeful that she would bring some good leftovers from the supper at Hibernia. Clearly there were two Hibernias during the days of the Fleming Winter Resort. There was the riverfront estate with the Big House, the cottages, and leisure activities where many servants and employees pampered the family and their paying guests. There was also the Hibernia away from the river, where African American laborers, housekeepers, waitresses, and farmers lived their own lives. One former employee said that the

Scott Ritchie

Flemings and the African American community relied on each other,
and that relations were cordial and respectful between the family
and their employees. Black children played with white children, both
the Fleming children and the children of guests. There was a barrier
between the two communities, though, with invisible lines drawn that
everyone knew they must not cross.

Fire in Hibernia Once Again

In early April of 1910 Miss Fanny Brown fired her longtime house
servant at The Myrtles. The young woman was pregnant, and at
seventy-three years old, Miss Brown had no tolerance for the prospect
of a crying baby in her home, nor did she want a distracted servant
constantly worrying about a newborn. A few days later the African
American community held one of their regular dances at the location
of an old cotton gin across the small creek just south of the Hibernia
Golf Club. After the dance the servant's angry husband recruited an
accomplice. They sneaked up to Miss Brown's property in the dead
of night and set fire to everything, including her home, the carriage
house, and a barn. The blaze quickly engulfed the structure, destroying
Miss Brown's beautiful winter home and practically everything in it.
She was lucky to escape with her life. Authorities apprehended both
"incendiaries," to use a term of the day. The accomplice testified against
the servant's husband, who was sentenced to twenty years in prison.
Miss Brown never rebuilt at Hibernia, and all that remains today of her
lovely home is a small swimming pool, really nothing more than the
size of a modern hot tub, filled with algae, goldfish, and frogs.[14]

Fanny Brown hosted the eleventh annual Hibernia Golf Tournament
as scheduled just two weeks later. Each year the tournament included
several contests designed to attract players of all ages and skill levels.
One of the most popular events was "Clock Putting," an event on a
circular putting green with stations around the circumference like
the hours of a clock. Miss Brown bought the trophies and presented
them in an elaborate post-tournament ceremony. The golf tournament
lasted almost as long as the Hibernia Winter Resort. The tradition
carried on for many years after Fanny Brown's death on April 4, 1916,
at her sister's home in Philadelphia.[15]

During her life Fanny Brown engineered two remarkably generous
land deals for the benefit of the Fleming family. The first involved
Frances Canby Biddle Griscom, mother of golfing champion, Miss
Frances Griscom, and the wife of Clement Acton Griscom. Mr. Griscom

died in 1912 shortly after the disaster of the *Titanic*. Within weeks Miss Brown purchased their Hibernia property and cottage for one hundred dollars, and ten days later she sold it to Frederic Fleming for the same price. Frederic wasted no time enlarging and modifying the structure to accommodate winter guests. It became known as Holly Cottage, and for the next twenty-seven years was a popular residence at the Hibernia Winter Resort. The second transaction involved the golf course. The Fleming family recently had incorporated their business, and in her will Fanny Brown bequeathed the entire Hibernia Golf Club, including all of her land and the clubhouse, to Hibernia, Inc., for "as long as said lands should be used as a golf course." What is even more remarkable, though, is that she directed her niece, Fanny Brown Coleman, to use the residuary estate to pay the cost of maintaining the golf course in perpetuity. If Hibernia, Inc., ever stopped using the property as a golf course then her nephew, Edward Riou Coleman, would receive the land. Miss Coleman honored that bequest until 1925, when she and Edward Coleman both wanted out of the deal. They relinquished any claim to the land and golf course in exchange for relief from the obligation to maintain the course. For a mere one hundred dollars each, the Colemans conveyed all Fanny Brown's Florida property to Hibernia, Inc., and substantial acreage from George Fleming's original Spanish Land Grant once again returned to the family fold.

Fanny Brown's financial support of the Flemings in Hibernia underscores an important point. For many years the boarding business enabled the family to live a privileged lifestyle, but it never made them wealthy. Among Margaret Seton Fleming's assets at her death were land, a beautiful mansion, a great deal of furniture, a cottage, multiple outbuildings, equipment, and supplies. There were no stocks, no bonds, no amassed wealth, and no cash. Times got lean during summers when the family had no income from the boarding business. During Fred Fleming's years as host at Hibernia he resorted to mortgaging tracts of land several times to raise cash. For a few summers Fred Fleming moved his family to Clarksville, Georgia, where he worked as proprietor of the Mountain View Hotel to supplement their income.[16] He and his siblings gradually sold off portions of their Hibernia land to winter guests and to their African American neighbors. After years of housing, entertaining, and feeding affluent guests, Fred Fleming, like his mother before him, had no stocks, no bonds, no amassed wealth. Fanny Brown's generous bequest likely enabled the family business to survive because Hibernia and golf had become practically synonymous. Without the golf course it is entirely possible that many guests would seek a new winter haven.

Fanny Brown (right) with
her friend Mrs. Morris on
the river road in Hibernia
in 1913. *RA Collection*

On March 29, 1917, Frederic Alexander Fleming Sr. died in his home. He was seventy-three years old. Like his father's before him, Fred's death came suddenly. He succumbed to heart failure after just two days of illness. During his lifetime Frederic Fleming always indicated "hotel keeper" as his occupation, but he was also a dedicated public servant. Frederic was postmaster at Hibernia for many years, justice of the peace for Clay County and a Clay County commissioner, and he was elected to the Florida Senate in 1892. Fred was the last of the patriarchs among the Fleming family born during a time of slavery and raised in a plantation culture.[17] He grew up with slaves that were his friends, but also were the family's property. Despite that upbringing, or perhaps because of it, a former employee at Hibernia once described Mr. Fleming as openhearted and even generous to the African American community at Hibernia. Upon his death George Gray, an African American businessman in Jacksonville, published a small newspaper column titled "A Colored Man's Tribute." Mr. Gray wrote that Fred Fleming was "a staunch friend to the unfortunates and was always ready to do something for the happiness of my race." He added that Mr. Fleming's grandparents, George and Sophia Fleming, "were owners of my grandparents and allowed them to purchase their freedom, to enjoy their privilege." Mr. Gray expressed appreciation that L. I. Fleming was once his guardian.[18] This public eulogy supports a family oral tradition of kindness towards slaves and free Negroes, but cannot negate the fact that the Flemings owned other human beings. No honest telling of their story can omit what is known about that shameful legacy.

Frederic Alexander Fleming. *MWF Collection*

Endnotes

1. www.colemanmemorialpark.org. George Dawson Coleman and his brother, Robert, built the North Lebanon Furnaces in Lebanon, PA, and were successful iron and steel producers.

2. *Sunday Herald* (Boston), September 2, 1900, 39.

3. Dorothy Fleming Austin interview, Samantha Bryant interview, and Margaret Frazier interview, *MWF Collection*; *LCA Collection*.

4. Mary Augusta Biddle Scheetz, telephone interview by the author, April 30, 2013. Samuel Hopkins Adams is probably best remembered as the author of the short story "Night Bus," which Hollywood director Frank Capra adapted into the multi-Oscar-winning movie *It Happened One Night* starring Clark Gable and Claudette Colbert.

5. Margaret Frazier to Scott and Margot Ritchie, personal conversation.

6. B. A. Wikström, *The Fleming's Island Gazette*, *MWF Collection*.

7. Christopher Klein, *The Man Who Shipped New England Ice Around the World*, August 29, 2012, www.history.com.

8. *Philadelphia Inquirer*, March 18, 1901.

9. *New York Times*, November 1, 1901.

10. Unattributed newspaper article, Dorothy Fleming scrapbook, *LCA Collection*.

11. Ibid.

12. Ibid., 1906 newspaper article without citation.

13. Clay County, Florida, Deed Book CC, L. I. Fleming to Pompey Jenkins, April 27, 1878, 242-45; Deed Book M, L. I. Fleming to George Norton and wife, November 3, 1881, 111-12.

14. *MWF Collection*; *Lexington Herald* (KY), March 20, 1910, www.genealogybank.com; Clay County, Motion Docket, 1885-1950, Book 1. "Miss Brown's pool" sits on private property owned by a member of the seventh generation of Flemings in Hibernia.

15. *Philadelphia Inquirer*, April 6, 1916, 19. Fanny Brown is buried in a family plot at Laurel Hill Cemetery in Philadelphia.

16. *Macon Telegraph* (GA), July 1, 1896.

17. His brother, William, was still living at this time. He was never directly involved in the management of Hibernia, though, and was never considered an authority figure or a leader in the family.

18. Unattributed newspaper clipping, Dorothy Fleming Scrapbook, *RA Collection*.

The Flemings and Slavery

Over a span of seventy-five years the Flemings of Fleming Island owned many slaves, but we know very little about these people. Slave census records for Florida include only an age range, gender, and in some years a differentiation between full-blooded Negroes and mulattos. Slave census records never included the individuals' names or other personal information. Probate records often list men, women, and children by name, but to date, research has yielded just two such probates from the Flemings. Available records provide information about slaves owned by the following eight family members: George and Sophia Fleming; their children, Lewis, George Jr., and Mary; Lewis's children, L. I., George C., and little Matilda; and George Jr.'s daughter, Sophia Fleming Floyd, who inherited several of his slaves.

George Fleming may have owned a few slaves before marrying Sophia Fatio in 1788 when his father-in-law's gift of approximately thirty slaves vaulted him to considerable status. He owned at least thirty-three slaves in 1816, but unless his probate record is discovered we will not know how many he owned through the remainder of his life. During the first U.S. federal census of Florida in 1830, Sophia Fleming owned thirty slaves. Her son George owned ten slaves, bringing the family total to forty. Sophia included thirteen free Negroes for the 1830 Slave Census, seven of them less than ten years old. The data suggest that by 1840 Sophia Fleming had given her daughter, Mary Fleming, several of her Negroes, both free and enslaved. Sophia's ownership was down to twelve slaves in 1840, plus one free Negro. Mary now owned ten slaves and counted seven free Negroes as a part of her household. George's nine slaves brought the family total to thirty-one, along with eight free Negroes. The downward trend continued at the same pace ten years later. Lewis Fleming appears as a slave owner for the first time in 1850 with eight slaves to his name.[1] George Jr. increased his holding to fourteen slaves, and George C. Fleming owned one slave, for a family total of twenty-three. Neither Mary Fleming Halliday nor her husband appears in the 1850 census. Free Negroes were not included in the 1850 census so we don't know how many, if any, lived under Fleming sponsorship.

Three slaves among the 1850 census are identified through family oral traditions and a deed of ownership. Margaret Fleming's personal maid was a woman named Betty, who through the years took on the nickname "Mum Betty." Her husband, identified only as "Old July," was Lewis Fleming's personal servant. Old July was born in Africa on the Guinea coast and remembered his trip to America aboard a slave ship. In 1850 Mum Betty gave birth to a daughter named Rina. As each of the Fleming children was born, their father gave the new son or daughter a Negro child close in age. The intention was that the Negro child and the Fleming child would grow together, and that eventually the Negro child would become a loyal and faithful personal servant.[2] This was Rina's fate. To demonstrate his "natural love and affection" for his baby daughter Matilda, Lewis Fleming gave her a gift: "All that certain female negro slave named Rina about eight-months old *with her increase.*"[3] To be clear, this meant that little Matilda, just one year old at the time, now held title to Rina and would automatically own all of Rina's future children. Over 165 years later, this is difficult to comprehend.

A probate record and the 1860 federal census provide the last raw data about Fleming slaves. Shortly after George Fleming Jr.'s death in 1851, his son-in-law, Davis Floyd, bought three slaves from his estate, and his daughter, Mary Fleming Floyd, received the other nine as her inheritance. Historical records tell us a great deal about two of these slaves, and that information will be presented later. In 1860 Lewis Fleming was the last surviving member of the family who had once been a Spanish subject. He now owned just two slaves: an elderly man and a girl less than ten years old. This probably was little Rina, because even though Matilda was the owner, her property would have been tallied under her father's name as head of the household. Lewis's eldest son, L. I., now an attorney in Jacksonville, joined the ranks of family slave owners with ten to his name. The family total stood at twelve slaves on the eve of the Civil War and Emancipation.

To understand what is known beyond raw data about the Fleming family as slave owners, one must examine all available historical evidence. The following discussion of that evidence could be interpreted as a rather rosy picture of the Flemings as slave owners, but it is in no way a defense or an apology for their willing participation in the utterly deplorable institution of slavery. Make no mistake—the Fleming family chose to own slaves. Family members could have granted manumission to all their slaves, but they did not. They could have spoken out against the injustice of slavery, but there is no record of any family member ever doing this before Emancipation. To the contrary, Fleming family members supported the secession movement in 1861. Florida's "Declaration of Causes" for secession makes it abundantly clear that the right to own slaves was the core issue of the day.[4] A few enlightened, more highly principled, southerners risked the ire of their neighbors and took a stand against slavery. The Flemings did not.

George Fleming, the Irishman who became a Spanish subject and began the Fleming legacy in Florida, was not born into a slave culture. He may have first experienced slavery during his time in Charleston, South Carolina, but he didn't own slaves at that time. He arrived in St. Augustine as a young man about twenty-two years old, accompanied by a white male servant. George came to understand slavery in a Spanish realm dominated by Catholicism in East Florida. This was an altogether different system of bondage than what is most commonly understood. Historian Daniel Schafer encapsulated Spanish slavery in East Florida with the title of his scholarly article: "A Class of People Neither Freemen Nor Slaves." These men and women were not slaves in the way that most of us have come to understand through American history, nor were they free. Schafer argued that the Spanish instituted a mild and flexible system of slavery and race relations in East Florida.[5] Enslaved persons of African heritage had free time for their own pursuits and many earned wages for their labor. They possessed legal rights, could bring suit in courts against their owners, and sometimes prevailed in those court cases. The entire system was a paradox in that the Spanish believed slavery was an unnatural state of man and encouraged slave owners to grant manumission or permit their slaves to buy freedom, yet they allowed slavery to persist. Spanish treatment of slaves was a source of conflict with the British colonies, and later with the United States, because slaves repeatedly escaped to East Florida for a better way of life, where many were accepted as free men and women. To be sure, East Florida culture was not void of racial prejudice. There clearly existed a caste system in which both free and enslaved persons of color were of lower status than whites. Even within that system, though, a leading scholar on the subject wrote that "acknowledgement of a slave's humanity and rights" significantly impacted Spanish culture and black society.[6] This is the culture in which George Fleming first owned other human beings. It influenced his interactions with both free and enslaved African Americans throughout his life, which in turn impacted the attitudes of his slave-owning children and grandchildren.

George Fleming learned to manage slaves through his association with his father-in-law, F. P. Fatio. Both of these men developed reputations as fair and decent owners. One historian went so far as to call their slaves "pampered."[7] This seems an overstatement, but underscores the fact that bondage under the rule of the extended Fatio-Fleming family was much more bearable than under typical Southern slave masters. The Fatios and Flemings stood as godparents for many of the adult slaves and their children, which established spiritual relationships. Each godparent and godchild pair became *compadres* and expected "trust, confidence, respect, and mutual assistance from the relationship."[8]

The ultimate act of kindness a master could bestow upon a slave was to grant manumission. One historian wrote that the Fleming family apparently had a tradition of granting freedom to their slaves.[9] Sophia Fleming granted the first known act of manumission within the family. On February 8, 1812, she freed an elderly woman named Magdalena for her years of service.[10] Approximately thirty years later Sophia granted freedom to her personal servant, Lucy, who was around seventy years old at the time. Sophia also granted freedom to four children, Adele, Mary, Frank, and George, as well as an eighteen-year-old named Nancy.[11] Lewis Fleming granted freedom to a man named Pompey and made him overseer at Hibernia while he and Margaret lived in Panama Mills, and his brother George once freed a slave.[12] These documented acts of manumission over the course of decades might not be enough to support a "tradition," but census data suggest the possibility that there may have been more. In 1830 more free Negroes lived among the Flemings at Hibernia than anywhere else in Duval, St. Johns, or Nassau counties, which comprised the population center of northeast Florida at the time. The thirteen free Negroes at Hibernia accounted for fifteen percent of the free Negro population in all of Duval County.[13] This set the family distinctly apart from other slave owners at the time. No records reveal how most of these individuals gained their freedom, but we do know about one family among them.

George Fleming once owned a man named David Fleming and his wife, Barbara. Around the year 1820 David Fleming earned enough money on his own time to purchase his freedom. Soon thereafter he negotiated an installment plan to purchase freedom for his wife and children. Between 1824 and 1829 David Fleming paid $500 to the Flemings, and in return his family became free forever. David Fleming later changed his name to David Gray and became the most prosperous Negro in St. Johns County.[14] His grandson, George Gray, was the merchant in Jacksonville who published the eulogy to Frederic Fleming in 1917. Another of David and Barbara Gray's grandchildren, Edward Lycurgas, reported that slaves were inherited from generation to generation within the Fleming family. They never experienced the cruelties suffered by far too many African Americans throughout the South, and the Flemings never considered selling a slave except as punishment or out of economic necessity.[15] Sadly, this seemingly benign statement indicates that it is possible, and even probable, that at one time or another, a member of the Fleming family sold someone's son, daughter, mother, or father. The truth is that we have precious little information about slaves under Fleming ownership. The voices of many other slaves and generations of their descendants remain silent.

The Question of Interracial Children

It was not unusual in Spanish East Florida for a white slave owner to have a child with a Negro woman. In fact, several slave owners had open relationships with African women and "recognized their mulatto children, educated them, and provided for them in their wills."[16] A superficial examination of historical evidence could lead to a conclusion that George Fleming fathered mulatto children, because some East Florida slaves and free Negroes were named Fleming. The shared surname certainly raises eyebrows, but it does not necessarily indicate a genetic relationship. David Fleming (who later changed his name to David Gray) is one example. F. P. Fatio owned a female slave named Felicia who used the Fleming surname for a period of time. She gained her freedom, married a free Negro, and went by the name Felicia Fleming Robio. Her free daughter, Rosa, also used the Fleming surname at various times, even though her father's surname was Espinosa.[17] George and Sophia Fleming had a decades-long association with a free black man known as Scipio Fleming. Scipio's parents were free Negroes employed by F. P. Fatio, who allowed them to cultivate crops on land he owned. In 1803 Miccosukee Indians abducted Scipio's parents, his brother, Moses, and other siblings. Moses eventually escaped and returned to live with Scipio and his wife, who was a slave at New Switzerland. In 1806 Scipio began extended employment with George Fleming and frequently worked at his Hibernia plantation. Three years later Scipio petitioned Governor White for one hundred acres of public land equidistant from Six Mile Creek and Picolata, about five miles south of Fatio's New Switzerland plantation. George Fleming spoke on Scipio's behalf, calling him "a sober boy and of good conduct."[18] Within days Governor White awarded Scipio twenty-five acres known as *Padam Aram*. In the ensuing years Scipio became generally known as Scipio Fleming, but there is no evidence to suggest he was George Fleming's son. Rather it seems he was a trusted associate who probably chose the Fleming surname out of respect for his superior. His relationship with the family many years later was such that Sophia and Lewis Fleming, both testifying under oath, described Scipio as "an excellent character for truth and veracity." Sophia Fleming went so far as to say that "she would place the most implicit confidence in his statements."[19] Shared surnames between slaves or freemen and the white men who ruled over their lives were common throughout the South. All known birth records for Fleming and Fatio slaves show that each of them was given their owner's surname at baptism.[20] There is no evidence suggesting a genetic relationship between these, or any African Americans in Spanish East Florida, and George Fleming.

On the other hand, one published account tells us that Lewis Fleming was the father of an illegitimate mixed-race daughter named Chloe.[21] The author's claim is based on speculation—and he is wrong—but evidence does suggest the possibility that either Lewis or George Jr. was the father of a different mixed-race child. The facts merit a brief discussion, if for no other reason than to draw attention to the life of Dr. Louise Cecilia Fleming, affectionately known as "Lulu" to her friends and family, who may be the most accomplished African American born into slavery in Hibernia. George Jr. owned her parents, David Fleming and Chloe Moses.[22] Upon his death Mary Fleming Floyd, his daughter, inherited both of them. At the time David Fleming was about twelve years old and Chloe Moses was perhaps fourteen. They married on the Floyd plantation in Hibernia on March 1, 1857, and their three children, William, Scipio, and Louise, were born there as slaves.

Sometime after little Louise was born early in 1862, David Fleming escaped Floyd's plantation to join the U.S. Colored Troops and fight for black emancipation. He actually ran off twice. The first time he was captured and returned to Floyd; the second time he never came back.[23] When he enrolled with Company G, 33rd U.S. Colored Troops, at Port Royal, South Carolina, on November 11, 1862, David Fleming was twenty-three years old and five feet, eight inches, tall with light skin and hair that suggest he was a mulatto—part Negro and part Caucasian. His military service was unremarkable. Sadly David Fleming was one of approximately 37,000 U.S. Colored Troops to die of disease during the Civil War. He succumbed to pneumonia on March 13, 1864 at the regimental hospital in Beaufort, South Carolina.[24]

The question is this: How did David Fleming get his last name? We know that he did, in fact, have a white father. William Still, the well-known abolitionist who is often called "The Father of the Underground Railroad," wrote a brief biography of Dr. Louise Fleming during her lifetime. Mr. Still and Dr. Fleming both lived in Philadelphia at the time, and the content of the biography suggests it was based on a personal interview. Mr. Still wrote that Dr. Fleming's mother was "half Congo" and that her father was "half Caucasian."[25] That is all we know. This evidence contradicts the claim that Lewis Fleming was Chloe's father; however, it does suggest the possibility—some might even say probability—that either George or his brother Lewis could have been David Fleming's father, but it is not enough to be sure.

A Jacksonville historian once wrote that there is no evidence to suggest that any member of the Fleming or Fatio family ever had a child with an African American partner.[26] However, historical research continually pushes the boundaries of the past. We now know that F. P. Fatio Jr. fathered a mulatto child with a slave named Isabel, and the mystery of David Fleming's parentage creates intrigue.[27] Many scholars conclude that Southern planters with illegitimate, mixed-race children were commonplace, so we shouldn't be surprised if the Fleming family tree includes descendants of African Americans.[28] To date, though, there is no conclusive evidence.

Regardless of the name of the white man who was her grandfather, Dr. Louise Cecilia Fleming was a remarkable woman. A few years after David Fleming's death, Chloe married Clem Hawkins. They returned to Hibernia with the children soon after the end of the Civil War, where they lived in a house located near the Floyd plantation and the Flemings' home.[29] Louise rose above her beginnings as a little slave girl to attend a normal school in Jacksonville, possibly with the encouragement and financial assistance of Mary Fleming Floyd.[30] She became a school teacher in St. Augustine, then valedictorian of her class at Shaw University in Raleigh, North Carolina. In 1866 she was the first African American woman selected by the Woman's American Baptist Foreign Mission Society to serve in the Congo. Louise served at Palabala Station until poor health forced her to return to the United States. During the next few years she attended the Women's Medical College of Philadelphia, where she graduated as a medical doctor. In 1895 Dr. Louise Fleming returned to the Congo, serving at Irebo and Bolengi, doing all she could both medically and spiritually to assist the native people. In 1899 she contracted African sleeping sickness, a parasitic disease caused by the tsetse fly, and once again was forced to return stateside. Despite the greatest care, she died on June 20, 1899. Dr. Louise Cecilia Fleming was the first African American woman to serve the Baptist Foreign Ministry in the Congo, and she was among the earliest African American women to earn a medical degree.[31] Dr. Fleming died childless, so the only way to prove or disprove a genetic link to the Flemings of Fleming Island would be to locate a direct ancestor of her brothers and conduct a DNA test.

Dr. Louise Cecilia "Lulu" Fleming was born a slave in Hibernia. Her master was David Floyd and his mistress was George Fleming Jr.'s daughter, Mary Sophia Fleming Floyd. *Courtesy of Clay County Archives*

Scott Ritchie

Endnotes

1. Lewis Fleming likely owned slaves in 1840 while living at Panama Mills, but he does not appear in the 1840 Federal Census.

2. Biddle, *Unreturning Tide,* 41.

3. Clay County, Florida, Deed Book H, Deed of Gift, Lewis Fleming to Matilda C. Fleming, October 12, 1850, 321-22. Copy in *MWF Collection.* Italics added for emphasis.

4. Florida Declaration of Causes, State Archives of Florida, Series 577, Carton 1, Folder 6, http://civilwarcauses.org/florida-dec.htm.

5. Daniel L. Schafer, "A Class of People Neither Freemen nor Slaves: From Spanish to American Race Relations in Florida, 1821-1862," *Journal of Social History* 26:3, (1993), 587-609.

6. Jane Landers, *Black Society in Spanish Florida* (Urbana: University of Illinois Press, 1999).

7. Frank Marotti, *The Cana Sanctuary: History, Diplomacy, and Black Catholic Marriage in Antebellum St. Augustine, Florida* (Tuscaloosa: University of Alabama Press, 2012).

8. Landers, *Black Society,* 121-22.

9. Schafer, "A Class of People," 587-609.

10. *Escrituras,* SAHS, 1795-1816, Book 377, 177.

11. Probate Packets, Duval County, Florida, Sophia Fleming, no. 627.

12. Biddle, *Hibernia: The Unreturning* Tide, 32; Schafer, "A Class of People," 587-609.

13. 1830 U. S. Federal Census. At that time Fleming Island was a part of Duval County.

14. Frank Marotti, *Negotiating Freedom in St. Johns County, Florida, 1812-1813,* (PhD diss., University of Hawai'i, 2003), 153, 252, http://www.lib.utexas.edu/. In the years immediately preceding the Civil War David Gray was the wealthiest African American in St. Johns County. Marotti attributed his success to hard work, industrious habits, and positive relationships with the influential Fleming and Fatio families.

15. Pearl Randolf, "Edward Lycurgas," in Federal Writer's Project, *Slave Narratives: A Folk History of Slavery in the United States From Interviews with Former Slaves, Vol. III, Florida Narratives,* The Federal Writer's Project, 1936-1938 (Washington, D.C.: Library of Congress Project, Work Projects Administration, 1941), www.gutenberg.org. The U.S. federal census from 1880 shows that George and Julia Lycurgas lived with Julia's mother, Barbara Gray, and their children in St. Johns County, Florida.

16. Marotti, *Cana Sanctuary,* 142-43.

17. Marotti, "Negotiating Freedom," 216.

18. Scipio (A Free Black) 25 Acres Confirmed Claim, Florida Memory Project, http://www.floridamemory.com/Collections/SpanishLandGrants/.

19. Scipio Fleming Patriot War Claim. This file also contains a translation of documents pertaining to Scipio Fleming's petition to Governor Enrique White for his land at Padam Aram.

20. Roman Catholic Parish of St. Augustine, Black Baptisms, Books I–III, St. Augustine Historical Society.

21. T. D. Allman, *Finding Florida* (Atlantic Monthly Press, 2013), 301.

22. This is not the same David Fleming who purchased his freedom from George Fleming in 1820.

23. Chloe Fleming Hawkins' Claim for a Widow's Pension, NARA, Washington, D.C., case No. 237, 637, can No. 373, bundle No. 11. The facts of Louise's parentage, her birthdate, and her father's escape from the Floyd Plantation were given under oath in her claim for a pension based on her husband's service with the U.S. Colored Troops during the Civil War.

24. David Fleming, *Compiled Military Service Records of Volunteer Union Soldiers Who Served with the United States Colored Troops: Infantry Organization, 31st through 35th,* National Archives and Records Administration, Microfilm publication M1992, Muster Rolls/Company Records, 33 UCST, Co. G., Washington, D.C., 2005.

25. William Still, "Miss Lulu C. Fleming," in L. A. Scruggs, ed., *Women of Distinction: Remarkable in Works and Invincible in Character* (Raleigh: L. A. Scruggs, Publisher, 1893).

26. Dena Snodgrass Notes, *MWF Collection.*

27. SAHS, Roman Catholic Parish of St. Augustine, Black Baptisms–Book II, 1793-1807. Maria Francisca Fatio was born in 1795 or 1796 and baptized on January 14, 1798, by Father Crosby. The father is listed as "Francisco Fatio of London." The mother, Isabel, is listed as property of "F. P. Fatio" (without reference to London) which seems to distinguish between the two Fatio men. F. P. Fatio Sr. was born and raised in Switzerland. F. P. Fatio Jr. was born in Switzerland, as well, but his family moved to London when he was a baby. He was about thirty-five years old and unmarried at the time of this child's birth.

28. Karen A. Getman, "Sexual Control in the Slaveholding South: The Implementation and Maintenance of a Racial Caste System," *Harvard Women's Law Journal*, vol. 7 (1984).

29. *1870 United States Federal Census* (Provo: www.ancestry.com).

30. Joseph R. Moss, "The Missionary Journey of Louise 'Lulu' Fleming, M.D.," (1996). An unpublished address given to the Florida Baptist Historical Society, May 4, 1996. This source indicates that "the former slave owner's wife" assisted Lulu's education.

Scott Ritchie

31. Larry Eugene Rivers, "Louise Cecilia Fleming," in Larry Eugene Rivers and Canter Brown Jr., eds., *The Varieties of Women's Experiences: Portraits of Southern Women In The Post-Civil War Century* (Gainesville: University of Florida Press, 2010).

The Last Years of the Hibernia Winter Resort

After Frederic Fleming's death in 1917, his wife, Margaret Baldwin Fleming, married longtime guest and Hibernia Golf Club greenskeeper, Reginald Woolston. Mr. Woolston had a drinking problem and became an embarrassment to the business, so after Margaret died in 1921, the family essentially evicted him from Hibernia.[1] By that time three of the Fleming children had moved away. Margaret Seton "Peg" Fleming married Henry Canby Biddle, whose ancestors first visited Hibernia back in 1868. She and her husband lived in Riverton, New Jersey. Dorothy "Dorrit" Fleming married Lawrence Austin, a businessman she met during his first visit to Hibernia. Mr. and Mrs. Austin lived in Hartford, Connecticut. Frederic "Fritz" Fleming Jr. served the U.S. Army as a communications officer for the Wildcat Division in World War I, earned his law degree at the University of Denver, and worked as a land agent in Denver, where he met his future wife, Lillian Giddings Wilkin. Augusta "Honey" Fleming left home briefly to serve as an ambulance driver in New York during World War I. After the war she was the only member of the family who remained a full-time resident of Hibernia. Augusta Fleming operated the Hibernia Winter Resort for almost twenty years, though at various times all members of the extended Fleming family helped with one aspect or another of the business. The guestbook during Augusta's time as proprietress shows regular visits by her siblings, their families, and their extended families. Among the other guests who visited Hibernia during the twentieth century were American stained glass master, D. Maitland Armstrong; silent film star, Alice Brady; pioneering author of American scientific detective stories, William MacHarg; and celebrated author, E. B. White, whose stepson, Roger Angell, a regular contributor to the *New Yorker* best known for his stories about baseball, visited Hibernia as a child. The guestbooks for the years 1909 to 1940 identify nearly two thousand visitors, including academicians, businessmen, writers, artists, and socialites from over twenty states and at least three countries.[2]

Scott Ritchie

The Hibernia Winter Resort closed after the 1939–40 season, chiefly because Augusta Fleming married longtime guest Louis Reineman and no longer had the financial need or the desire to run the business. Shortly thereafter the four Fleming siblings dissolved Hibernia, Inc., and divided the property. Dorothy and Augusta shared all of Fanny Brown's former property, where Augusta and her husband built their home. Frederic Fleming Jr. and his sister Margaret became owners of the "Old Place." This included the Big House, the Big Cottage, Palm Cottage, and Holly Cottage.

By now Frederic Fleming had married Lillian Giddings Wilkin and was a businessman in Houston. He purchased his sister's share of the property and became sole owner of the heart of Hibernia. It seems Frederic inherited the mantle of "Stick to the Old Place." His greatest wish in life was to return to Florida, update the family home for modern times, and reopen the family business. While studying that possibility he settled on a temporary measure. In 1942 Mr. Fleming entered into a summer lease agreement with the Protestant Episcopal Church in the Diocese of Florida, allowing the diocese to use all of the Old Place as its retreat, Camp Weed.[3] He later negotiated a long-term lease with the diocese that extended through January of 1946. During those years diocesan clergy and personnel used Holly Cottage for their accommodations and business operations.[4]

Tragically, Frederic Fleming Jr. was killed in an automobile accident outside of Green Cove Springs on December 17, 1945. Any dream of resurrecting the Hibernia Winter Resort died with him. He left all of his Hibernia property to his wife, Lillian Wilkin Fleming. Mrs. Fleming found a tenant, Allen Scarbrough, who lived rent-free in Holly Cottage for several years with no electricity, no kitchen, and no heat in return for providing minimal services to maintain the entire property. After consultations with her in-laws, Mrs. Fleming decided to sell the old family home, but her terms of sale made it clear that she would not sell Holly Cottage. In April 1950 a devastating fire swept through Hibernia threatening every building on the property, including St. Margaret's Episcopal Church. Thanks to the combined efforts of many neighbors, the Green Cove Springs Fire Department, and the U.S. Naval Fire Squad, most buildings escaped with little or no damage. However, a few outbuildings were destroyed and the Palm Cottage was lost forever.[5] On May 14, 1955, Mrs. Fleming finally sold the Big House, the Big Cottage, the swimming pool, associated outbuildings, and six hundred feet of St. Johns riverfront property to Mr. and Mrs. Ralph Gibson. The Gibsons expressed a desire to renovate and remodel the

Big Cottage or the Big House and make it their home. Years of neglect and termites had done too much damage, though, so the Gibsons demolished both buildings. Fortunately, they salvaged many of the original building materials and incorporated them in the construction of a new home on the property.

Today Holly Cottage and St. Margaret's Episcopal Chapel are all that remain from nineteenth-century Hibernia.[6] Both are listed on the National Register of Historic Places. Holly Cottage is a private residence still owned by members of the Fleming family. St. Margaret's Episcopal Church thrived for many years, in part because of a land donation to the Episcopal Diocese by Frederic Fleming Jr.'s widow, and another land donation years later by his daughter, Marian Wilkin Fleming. St. Margaret's Episcopal Church eventually included an excellent preschool created by her daughter, Margot Fleming Ritchie, who is one of George Fleming's great-great-great-granddaughters.

Sadly, church attendance dwindled after the construction of a large, new worship space. Officers in the Episcopal Diocese of Florida and longtime members of St. Margaret's Church could not agree on issues related to leadership and church management, and after one hundred thirty-four years the Diocese shuttered its ministry at St. Margaret's and closed the doors to the school. Thankfully, the Episcopal Diocese continues to care for the historic chapel and cemetery.

Margaret Seton Fleming Biddle wrote her book, *Hibernia, The Unreturning Tide,* in 1947 as a tribute to her ancestral home and to preserve family memories of days gone by. She chose the title well because the Hibernia she knew as a young woman is, indeed, gone forever. Once there stood a long wharf to welcome steamers carrying guests and supplies to the magnificent antebellum home that dominated a bluff along the St. Johns River. Now only a few jagged old pilings mark that spot, and many large homes line the deeply wooded riverbank. U.S. Highway 17 has replaced the St. Johns River as the main route to Fleming Island, where six lanes hum with traffic throughout the day and cars whiz along at speeds unimaginable when Hibernia was an idyllic winter escape for northerners. Fleming Island is home to shopping centers, restaurants, big box stores, and nearly thirty thousand residents. Despite the development, it is also home to bald eagles, ospreys, turkeys, pileated woodpeckers, red-shouldered hawks, deer, and even a few remaining gopher tortoises. Manatees and alligators still thrive in the wide St. Johns River.

To get a sense of what Hibernia once was, you must visit St. Margaret's—the beautiful carpenter gothic chapel on Old Church Road on Fleming Island. Park the car and take a walk through the cemetery. You will see the resting places of five generations of the Fleming family, many generations of African American families who made their lives in Hibernia, and quite a number of winter guests who chose to make Hibernia their final stop. At the back of the cemetery you will see dozens of unmarked graves. There are no burial records for these gravesites, but oral traditions tell us these are the final resting places of Fleming slaves. Sit quietly for a while and take in the sights, the scents, the sounds, and the *feel* of this sacred ground. Take a walk down Old Church Road and look toward the river, but respect private property. This is Hibernia—the Old Place where the Flemings of Fleming Island staked their claim more than two hundred years ago, and where a few descendants of George Fleming, the Irishman who came to Florida in 1783, still live today.

Endnotes

1. Samantha Bryant interview, *MWF Collection*.

2. *MWF Collection*, Hibernia Guestbooks for years 1909–1940.

3. Ibid., Lease agreement between Frederic A. Fleming and the Episcopal Diocese of Florida, May 11, 1942.

4. Ibid., Bishop Frank Juhan to Frederic A. Fleming, December 1, 1944.

5. Ibid., Allen Scarbrough to Lillian W. Fleming, April 14, 1950.

6. The old clubhouse from Hibernia Golf Club still stands, but not on Fleming Island. In 1976 a preservation-minded Orange Park resident, Frica Massee, purchased the dilapidated clubhouse and moved it to Club Continental, where it is now a popular riverfront club.

Appendices

Appendix I: George Fleming's Patriot War Claim with Awards

George Fleming's Original Claim in 1817

burning of fences, orange grove, Houses, etc	$1,000.00
six cotton gins with a quantity of cotton destroyed	$250.00
one hundred head of cattle and a number of hogs, etc	$1,200.00
tools and a set of kitchen utensils	$50.00
provision, poultry etc	$150.00
two young mares stolen by the bandetti from Georgia	$100.00
a number of squared pine logs destroyed at Roses Bluff	$800.00
Loss caused by the invasion of the American troops which prevented my fulfilling my contract with Hibberson & Yonge for some cargoes of pine timber	$3,000.00
four yoke of oxen taken from Roses Bluff in 1812	$160.00
carts, lumber, chains, yokes etc, etc	$100.00
a four oared canoe complete	$80.00
a large flat chains, etc	$120.00
three working horses	$240.00
saddles, bridles, trace	$50.00
axes and tolls of different kinds: grindstone, camp utensils, provisions, etc	$200.00
Loss of a valuable negro by the insurrection	$600.00
Maintainance [sic] clothing etc for 30 negroes for one year in St. Augustine with the loss of their labor when the province was invaded in 1812 & this garrison besieged buy U.S. troops commanded by Col. Smith	$1,520.00

Scott Ritchie

Total of George Fleming's Claim	**$9,620.00**
Totals indicated on the Claim itself are	**$9,680.00**

Lewis Fleming's Amended Claim in 1834

burning of dwelling & negro houses	$1,000.00
destruction of orange grove	$1,250.00
burning of fences etc	$1,000.00
six cotton gins	$300.00
cotton crop for 1812	$2,500.00
cotton crop for 1813	$2,500.00
one hundred head prime stock cattle	$1,200.00
fifty head of large hogs	$300.00
provision crop of 1812	$500.00
provision crop of 1813	$500.00
two young mares stolen by the bandetti from Georgia	$1,100.00
1000 feet of pine timber at $.12	$1,200.00
120 cord of lath wood $.50	$600.00
[illegible] & other miscellaneous timbering not recollected	$1,200.00
four yoke of oxen taken from Roses Bluff in 1812	$300.00
poultry etc	$100.00
[illegible] & clothing 30 negroes during the invasion of 1812, when the post of St. Augustine was besieged by American troops under Col. Smith and corn was at $4 per bushel	$1,500.00
carts, lumber, chains, yokes, etc	$100.00
on large flat & chain	$120.00
three working horses	$240.00
three saddles, bridles & harnesses, etc	$150.00
axes & tool of different kinds: grindstone, camp furniture, etc	$250.00
Loss of valuable negro (a sawyer) by the insurrection	$600.00
Total of Lewis Fleming's Claim	**$18,510.00**
Totals indicated on the Claim itself are	**$17,650.00**

Awarded By Judge Robert Raymond Reid

dwelling house & other houses	$600.00
the orange grove	$200.00
the fences	$200.00
cotton crop of 1812	$2,000.00
provision crop	$300.00
crop of 1813	$1,534.00
cattle (100 at $8)	$800.00
hogs (20 at $3)	$60.00
lumber loss	$500.00
oxen (2 yoke)	$100.00
poultry	$25.00
cart chains etc	$60.00
	$6,379.00

Revised by United States Treasury Secretary J. C. Spencer in 1843

Judge Reid's award	$6,329.00
Deduct cops losses	$3,434.00
Revised Award	$2,895.00

Awarded by United States Treasury Secretary George Bibb in 1844

$6,379.00

Scott Ritchie

Source: NARA, Patriot War Claim of George Fleming, RG 217, Entry 347, Box 1390, Washington, D.C.

Note: These figures are exactly reproduced from documents in the referenced Claim. I cannot explain the discrepancies between the totals indicated on the Claims of George and Lewis Fleming with the actual totals.

Appendix II: Sophia Fleming's Assets at the Time of Her Death

Slaves / Age	Value
*Lucy-75	none
Abby-65	$75.00
Sukey-60	$150.00
Phyllis-42	$300.00
Georgianna-18	$400.00
*Nancy-18 (sick at the time)	$300.00
*Addel-4	$200.00
*Frank-2	$150.00
*Mary-1	$100.00
*George-8	$300.00

Other Property

1 bureau	$6.00
12 cane bottom chairs, 2 broke	$10.00
2 chairs	$1.00
2 leaf tables	$6.00
1 rocking chair	$1.50
1 fender	$1.50
1 clock	$5.00
1 couch and cushions	$3.00
6 German silver tea spoons	$3.50
1 fish knife, 1 fruit basket, 2 stands	$3.00
5 9/16 lbs. old silver ware	$89.00
2 glass lamps and 2 glass candlesticks	$1.00

Scott Ritchie

[illegible] glass objects	$5.00
[illegible]	$2.00
5 pots and kettles, one waffle iron	$5.00
1 lot old knives and forks	$0.50
2 brass candlesticks	$0.50
1 steel corn mill	$1.00
1 feather bed	$10.00
9 feather pillows	$6.75
4 moss mattresses	$8.00
6 blankets	$8.00
3 quilts	$4.00
5 pairs sheets	$5.00
5 pairs pillow cases	$1.50
12 towels	$1.50
1 pine bed sted	$1.50
1 cot	$0.50
1 old chest of drawers	$2.00
1 wash stand	$1.50
2 pitchers and basins	$1.00
2 old carpets	$3.00
8 window curtains	$0.50
2 old tables	$1.00
12 towels	$1.50
1 pine bed sted	$1.50
1 cot	$0.50
1 old chest of drawers	$2.00
1 wash stand	$1.50
2 pitchers and basins	$1.00
2 old carpets	$3.00
8 window curtains	$0.50
2 old tables	$1.00
Total Slaves and Other Property	**$3170.25**

Real Estate

Half the value of house and lot in Jacksonville	$250.00
Hibernia - 360 acres	none given
Remaining Nassau River Acreage	none given
Grand Total	**$3420.25**

*Prior to her death, Sophia granted manumission to these slaves. Her estate appraisers, Isiah Hart and Oliver Wood, apparently did not know that at the time of their accounting and included them as her property. Source: Sophia Fleming Probate Record 627, Duval County, Jacksonville, Florida.

Appendix III: George Fleming Jr.'s Assets at the Time of His Death

Slaves	Gender	Value
George	man	$600.00
Scippio	man	$600.00
Mary	woman	$350.00
Louisa	woman	$500.00
Elsy	woman	$500.00
Matilda	woman	$500.00
Chloey*	girl	$350.00
Emma	girl	$250.00
Diana	girl	$250.00
John	boy	$200.00
Davy*	boy	$400.00
Charles	boy	$100.00
Total		**$4,600.00**

Personal Property

one boat and oars	$75.00
one cart	$15.00
one double barrel gun	$15.00
about 500 weight sugar	$30.00
two saddles	$12.00
about 100 pounds coffee	$12.00

about 20 bushels of corn	$20.00
one corn sheller	$3.00
one thermometer	$1.00
39 head stock cattle @ $4 each	$156.00
one sorrel mare	$75.00
one bay mare colt	$25.00
one yoke oxen	$35.00
six head hogs @ $1 each	$6.00
one cotton gin	$35.00
one gin band (old)	$6.00
one spinning wheel	$2.00
one cross cut saw	$3.00
one plough	$1.50
two hoes (old) @ 25¢ each	$0.50
one iron wedge	$0.50
one cart	$10.00
150 lbs. fodder	$1.50
20 bushels peas in hull @ 6¢ each	$1.20
one ox yoke	$2.00
one lead chain	$1.50
assorted tools, etc	$18.50
Total	**$563.20**

*These are Chloe Moses and David Fleming, who later married and became the parents of Dr. Louise Cecilia Fleming.

Source: George Fleming Jr. Probate Record 911, Duval Country, Jacksonville, Florida.

Appendix IV: Margaret Seton Fleming's Assets at the Time Of Her Death

The Big Cottage

8 double sets furniture @ $25	$200.00
4 single sets furniture @ $10	$40.00
8 sets of toilet ware @$4	total omitted
14 window shades	$2.80
6 moss mattresses @ $15	$90.00
1 hair mattress, double	$15.00
16 feather pillows @ 40¢	$6.40
8 pieces oil cloth @ 30¢	$5.00
7 bolsters @ 25¢	$2.40
7 sets fire irons @ $2	$14.00
1 set brass & fender	$6.00

The Big House

Garrett

2 cots @ $2	$4.00
2 mattresses @ $1	$2.00
2 bolsters @ 20¢	$0.40
1 beaureau	$1.00
washstand, pitcher, bowl, etc	$0.75
2 chairs	$0.50
set furniture bedstead, beaureau table, washstand, mattress, etc	$6.00

3rd Story

Room No. 1

Set furniture, fire set, table, washstand, bowl, pitcher,
  soap dish, two shades $20.00

Room No. 2

Bedstead, cot, beaureau, washstand bolster, pitcher, bucket,
  table, chair chair towel rack, fire set, mattress $15.00

Room No. 3

bedstead, spring, washstand, bowl, pitcher, 2 foot tubs, table,
  mattress, pillow, bolster, fire set $8.00

Room No. 4

bedsted, beaureau, table, washstand,mattress, pillow, bolster $8.00

Room No. 5

bedsted, spring, beaureau, washstand, set table, chair,
  mattress, pillows $8.00

Room No. 6

double bedstead, springs, beaureau, table stand, 2 rockers,
  2 plain chairs, mattress pillows, bolster $20.00

Room No. 7

bedstead, beaureau, table, chairs, washstand, bowl, pitcher,
  fire set, mattress, bolster, pillows $15.00

Room No. 8

vacant

Fred's Cottage

beaureau, washstand, etc $5.00

Room No. 2

bedrooms set furniture $15.00

Implements

1 ox wagon	$40.00
1 oxen cart	$10.00

Stock

7 head of cattle	$52.50
1 horse	$50.00

2nd Story

Room No. 1

Sette on porch set furniture complete	$12.00

Room No. 2

Set furniture complete	$12.00

Room No. 3

Set furniture complete	$8.00

Room No. 4

set furniture, fire set, bolsters, pillows	$15.00

Room No. 5

set furniture, mattress, pillows	$20.00

Room No. 6

set furniture walnut	$75.00

Room No. 7

folding couch, hair mattress, cot, 2 centre tables, 2 marble tops, stands, 1 folding walnut table, lamps, stands, 4 cane chairs, rocking walnut chair, 1 cane rocker, 1 folding 1 camp chair, toilet set, fire set of brass, 1 book rack, 1 fancy walnut water cooler $200.00

Room No. 8

set furniture, cot, mattress	$30.00

Scott Ritchie

Room No. 9

sofa lounge, 2 beaureaus, bedstead & spring, 2 washstands, 2 tables, toilet set, fire set, 3 chairs, rocker, 2 bolsters, 3 pillows, matting, slop tub, bucket	$60.00
bedstead, cot, 2 beaureaus, 2 washstands sets, 2 tables, 2 chairs, 2 mattresses, 4 pillows, stove & matting	$22.50

Ground Floor

Room No. 1

washstand, mattress, etc	$4.00

Room No. 2

2 beaureaus, springs, bedstead, washstand, etc	$12.00

Room No. 3

41 prs blankets @ $4	$164.00
5 comforts @ $1	$5.00
5 mattresses @ $4	$20.00
3 pillows @ 40¢	$1.20
30 carpets	$150.00
3 chairs @ 50¢	$1.50
1 rocker	$0.50
mattress, bolster, pillows	$3.00
2 lamps	$3.00
1 set fire irons	$1.50
1 bath tub & cloth rack	$0.60

Room No. 4

set furniture, spring, mattress, pillows	$25.00

Room No. 5

bedstead, mattress, beaureau, table, washstand, bowl, pitcher, 2 chairs, rocker, pillows, bolsters, looking glass	$20.00

Parlor

2 res sofas	$10.00
1 old style sofa	$5.00
2 res lounges	$10.00
2 marble top tables	$20.00
1 centre table	$2.00
7 chairs @ 50∞	$3.50
1 rocking chair	$0.75
6 pictures	$10.00
chandeliers	$10.00
cornice & curtains	$3.00
brass fender & irons	$5.00
wall brackets	$1.00
piano	$120.00

Linen

100 towels	$10.00
100 pillow cases	$5.00
100 sheets	$15.00
8 table cloths	$24.00
50 bed spreads	$50.00

Mrs. Fleming's Room

writing desk	$15.00
bedstead walnut	$10.00
mattress & Spring	$5.00
2 pillows	$0.80
1 bolster	$0.50
1 old ottoman	$1.00
1 beaureau	$3.00
1 small table	$4.00
2 rockers	$1.50
4 chairs	$2.00

Scott Ritchie

1 fancy clock	$10.00
2 fire sets	$2.00
1 toilet set	$0.75
1 wash stand	$0.25
1 students lamp	$2.00

Dining Room

36 dining chairs @ 50¢	$18.00
2 extension table $15	$30.00
1 old extension table	$3.00
1 side boardt	$15.00
1 water stand	$0.50
1 common clock	$1.50
8 lamps	$4.00
1 wire safe [for food storage]	$5.00
1 bell	$1.00
1 picture	$1.00

Pantry

lot of old articles	$5.00
china ware	$30.00

Kitchen

2 stoves & utensils	$50.00

Silver Ware

Punch Bowl*	$200.00
set spoons, cream, pots, etc	$30.00

Plated Ware

3 casters, 3 cake baskets, 5 doz. knives, 5 doz. forks, 3 doz. table spoons, 5 doz. tea spoons	$75.00

Back Parlor

bedstead, washstand, beaureau, table, lounge rocker, chamber set, fire set	$15.00

*This is a silver bowl that was known in the family as the "Seton Bowl." It is now on display at the Fine Arts Museums of San Francisco, Legion of Honor. A picture is available at https://art.famsf.org/hugh-wishart/punch-bowl-197946.

Source: Margaret Fleming Probate Record, Clay County Archives

Appendix V: George Fleming's Slaves

On March 2, 1800, F. P. Fatio gave George Fleming the following slaves as a part of his wife's dowry. Their collection value at the time was $4000. Fleming also received slaves named Susannah, Jack, Simeon, all considered of no value.

Madalena	David	Lukey	Esther
Lucy	Lancaster	Jacob	Will
Peggy	Manuel	Phillis	Mary

One of George Fleming's earliest documented slaves, Felicia, gave birth to a son, Marcelino Fleming, on October 8, 1800. He died and was buried four days later. The father was a mulatto named Marcelino who was the property of Sebastian Espinosa. Another Fleming slave named Margarita gave birth to a son, Enrique McQueen, in February 1802. The father, Harry, belonged to Juan McQueen. Enrique lived just six months. He was buried on August 24, 1802. The owner of the mother was the de facto owner of the child in East Florida.

In 1816 Fleming's friend, William Lawrence, conducted an inventory of his slaves that includes only their first name and age. No doubt some of these men and women had children, but they are not included in the inventory.

Davy (29)	Will (35)	Jacobo (60)	Simon (44)	Manuel (18)
Dick (40)	Charles (20)	Peter (19)	James Mason (21)	Hercules (18)
Friday (19)	Ned (40)	Joe (38)	Alick (31)	Lewey (33)
George (29)	Juba (63)	Tony (40)	Philip (31)	Elsy (26)
Madalena (45)	Suky (23)	Georgiana (16)	Peggy (35)	Mary China (18)
Molly (37)	Pamella (32)	Mary Ann (26)	Sofia (17)	Mirtilla (34)
Rose (40)	Abagail (26)	Hannah (25)		

Over the years "the Indian Nation" spirited away many Fleming and Fatio slaves. During the settlement of F. P. Fatio's estate, the family recovered more than thirty-five of these people, and in 1820 they were divided among the heirs. George Fleming received the following individuals (their values in parentheses) on behalf of his wife, Sophia Fatio Fleming:

Frank	($350)
Prince	($200)
Abby	($400)
Susan	($50)
Judy	($250)
Lucy	($250)
Moses	($250)

Sources: L'Engle, *A Collection of Letters*, 1:194-195; SAHS, Roman Catholic Parish of St. Augustine, Black Baptisms–Book II, 1793-1807; George Fleming's *Langley Bryan* Spanish Land Grant, Florida Memory Project.

Appendix VI: Fleming Family Slave Ownership from U.S. Federal Census Data

See illustration next page.

Note that in 1830 and 1840 the Federal Slave Census included the numbers of free Negroes who lived under a white man or woman's sponsorship. The Federal Censuses of 1850 and 1860 did not include free Negroes.

Fleming Slave Ownership from U.S. Federal Slave Census Data

1830 and 1840

Year	Sex	Age	Sophia Fleming (Free)	Sophia Fleming (Slaves)	George Fleming Jr. (Slaves)	Mary J. Fleming (Free)	Mary J. Fleming (Slaves)
1830	female	55-99		1			
1830	female	36-54		2			
1830	female	24-35	4	1	1		
1830	female	10-23	1	6	1		
1830	female	less than 10	5	7	3		
1830	male	55-99	1	2			
1830	male	36-54		2	1		
1830	male	24-35		2			
1830	male	10-23		3	2		
1830	male	less than 10	2	4	2		
1840	female	55-99	1	1			2
1840	female	36-54		1		1	
1840	female	24-35		1	1		1
1840	female	10-23		4	2		3
1840	female	less than 10		1	3	2	2
1840	male	55-99					
1840	male	36-54					
1840	male	24-35			3		
1840	male	10-23			2	1	1
1840	male	less than 10		1	1	2	1

1850 and 1860

Year	Sex	Age	Lewis Fleming (Slaves)	George Fleming Jr. (Slaves)	George C. Fleming	L. I. Fleming (Slaves)
1850	female	55-99				
1850	female	36-54	2	1		
1850	female	24-35		1		
1850	female	10-23	1	3		
1850	female	less than 10	2	3		
1850	male	55-99	1			
1850	male	36-54	1			
1850	male	24-35	1	2		
1850	male	10-23	1	2		
1850	male	less than 10				
1860	female	55-99				
1860	female	36-54				1
1860	female	24-35				2
1860	female	10-23				3
1860	female	less than 10	1			2
1860	male	55-99	1			
1860	male	36-54				
1860	male	24-35				
1860	male	10-23				
1860	male	less than 10				2

Bibiliography

Collections

Florida Historical Society:
    Francis P. Fleming Papers 1694–1912

Florida Memory Project (FMP):
    An archive of documents related to Spanish Land Grants from the Second Spanish Period, 1784–1821, is available online. Land grants are cited by the name of the claimant on the particular property claimed. Unless otherwise noted, all references to Spanish Land Grants from the Florida Memory Project were accessed at www.floridamemory.com/Collections/SpanishLandGrants.

Library of Congress:
    The East Florida Papers (EFP): Cited as *EFP*, reel/section, date. Some documents did not include a section number. Those are referenced by reel number only. Other documents without a section number sometimes include an item number. Dorman, Orloff M. *Memoranda of Events That Transpired at Jacksonville, Florida.* Library of Congress, Manuscript Division, MMC-1884.

Marian Wilkin Fleming Collection (MWF):
    This is a collection of Fleming family documents and photographs preserved by Marian Wilkin Fleming, who is one of George Fleming's second great- granddaughters. It includes extensive notes compiled by Jacksonville historian Dena Snodgrass. The collection is in the possession of the author.

National Archives and Records Administration (NARA):
    Record Group 217, Settled Miscellaneous Treasury Accounts, 9/6/1790–9/29/1894, Office of the First Auditor, Records of the Accounting Officers of the Department of the Treasury. These accounts

include the Patriot War Claims of East Florida residents that resulted from the Florida invasion by combined U.S. and "Patriot" troops from 1812 until 1813. The following claims are of particular importance and are referenced by each parenthetical abbreviation:

George Fleming, Account 89454, RG 217, Entry 347 (Fleming, Patriot War Claim)

Francis P. Fatio Sr., Account 76445, RG 217, Entry 347 (Fatio, Sr., Patriot War Claim)

Francis P. Fatio Jr., Account 89602, RG 217, Entry 347 (Fatio, Jr., Patriot War Claim)

Scipio Fleming, Account 99008, RG 217, Entry 347 (Scipio Fleming Patriot War Claim)

State Claims Relating to the Florida Indian Wars, Record Group 217, Entry 756, is a collection of nineteen file boxes, most of them full of documents ranging in date from as early as the 1830s through the 1850s.

Compiled Service Records of Confederate Soldiers Who Served in Organizations from the State of Florida. NARA, RG 360, M251. Records of Chs. Seton Fleming, F. P. Fleming, Fred Fleming, L. I. Fleming, and William H. Fleming.

Compiled Military Service Records of Volunteer Union Soldiers Who Served with the United States Colored Troops: Infantry Organization, 31st through 35th. National Archives and Records Administration, Microfilm publication M1992, Muster Rolls/Company Records, 33 UCST, Co. G., Washington, DC, 2005. Record of David Fleming.

Chloe Fleming Hawkins' Claim for a Widow's Pension, NARA, Washington, D.C., case no. 237,637, can no. 373, bundle no. 11.

Notre Dame University Archives:
The letters of Mrs. Christine Nostrond Tiers, who visited Hibernia during the 1856–1857 winter season.

Lurana Crowley Austin Collection (LCA Collection):
Mrs. Rainey Austin is the widow of George Fleming's second great-grandson, Lawrence Austin. Her privately held collection includes several family photo albums, copies of deeds, and a few family letters.

St. Augustine Historical Society Research Library (SAHS):
East Florida Papers, Transcriptions of *Escrituras*

St. Johns County, Florida: Civil Cases

Roman Catholic Parish of St. Augustine, Black Baptisms, Book 2, 1793–1807

Roman Catholic Records of St. Augustine Parish, White Baptisms, Register Books 2 and 3

South Carolina Department of Archives and History

University of Florida Digital Collections:
Florida Digital Newspaper Library (FDNL)

Florida Department of Military Affairs, Special Archives Publication no. 69, vol. 5, Florida Militia Muster Rolls, Seminole Indian Wars

University of Florida, Smathers Libraries:
Francis P. Fleming Papers, MS 243

Dena Snodgrass Collection, MS 156

Mahon, John. "The First Battle of the Second Seminole War, Black Point, 18 December 1835." John K. Mahon Papers

University of North Florida:
Fleming Family Letters, Collection M02-3

Books

Acts and Resolutions Adopted By the Legislature of Florida at its Extra Session, Under the Constitution of A.D. 1885, The. Tallahassee, FL: N. M. Bowen, Printer, 1889.

Adams, Charles S., ed. Report of the Jacksonville Auxiliary Sanitation Association of Jacksonville, Florida. Covering the work of the Association during the Yellow Fever Epidemic, 1888. Jacksonville, FL: Times-Union Print, 1889.

Alexander, E. P., and Gary W. Gallagher, eds. *Fighting for the Confederacy: The Personal Recollections of General Edward Porter Alexander.* Chapel Hill: University of North Carolina Press, 1989.

Allman, T. D. *Finding Florida.* Atlantic Monthly Press, 2013.

Bennett, Charles E. *Florida's "French" Revolution, 1793–1795.* Gainesville: University Presses of Florida, 1981.

Bicheno, Hugh. *Gettysburg.* London: Cassell, 2001.

Biddle, Margaret Seton Fleming. *Hibernia: The Unreturning Tide.* New York: Vantage Press, 1971.

Scott Ritchie

Blakey, Arch Frederic, Ann Smith Lainhart, and Winston Bryant Stephens Jr. *Rose Cottage Chronicles: Civil War Letters of the Bryant-Stephens Families of North Florida.* Gainesville: University Press of Florida, 1998.

Carter, Clarence Edwin, ed. *The Territory of Florida, 1821–1824. Vol. 22 of Territorial Paper of the United States.* Washington, D.C.: USGPO, 1956.

Catalogue of the Alumni of the Medical Department of the University of Pennsylvania 1765–1877. Published by the Society of the Alumni of the Medical Department. Philadelphia: Collins, Printer, 1877.

Chase, George Wingate. *The History of Haverhill, Massachusetts, From Its First Settlement in 1640 Through the Year 1860.* Published by the author, 1861.

Congressional Globe, The. *New Series: Containing Sketches of the Debates and Proceedings of the First Session of the Twenty-Ninth Congress.* City of Washington: Blair and Rives, 1846.

Cusick, James G. *The Other War of 1812: The Patriot War and the American Invasion of Spanish East Florida.* Athens: University of Georgia Press, 2007.

Daniel, R. P. "Report on Yellow Fever in Jacksonville, Fla. in 1877." *Proceedings of the Florida Medical Association, Session of 1878.* Jacksonville, FL. MWF.

Davis, T. Frederick. *History of Early Jacksonville Florida.* Jacksonville, FL: H. & W. B. Drew, 1911.

———. *History of Jacksonville and Vicinity 1513 to 1924.* A Facsimile Reproduction of the 1925 Edition. Gainesville: University of Florida Press, 1964.

Denham, James M., and Keith L. Huneycutt, eds. *Echoes from a Distant Frontier: The Brown Sisters' Correspondence from Antebellum Florida.* Columbia: University of South Carolina Press, 2004.

Dodd, Jordan. *Early Georgia Marriage Index 1786–1850.* www.ancestry. com.

Duval, John P. *Compilation of the Public Acts of the Legislative Council of the Territory of Florida, passed prior to 1840.* Tallahassee, FL: Samuel S. Sibley, Printer, 1839.

Eicher, David J. *The Longest Night: A Military History of the Civil War.* New York: Simon & Schuster, 2001.

Evidence Taken by the Authority of the Honorable, the Secretary of the Treasury, Under a Report of the Committee of Claims, and a Resolution Concurred in by the House of Representatives of the United States of

America, In the Case of Indemnity of Charles F. Sibbald, of Philadelphia. Philadelphia: John Richards, 1837.

Fleming, Francis P. *Memoir of Capt. C. Seton Fleming, of the Second Florida Infantry, C.S.A.* Jacksonville, FL: Times-Union Publishing House, 1881.

Fleming, Margaret Baldwin. *An Emerald Isle.* New York: Broadway Publishing. Privately published, n.d.

Forbes, James Grant. *Sketches, Historical and Topographical, of the Floridas; More Particularly of East Florida.* New York: C. S. Van Winkle, 1821.

Furgurson, Ernest B. *Not War But Murder: Cold Harbor 1864.* New York: Vintage Books, 2000.

General Catalogue of Amherst College, Including the Officers of Government and Instruction, the Alumni, and All Who Have Received Honorary Degrees, 1821–1890. Amherst, MA: Published by the College, 1890.

Gifford, George E., Jr., ed. *Dear Jeffie: Being the letters from Jeffries Wyman, first director of the Peabody Museum, to his son, Jeffries Wyman, Jr.* Cambridge, MA: Peabody Museum Press, 1978.

Hooper, Kevin S. *The Early History of Clay County: A Wilderness That Could Be Tamed.* Charleston, SC: History Press, 2006.

Howe, M. A. DeWolfe. *Memoirs of the Life and Services of the Rt. Rev. Alonzo Potter, D.D., LL.D. Bishop of the Protestant Episcopal Church in the Diocese of Pennsylvania.* Philadelphia: J. B. Lippincott, 1871.

Hubbell, W. S., A. M. Carne, and D. D. Brown, eds. *The Story of the Twenty-First Regiment, Connecticut Volunteer Infantry, During the Civil War, 1861–1865.* Middletown, CT: Press of the Stewart Printing Co., 1900.

Jarvis, Grace H. *A Spanish Census of Florida in 1783.* Jacksonville, FL, n. d.

Kirkland, Thomas J., and Robert M. Kennedy. *Historic Camden.* Columbia, SC: The State Company, 1905, 300.

Landers, Jane. *Black Slavery in Spanish Florida.* Urbana: University of Chicago Press, 1999.

———. *Black Society in Spanish Florida.* Urbana: University of Illinois Press, 1999.

Landers, Jane G., ed. *Colonial Plantations and Economy in Florida.* Gainesville: University Press of Florida, 2000.

L'Engle, Gertrude N. *A Collection of Letters, Information, and Data on Our Family*, volumes 1 and 2. Jacksonville, FL, privately published, 1951.

L'Engle, Gertrude Nelson, and Katherine Tracy L'Engle, eds. *Letters of William John L'Engle, M.D. and Madeleine Saunders L'Engle, his Wife 1843–1863.* Jacksonville Public Library, Jacksonville, FL.

L'Engle, Susan Fatio. *Notes of My Family And Recollections of My Early Life.* New York: Knickerbocker Press, 1888.

Lockley, Joseph Byrne. *East Florida 1783–1785: A File of Documents Assembled, and Many of Them Translated.* Berkeley: University of California Press, 1949.

Marotti, Frank. *The Cana Sanctuary: History, Diplomacy, and Black Catholic Marriage in Antebellum St. Augustine, Florida.* Tuscaloosa: University of Alabama Press, 2012.

Mills, Donna Rachal. *Florida's First Families: Translated Abstracts of Pre-1821 Spanish Censuses,* vol. 1. Berwyn Heights, MD: Heritage Books, 2011.

Price, Eugenia. *Margaret's Story.* New York: Lippincott & Crowell, 1980.

Randolf, Pearl. "Edward Lycurgas," in Federal Writers' Project, *Slave Narratives: A Folk History of Slavery in the United States From Interviews with Former Slaves,* vol. 3, *Florida Narratives.* The Federal Writers' Project, 1936–1938. Washington, D.C.: Library of Congress Project, Work Projects Administration, 1941.

Rollins, Richard, ed. *Pickett's Charge: Eyewitness Accounts.* Redondo Beach, CA: Rank and File Publications, 1994.

Roman Catholic Records, St. Augustine Parish, White Baptisms, Register Books 2 and 3. St. Augustine, FL: St. Augustine Historical Society Research Library.

Sears, Stephen W. *Gettysburg.* Boston: Houghton Mifflin, 2003.

Senate Journal. A Journal of the Proceedings of the Senate of the Extra Session of the Legislature of the State of Florida. Tallahassee, FL: N. M. Bowen, Printer, 1889.

Snodgrass, Dena. *The Island of Ortega: A History.* Jacksonville, FL: Ortega School, 1981.

Sprague, John T. *The Origin, Progress, and Conclusion of the Florida War.* New York: D. Appleton, 1848.

Stagg, J. C. A., Jeanne Kerr Cross, and Susan Holbrook Perdue, eds. *The Papers of James Madison, Presidential Series,* vol. 3. Charlottesville: University of Virginia Press, 1996, 123-4.

Still, William. "Miss Lulu C. Fleming," in Scruggs, L. A., ed. *Women of Distinction: Remarkable in Works and Invincible in Character.* Raleigh, NC: L. A. Scruggs, 1893.

Stillman, William James. *The Autobiography of a Journalist,* vol. 1. Cambridge, MA: Riverside Press, 1901.

Tanner, Helen Hornbeck. *Zéspedes In East Florida 1784–1790.* Jacksonville: University of North Florida Press, 1989.

United States War Department. *The War Of The Rebellion: A Compilation of the Official Records of the Union and Confederate Armies,* series 2, vol. 4, serial 117, 442. Washington, D.C.: GPO, 1880-1901.

U.S. and International Marriage Records, 1560–1900. Provo, UT: Yates Publishing, 2004. www.ancestry.com.

Williams, John Lee. *The Territory of Florida, or, Sketches of the Topography, Civil and Natural History of the Country, the Climate, and the Indian Tribes, from the First Discovery to the Present Time.* New York: A. T. Goodrich, 1837.

Wilson, Emily J., ed. *Florida Historical Records Survey, Selected Abstract from Superior and Circuit Court Case Files,* vol. 1. St. Johns County, FL, 1939.

Wilson, John Simpson. *The Dead of the Synod of Georgia: Necrology: or Memorials Of Deceased Ministers Who Have Died During the First Twenty Years After Its Organization.* Atlanta, GA: Franklin Printing House, 1869.

Journal Articles

Cusick, James G. "Hello, Sailor!" *El Escribano*–The St. Augustine Journal of History 47 (2010).

Davis, T. Frederick. "MacGregor's Invasion of Florida, 1817." *Florida Historical Quarterly* 7, no. 1 (1928).

Hammond, E. A., ed. "Benrose's Medical Case Notes from the Second Seminole War." *Florida Historical Quarterly* 47 (April 1969).

Jones, William M. "A Report on the Site of Camp Finegan," *Florida Historical Quarterly* 39, no. 4 (1961).

Lowe, Richard G. "American Seizure Of Amelia Island." *Florida Historical Quarterly* 45, no. 1 (1966).

Murdoch, Richard K. "The Return of Runaway Slaves, 1790–1794." *Florida Historical Quarterly* 38, no.2 (1959).

Parker, Susan R. "I Am Neither Your Subject Nor Your Subordinate," in Fretwell, Jacqueline K. and Susan R. Parker, eds. "Clash Between Cultures: Spanish East Florida, 1784–1821." *El Escribano*–The St. Augustine Journal of History (1988).

Schafer, Daniel L. "A Class of People Neither Freemen nor Slaves: From Spanish to American Race Relations in Florida, 1821–1862." *Journal of Social History* 26, no. 3 (1993), 587-609.

Waterbury, Jean Parker. "Where Artillery Land Crosses Aviles Street: The Segui/Kirby House." *El Escribano*–The St. Augustine Journal of History 24 (1987).

Willis, William Scott. "A Swiss Settler In East Florida: A Letter of Francis Philip Fatio." *Florida Historical Quarterly* 64, no. 2 (1985).

Contemporary Newspapers

Cox, Jeremy. "An Uphill Battle to Save Civil War Site Camp Finegan." *Florida Times-Union, Community/Westside* (Jacksonville), March 27, 2010. http://jacksonville.com/community/westside/2010-03-28/story/uphill-battle-save-civil-war-site-camp-finegan.

Farrington, Brendan. *Associated Press,* 2002. http://www.cbsnews.com/news/a-measure-of-justice/.

Parker, Susan. "Invasion Scare Terrorized Residents in 1794." *St. Augustine Record,* January 15, 2006. http://staugustine.com/stories/011506/com_3578636.shtml#.VnhgT1I67dw.

Historic Newspapers

All historic newspapers were accessed online at University of Florida Digital Newspaper Library (FDNL) or www.geneaologybank.com.

Boston Daily Advertiser, February 16, 1876.
Boston Evening Transcript, October 25, 1858.
Boston Traveler, December 20, 1855.
Charleston Courier (SC), May 31, 1858; November 2, 1858.
*City Gazette and Daily Advertiser (*Charleston, SC), November 6, 1821.
Daily Constitutionalist (Atlanta), June 7, 1864; July 2, 1864.

Daily National Intelligencer, October 3, 1817.
Daily Picayune (New Orleans), May 26, 1858.
Enquirer (Richmond, VA), July 29, 1836.
Federal Intelligencer and Baltimore Daily Gazette, September 1, 1795.
Florida Herald (St. Augustine), January 10, 1835; April 1, 1835; April 15, 1835; June 17, 1835; July 1, 1835; August 6, 1835; September 10, 1835; July 9, 1836.
Florida Herald & Southern Democrat (St. Augustine), December 16, 1829.
Florida News (Jacksonville), October 27, 1855; June 8, 1858.
Florida Republican (Jacksonville), January 1, 1852; July 29, 1852.
Florida Union (Jacksonville), February 3, 1866.
Floridian and Advocate (Tallahassee), January 30, 1838; March 31,1838.
Independent Chronicle & Boston Patriot, December 14, 1836.
Jacksonville Courier (FL), December 3, 1835.
Macon Telegraph (GA), June 1, 1888; July 1, 1896.
Newport Mercury (RI), July 6, 1867; February 22, 1868.
News (Jacksonville, FL), January 23, 1846.
News (St. Augustine, FL), September 27, 1839.
New York Times, June 8, 1864.
Palatka Daily News (FL), n.d.
Pensacola Daily Commercial (FL), September 19–October 3, 1888.
Philadelphia Inquirer, March 18, 1901; April 6, 1916.
Pilot (Cazenovia, NY), October 15, 1817.
St. Augustine Examiner, June 8, 1861.
Sun (Baltimore), October 31, 1856.
Weekly News and Courier (Charleston, SC), March 24, 1897.
Yankee (Boston, MA) vol. 6, iss. 33, August 8, 1817.

Unpublished Works

Klein, Christopher. *The Man Who Shipped New England Ice Around the World*. August 29, 2012. www.history.com.

Marotti, Frank. *Negotiating Freedom in St. Johns County, Florida, 1812–1813*. PhD diss., University of Hawai'i, 2003.

O'Riordan, Cormac A. "The 1795 Rebellion in East Florida." Masters thesis, University of North Florida, 1995, 99. https://digitalcommons.unf.edu/etd/99.

Scott Ritchie

Turner, Shane Micah. "Rearguard of the Confederacy: The Second Florida Infantry Regiment." Masters thesis, Florida State University, 2005, 1459. https://diginole.lib.fsu.edu/etd/1459.

Wikström, B.A. *The Fleming's Island Gazette.* MWF Collection.

Public Records

House of Representatives, 32nd Congress, 2nd Session, Ex. Doc No. 68.

United States Federal Census. Provo, UT, USA: www.ancestry.com.

Clay County, Florida:

> Index to Duval Marriages to 1860, Clay County Archives, Clay County, Florida.
>
> Marriage Records
>
> Deed Books
>
> Motion Docket, 1885–1950, Book 1.
>
> Lewis Fleming Probate Record, Clay County Archives.
>
> Margaret Fleming Probate Record, Clay County Archives.

Duval County, Florida:

> Probate Packets: Sophia Fleming, No. 627; George Fleming Jr., No. 911; Louis I. Fleming, No. 688.

Nassau County, Florida: Land Records

St. Johns County, Florida: Land Records

Index

Battle of Cold Harbor 7, 119, 132, 133–136

Battle of Gettysburg

Cemetery Ridge 121

command of Capt. Seton Fleming 119–123

death of Major Moore 120

Pickett's Charge 121–123

Second Florida Regiment routed 119–123

Battle of Jonesboro 137

Battle of Olustee 125, 126, 137

Battle of Seven Pines 118

Battle of Wahoo Swamp 70, 71, 75–77

Battle of Williamsburg

death of Colonel George T. Ward 116

Seton Fleming wounded and captured 116–118

Battle of Yorktown 116

Beggs, James D. 164

Bell, Thomas

convicted of piracy 22

Bennett, Mary O.

wife of George C. Fleming 113

Bethune, Farquhar

administrator of Sophia Fleming estate 81, 86, 87

Bibb, George M.

U.S. Secretary of Treasury 83, 229

Biddle, Henry Canby 219

Biddle, Mary Augusta "Dusty"

Fleming family member 193

Biddle, Miss Helen

Hibernia guest 198

Big House. See Fleming Mansion

Bird, Major Pickens

killed at Cold Harbor 134, 135

Birney, Brig. Gen. William

allows Margaret Fleming to reclaim Hibernia 147, 148

orders assault on Fleming Island 129, 130

Black, Christian 154, 188

Black, Mary

wife of Christian Black 188

Blair, Henry

U.S. Congressman 152

Bleach, Lt. Elijah 70

Bolivar, Simon 65

Bowden, John M. 82

Brady, Alice

silent film star and Hibernia guest 219

Brantley, John

Fleming neighbor 130

Breckenridge, Maj. Gen. John C.

Davis Creek 42

Davis, T. Frederick

historian 48, 168

Dean, James

African American judge removed
from office 177, 179

Delgado, Sergeant Antonio 23, 24

Dell, Captain James 71, 77

de Lono, Angel 179

Derby, E. H. 152

Doctor's Lake 171

Dominique (slave) 86

Dorman, Orlando M. 97

Dorman, Rodney

attorney 82

Downing, Charles 82

Drew, George 161, 162

Drysdale, John

attorney for Lewis and George
Fleming 62

Dublin (slave) 69

Duncan, James H.

recommends Fleming boarding
house in Boston 99

Duval Conservative Democratic Party Executive Committee 161

E

Easter

Frank Fleming family servant 168

Elliot, Charles G.

honored by JASA for service during
1888 yellow fever epidemic 177

Elsy (slave) 96, 235, 245

Escape

pirate schooner 22

F

Fairlie, James M.

honored by JASA for service during
1888 yellow fever epidemic 177

Fatio, Francis Philip

cattle contracts 22, 23, 32

desecration of his body 44

New Switzerland manor house 10,
20, 37

summary of his life 22, 23, 40

wine/brandy sales 27

Fatio Jr., Francis Philip

joins father in East Florida 27

leases land from John Forbes 46

New Switzerland during Patriot War
43, 44

rebuilds New Switzerland 49

Fatio, Louisa

boarding house 99

daughter of F. P. Fatio Jr. 81

Fatio, Maria Magdalena Crispel

wife of F. P. Fatio Sr. 40

263

medical school 95

seminary 95

Fleming, George Philip 207

    creditors and civil suits 60, 62, 82

    death and administration of estate 96, 97

    default on St. Augustine mortgage 60–62

    divorce 96, 97

    Second Florida Mounted Volunteers 75

    Second Seminole War service 7, 70

    son of George and Sophia Fleming 4, 26

Fleming Hotel prior to 1858

    1855 description 99, 101–103

    1856 guests and activity 102–105

    destroyed by fire 105, 106

    first known guests 99

Fleming, Isabella Frances

    baptism 153

    daughter of Lewis and Margaret Fleming 99

Fleming Island

    Hibernia Mound 33

    Native Americans 33

Fleming Jr., Francis P.

    son of Francis P. Fleming 179

Fleming Jr., Frederic Alexander

    son of Frederic and Margot Fleming 187

Fleming Jr., Louis Isadore

    son of L. I. and Mary L'Engle Fleming 149

Fleming Jr., Margaret "Maggie"

    daughter of Lewis and Margaret Fleming 96

    description 154

    dies of yellow fever 154

Fleming Jr., Margaret Seton

    daughter of Lewis and Margaret Fleming 96

Fleming, Lewis Michael

    assists his father for Fernandina counterattack 47

    Battle of Wahoo Swamp 70, 71, 75, 76

    creditors and civil suits 50, 60–63

    death at Hibernia 107, 118

    default on St. Augustine mortgage 60

    fiction of wound during war 77

    last service during Second Seminole War 77, 100

    marriage to Margaret Seton 80

    married in Cuba 59

    Panama Mills 83–85

    pecuniary embarrassments 82–84, 85

    Second Florida Mounted Volunteers 75

About the Author

Scott Ritchie lives in Austin, Texas, but often returns to his extended family's ancestral home on a high bluff along the St. Johns River in northeast Florida. This is where he and his wife began their careers together, where their four children were born, and where he developed an obsession for the history of Hibernia and the Flemings of Fleming Island. After 36 years as an educator in elementary schools, colleges, and universities, Scott "retired" to take up historical research full time. When his isn't at some archival collection surrounded by old documents or crafting a narrative to tell a long-forgotten story, you might find him fishing, hiking, playing his guitar, or turning a decorative bowl on the lathe in his woodshop.

On the wall above his desk hangs an oil painting—a landscape of the St. Johns River. A family member captured this scene looking northeast from Hibernia. It serves as a constant reminder of the natural beauty of Florida, as well as a catalyst that allows his imagination to drift back over two hundred years ago when his children's fourth great-grandfather, George Fleming of Ireland, first claimed the land as his own.

He admits the family connection might bias his interpretation of the historic record, but hopes that his education has taught him enough to recognize when it does. As a lifelong educator, he is also a lifelong student, with a bachelor's degree from the University of Northern Colorado, two master's degrees from Jacksonville University, a Ph. D. from the University of Texas at Austin, and an insatiable desire to keep learning new things.